FOR THE CHILDREN

DOUBLEDAY

NEW YORK

LONDON

TORONTO

SYDNEY

AUCKLAND

for the CHILDREN

LESSONS FROM A VISIONARY PRINCIPAL

Madeline Cartwright
&
Michael D'Orso

PUBLISHED BY DOUBLEDAY

a division of Bantam Doubleday Dell Publishing Group, Inc.
1540 Broadway, New York, New York 10036

DOUBLEDAY and the portrayal of an anchor
with a dolphin are trademarks of Doubleday,
a division of Bantam Doubleday Dell
Publishing Group, Inc.

All dates, place-names, titles, and events in
this account are factual. However, the names
of certain individuals have been changed in
order to afford them a measure of privacy.

The poem "Tomorrow" by Rhonda Johnson used by
permission of the author.

Library of Congress Cataloging-in-Publication Data

Cartwright, Madeline.
For the children : lessons from a visionary principal /
Madeline Cartwright and Michael D'Orso. — 1st ed.
p.   cm.
1. Children—Education (Elementary)—Pennsylvania—
Philadelphia—
Case studies.   I. D'Orso, Michael.   II. Title.
LC5132.P4C37   1993
372.9748'11—dc20   92-21196   CIP

ISBN 0-385-42372-1

Interior design by Susan Yuran

Printed in the United States of America

September 1993

First Edition

1 3 5 7 9 10 8 6 4 2

Dedicated
to
my lovely daughter
Jill
and my grandson
Jared
who are my very special therapy
that keeps all problems
in perspective

Acknowledgments

I thank God and all of the people who made this book possible. Thanks to my father who never allowed me to think that I could not achieve and to my mother who worked so hard to teach us values necessary to success; to my sisters and brothers who reminded and told me of the days on the farm.

A heartfelt thanks to my husband, Earl, who always supported my efforts for the children. My sincere appreciation to our daughter Jill who unselfishly shared her home, clothes, her father and me with children who had less. A very special thanks to Jill for reading and typing far into many nights.

A special thanks to Dr. Ruth Hayre who inspired me with her words of wisdom. "It is easy to criticize what someone else is doing, but far better to work toward improving a situation. Before one begins to tear down what is, one should make sure there is something better to be put in its place."

Thanks to Dr. Jeanette Brewer who recommended me to be principal at Blaine and who helped, directed and encouraged me.

Thanks to Raymond Brooks, Allyson Marcus and the staff of the James G. Blaine School who worked so very hard for the children and me. Thanks to the parents, the children and the community who accepted my leadership and followed with unswerving faith.

Thanks to Vernon Loeb of the Philadelphia *Inquirer* newspaper staff who told me, ". . . write your story. It should be told and you can and should tell it yourself," and to Shirley Adams who listened, organized my material and helped with the direction for my first draft.

A most special thanks to Michael D'Orso who worked so hard and persevered to shape this book so that those who read it know we must do more for the children. Thanks to Mike's daughter Jamie whose words and smiles made me know that it could all come together.

Thanks also to David Black who helped to keep this project on course.

I deeply appreciate the help and encouragement from the Doubleday staff: Martha Levin, Ellen Archer and especially my editor, Casey Fuetsch.

Thanks to my agent, Faith Hampton Childs, without whose guidance, commitment and confidence this book would not have been completed.

And to Pat Krug who believed in the book and encouraged and worked with me daily during the last two and most crucial years of the writing and shaping of this book, I say Hallelujah.

And finally thanks to my idol, Dr. Constance E. Clayton, truly a woman of substance whose life demonstrates that we can do so much more for the children when we sincerely believe that we can do more and are guided by a commitment to making the children come first when considering changes and programs in education.

FOR THE CHILDREN

PROLOGUE

The little boy's name was Tyrone, but his classmates called him Ethiopia because he looked so much like the starving African children they had seen on television. He answered to the name and did not seem bothered by it.

It wasn't hard to understand why Tyrone was so underweight. He was the youngest of three children who lived with a mentally impaired mother. All too often, food and money in his home were exhausted before the next welfare check came. His home was like many others in a neighborhood of run-down apartments and crowded, often condemned, row houses, all thronged with children.

Like Tyrone's, an overwhelming majority of the homes were made up of single-parent families on welfare. Most were without fathers or proper role models. Most of the young mothers had been teenagers when they were lured or coerced into parenthood. The plight of these families trying to exist on an income far below the poverty level, compounded by the lack of experience, resources and counseling, made their children likely candidates for neglect, abuse and failure.

I knew Tyrone depended on the school to supply clean clothes and food. But I never realized how much school meant to this little seven-year-old until I arrived one morning to find him outside the front doors, cradling his left arm, his brown eyes wet with held-back tears.

His arm looked horrible. It hurt just to look at the raw third-degree burns exposed to the cold morning air. I could only imagine Tyrone's pain. I hurried him inside, asking him what had happened as I called Liz, our school community coordinator, to find his mother so that I could take her and Tyrone to the hospital.

He explained that he had been helping his mother pour hot grease from a frying pan into a glass jar to store for the next use. He was steadying the jar when it burst, spilling the scalding oil onto his arm.

There was no phone in the house to call for help. There was no transportation to the hospital. But there was the school. Tyrone knew when he went to bed that night, biting his lip to endure the pain, that morning would come and with it would come his teachers, his principal and the open doors of that building—and with them would come help.

Help and hope. As I sat with Tyrone, I could see there was no separating the two concepts for this little boy, nor for so many other children living the same kind of life.

Help and hope for the education of children in America is what this book is all about.

This is not just another book on educational theory and philosophy. God knows there are enough of those out there. I have shelves full of them myself, nearly a forty-year collection, as a matter of fact.

I have worked for the Philadelphia public school system for thirty-three years, both as a teacher and as a principal. Eisenhower was President when I stepped into my first classroom, and since then I've watched an entire generation of children spill in and out of these doorways, run up and down the halls, flock onto those playgrounds and, eventually—for better or for worse—make their way out into the streets.

For too many of these children, that way has been for the worse.

I have watched the educational system in this city and in cities across the country slowly and steadily crumble into crisis. Desperation and anger, abandonment and fear, hatred and hopelessness are feelings that have been swirling through our cities for thirty years now, gusting up and down the alleyways, whistling through the tenement houses, blowing into the dark cinder-block hallways of the public housing projects and back onto those forlorn streets. For thirty years—an entire generation—these winds have been gathering strength like a tornado, sweeping up our children, and their schools, and with those schools, much of our hope for the future.

If there is one thing America has always counted on and never questioned, it has been a better tomorrow, glowing and promising. That has been our birthright since this country was founded. We have always believed in the future.

But now, as never before, our country is standing on unsteady ground, facing a future we can hardly understand, much less predict. Questions of sheer survival are whirling around us. The world is shifting at a dizzying rate, and we are unsure of our place in it.

Look at the global picture: Old nations are falling apart; new ones are ascending. Which are our enemies? The challenges of an international community have let us know we no longer control the game, we no longer make the rules. Do we simply take our drumbeats of defense, formerly turned toward the Soviet Union, and pound them at the Japanese? Or do we turn our sights on ourselves and begin the painful task of redefining who we are and how we fit into a world that continues to shift and shrink before our very eyes?

Here at home, in a society swirling with complex economic, technological and environmental demands, with workplaces starving for the sophisticated skills and intellect necessary to carry us into the twenty-first century, we have a public education system that is in crisis as never before. How much longer can we afford to turn out children unable to comprehend and respond to the challenges that face us all?

These questions are as frightening as they are crucial, and they all direct attention to our schools, to the children who are, literally, our tomorrow. For the first time in our history, we have to wonder what the future holds for our children. They themselves wonder.

Thirty years ago few people paid much attention to what was happening to the children in our schools. There were scattered cries of alarm about the changes occurring in the lives of our children at home—in their families, in their neighborhoods, in their vision of the world. Warnings were sounded in suburbia, where the good life was beginning to take its toll, where the price of prosperity in many cases meant both parents had to work (if there were still two parents in the home), where time was becoming a commodity more precious than money, and where parents were spending less and less of that time with their children.

For kids in the city, the changes were even more acute, and they have accelerated with each day. Urban children have ugliness outside their doors that equals anything on the television screen—brutal, sudden violence that launches them belly-down on the floor, either tense with anxiety or numb with acceptance.

There are drugs around the corner, across the street, in their faces. Children in the suburbs see some of the same, but children in the city face more; they face poverty so real it can rip the hope from their tiny little souls. Both environments have parents who, by choice or necessity, don't have the time a child needs in so many ways.

Disconnection has frayed the fabric of our lives everywhere, among the well-to-do and the poor, among the minorities and the white. Although the most essential thread in that fabric remains the bond between parents and children and, by extension, schools, that bond has weakened drastically, if not disappeared altogether, among members of our families, and between too many of our families and their schools all across this country.

There is no mystery about what that bond means at home.

Every minute we spend with our children, we are teaching them something. If we're bending over a book together, we are teaching them to quest for knowledge. If we are sitting down to dinner together, we are teaching them about comfort, continuity, community and communication. If we simply hold them in our arms in silence, we're teaching them about love.

Schools have always depended on this bond at home to support the literal learning that takes place within the walls of our classrooms. It's no big mystery why schools suffer when that bond breaks down. If the load of what today is called "parenting" is shifted toward the teachers and staff in our schools, and if those teachers and staff are unable or unwilling to take it on—whether in the most prosperous suburban schools or in the most neglected classrooms of our inner cities—the system begins to tilt.

It strains. It cracks. Pretty soon it begins to crumble.

Ten years ago we sat bolt upright when the Department of Education released a report titled *A Nation at Risk*. Suddenly we had a certified, government-issued, honest-to-God crisis. Suddenly our schools were in dire need of drastic attention. Scores were down in the United States; other nations' were up. "Creative" educational programs begun in the 1960s were blamed, and "Back to the Basics" became the rallying cry of the eighties.

But those were just words, words that disguised a swing away from truly "public" education toward a system that basically said, "Teach the best and to hell with the rest."

With that, those in public schools became even more confused about their mission, their direction, their roles and their responsibilities. The system moved into more disarray. Test scores continued to drop. In math, science, languages, literature—America was falling behind the rest of the world. We were no longer in the top ten in some categories.

Here at home, jobs were suddenly drying up. College entry requirements became tougher to meet and, for many, unimaginably expensive. Throughout the 1980s the rich got richer, the poor stayed poor and more families joined the poorer ranks. The middle classes began feeling a strain just to stay afloat. Competition displaced community as people started scrambling for a slice of an ever-shrinking economic pie. Fewer people were bothering even to pay lip service anymore to words like "brotherhood," "opportunity" and "democracy." Only the most idealistic talked about those conditions anymore. More than ever, the name of the game became every man for himself.

The decline was felt, more than anywhere else, in our schools. Education was abandoned; surreptitiously in some places, blatantly in others. In most cases, it was as clear as black and white. Many families who could afford to flee the inner city did so, leaving the inner city and its public education behind.

But there can be no pulling out of this. There is no place to run, or to hide. If we turn our backs on the cities and public schools, we are putting ourselves in a precarious situation. Our cities are where the most neglected of our children live and attend the most neglected of schools.

There are nearly 13 million children living in poverty in America today, an increase of almost 25 percent from a decade ago. That is one out of every five children in this country.

If these children—these millions of boys and girls—are left behind, be assured they will not stay put. They may take out their desperation on one another for a time, but eventually they will aim their rage outward and there will be no ignoring them then.

The response must begin in the homes and the schools. Support and involvement from all of America is necessary to restructure inner-city schools and neighborhoods. For the past twenty years there has been a steady, concerted, almost conscious desertion of the principles and the programs that were at the heart of the civil rights movement of the 1950s and 1960s. The poor and the dispossessed, minorities and white alike, have been virtually forsaken by a government answerable almost exclusively to the interests of the privileged.

Much press has been given to the murder and chaos in our cities, but relatively few spotlights have been aimed at the schools. Oh, it happens. A newspaper or magazine reporter might venture in and write a story, maybe about something heart-warming, even inspiring. A television crew might follow with its cameras. A radio team may arrive armed with tapes and micro-phones.

But then the reporters leave. Middle America might mull over the stories over coffee. But nothing is done. Who has the time? Who has the money? Who has the plan?

Meanwhile, many children live in homes where they must feed and care for one another because their parents are away from home. For too many children, whose "home" is no more than a corner of a condemned building where they tear the boards off the windows, light a kerosene heater for warmth and fetch water in empty plastic soda bottles, life goes on.

For too many of them, living moment to moment with the reality of death on their doorsteps, with bodies—drunken or dead—littering their path to school, life goes on.

What does homework mean to an eight-year-old boy who has nursed his mother through an overdose the night before?

What does the threat of suspension mean to a ten-year-old girl who is selling herself on the street and is more at home there than she is anywhere else in her life?

What does discipline mean to a boy or girl who has been behind bars and found that situation better than home or the neighborhood? What does the "future" mean to a child who won-ders if he will live to or beyond the age of twenty-five?

This is a world unimaginable to most Americans. It is a world in which terms like "school," "teaching," "learning" and, most of all, "children" have definitions entirely different from the rest of society's. I know this world, I know it well.

For eleven years I was principal of the James G. Blaine Ele-mentary School in the heart of North Philadelphia, in the poorest and most dangerous part of that city. For eleven years I lived with these children and their parents. I climbed into their lives, outside the school as well as in the classrooms. I brought them, parents and teachers alike, into a place they had not believed belonged to them and made it a beacon in their lives. I learned from them, and they learned from me. And together—*together!*—we turned our little corner of this cruel and crippling world around.

What we did at Blaine can be done at any inner-city school in America.

It must be done, for the sake of every child who knows a life like Tyrone's, as well as for the children lucky enough not to know it.

It must be done, for the sake of us all.

Let me tell you how we did it.

CHAPTER

1

IT WAS EARLY MARCH. THE CHILL OF WINTER STILL hung in the air, but the morning sky looked like springtime as sunlight sparkled off the stripped carcasses of abandoned cars and bits of broken glass strewn over the street.

Above the old row houses and the crumbling Victorian walkups, over the empty lots ankle-deep with garbage and the walls sprayed with graffiti, the sky was bright blue.

But down on the cracked, crumbling sidewalks, it was still dark. The front stoops and basement steps were cloaked in shadows.

A few people were already sitting out on their porch steps, but it was still too early for school, so there wasn't a child in sight. Most of the little ones were just now climbing out of bed, rubbing their eyes, hunting for their clothes, for a toothbrush, maybe for some breakfast.

It was hard to imagine children living inside some of those buildings: doors hung crookedly off hinges or had been replaced by boards of plywood or thin, pocked sheets of metal.

There were real homes here and there, to be sure, tidy places painted the bright colors of fruit, with flower boxes in the windows and soft, warm lights glowing inside. But many more buildings looked as if they had been bombed. They were hollow, gutted, dangerous-looking places with floor-to-roof roaches and rats.

Yet these seemingly empty buildings were full of people, entire families. They were full of children.

It was for the children that I had come to North Philadelphia, but the first faces I passed that morning didn't know that. Not too many Cadillacs came rolling down those streets—not unless it was somebody's grandmother coming to visit. Or someone who had taken a wrong turn off Girard Avenue or Thirty-third Street in the direction of the park or the zoo and had wound up lost and petrified in this maze of boarded-up brownstones and narrow one-way streets.

I wasn't lost, and I wasn't frightened. As far as I was concerned, there was nothing to frighten me. I was no stranger to ghettos—I had spent about half of my young life in one. I was no stranger to the neighborhoods of North Philadelphia either, and I was set to make this one my home for years to come.

I was so happy! I was ecstatic. I couldn't keep my jaws down, I was smiling so hard. This was what I had worked toward for such a long, long time. It was my dream come true.

The people on their front steps had to wonder about this woman, wheeling her Cadillac so slowly up their street, waving at them as if she were a politician courting their votes.

"Good morning! Good morning!" I sang out, daring them not to respond. A crazy lady. That's what the people of Strawberry Mansion thought that first morning as I made my way toward their school.

Toward *my* school.

STRAWBERRY MANSION. TAKE ONE LOOK AT THE PLACE AND the name sounds like some sort of bad joke.

As with so many sections of so many cities all across America, the name is about the last thing left from a time when the community itself, along with the city surrounding it, was a totally different place. Nothing left in Strawberry Mansion today is the way it was when the place was created nearly two hundred years ago. Little is the same as it was fifty years ago.

Little but the name.

Strawberry Mansion began as an estate built back in the 1750s, one of a string of country houses that sprang up during colonial times on the bluffs overlooking the Schuylkill River north of Philadelphia. When the British occupied the city during the Revolutionary War, most of the estates were sacked and burned. This one was rebuilt in the 1790s by a friend of George Washington's, and it became known for its beds of strawberries, the first grown in the United States.

In 1808, the place became a combination dairy and restaurant, offering the first ice cream sold in the city of Philadelphia. An Italian named Bosio ran the operation. Picnickers rowing up the river on Sunday afternoons would stop to sample the strawberries and cream served in Bosio's garden. Daniel Webster, John Calhoun and the Marquis de Lafayette were among the early American celebrities who dropped in at Strawberry Mansion to taste some of that famous fruit.

But the leisure didn't last long. This was a nation in a hurry, on the move, changing fast: people swarming in, buildings going up, businesses burgeoning and pushing aside the peace of the past. It didn't take long for places like Strawberry Mansion to be swallowed by the speed.

By the 1870s the strawberries were gone and the place had become a beer garden. By 1890 the main house was an outdoor Italian restaurant, smelling of garlic and red wine, with a reputation as a good spot for a sailor to find female companionship.

By the end of the century it was hard to remember that Strawberry Mansion had been a sleepy countryside retreat just a hundred years before. Road crews and masons had begun building new neighborhoods as the city stretched north during the mid-1800s, and behind them came hundreds of Irish, Italian and African-American families looking for a home. They settled around the mansion and nearby Fairmount Park.

The 1890s saw a burst of new construction as developers responded to a huge wave of immigration from Eastern Europe. Impressive Victorian homes with soaring turrets and hallway tiles and affordable row houses with wrought-iron railings and wood ornamentation went up in the area across from the park, all quickly filled by these new Americans, most of them Jewish.

Trolley lines and a subway and new streets were built to link the neighborhood with downtown. By 1940, the little back streets and narrow alleys of Strawberry Mansion bristled with small shops and businesses, most bearing Jewish names. According to that year's census, 62 percent of the community's 51,000 residents were Jews.

By then, the Jewish businessmen were already leaving, keeping their shops but moving their families farther north to nicer, more newly developed neighborhoods in the northeast section of the city. They continued to do business in Strawberry Mansion. Business was good. But as their fortunes got better, they wanted bigger, better homes for their families.

As the Jews moved out, more African-Americans moved in. Mortgage money was easy after the war, and the neat, solid row houses in Strawberry Mansion were affordable for renters or buyers. Almost all of the new renters and buyers throughout the 1950s were African-American. This hurried the exit of almost all the old-timers who were not. By 1960, only 2 percent of the neighborhood population, which had dropped to 45,000, was Jewish. The rest had fled to whiter horizons.

With them went their money. Banks that had been collecting mortgages for ten or twenty years from African-American homeowners in Strawberry Mansion now said no to any loans for home improvements. As far as they were concerned, this neighborhood —this *black* neighborhood—was no longer worth investment or worth maintaining. Some savings and loan banks stayed in the area, but they were now there only to take money from depositors, not to lend money.

When the home improvement money disappeared, of course, so did the home improvements. Strawberry Mansion began to deteriorate, caving in on itself, a casualty of the classic process called "redlining" by everyone except the banks. Banks denied that it existed, since it was an illegal practice.

Redlining is basically economic abandonment, pure and simple. It is banks taking their cash to greener pastures, leaving a community to wither and die. If the community does not die, it comes very close to it. That's what happened in Strawberry Mansion. A person could stand at the edge of the neighborhood and look south, across the railroad tracks, toward the skyscrapers of downtown Philadelphia two miles away. Those skyscrapers seemed close enough to touch. But by the 1960s, those gleaming buildings were more distant than they had ever been. They seemed a world away.

Strawberry Mansion had become a deserted urban island. Landlords who owned property in the neighborhood saw the place going to seed; they knew there was no money available to turn the tide, so they kissed their equity goodbye and did not bother to make any more repairs.

With no repairs, the places fell apart. When the places got so bad that no one would live in them, the landlords simply walked away, leaving the rotten buildings as total losses, written off along with the lives still inside them.

When the landlords left, the places became prime targets for vandals. With no owners and in many cases no tenants to protect them, the buildings were ripped apart by scavengers who tore away anything and everything that could be sold, from bathroom fixtures to doorknobs.

It wasn't just those buildings that were affected. The rain and snow falling through a damaged roof would rot the joists and beams that connected the row house to those on each side. No matter that those adjoining properties might have been good, solid homes inhabited by good, solid families. Rats scurried from the empty houses into the occupied ones.

Conditions only worsened as the whites continued to flee. White flight is what happened in Strawberry Mansion. By the end of the 1960s, the Jewish businesses that were still hanging on in the neighborhood at the beginning of that decade had disappeared. Many left with the rioting that swept North Philadelphia in 1964. The rage that exploded that summer left most of the stores and shops charred and in ashes. When Martin Luther King, Jr., was shot in 1968, there were riots again, and Strawberry Mansion was left looking like Dresden.

The census figures tell what happened to this neighborhood —the same thing that happened to hundreds like it all across the country. The 1960 population figure of 45,000 dropped to 36,000 by 1970. African-Americans were leaving now, too, taking their families to bigger and better houses and neighborhoods. Among the residents left behind, many were dying. Too many were dying young.

The situation continued to decline in the 1970s, as gang wars swept through the streets, driving away even more of the good, solid people who had hung on until then. By 1979, the population of Strawberry Mansion, 98 percent of it African-American, was down to 25,000.

Almost everybody who could leave, white and African-American alike, left. There were still strong, defiant, proud homeowners left in this neighborhood, people who refused to surrender, who insisted on holding the line against the gangs and drugs and random violence that had come to rule their streets even if it killed them. They said as much, daring the gangs to shoot them along with each other, staring down the sons of their neighbors and friends, staring down their own sons.

They formed coalitions and community groups, town watches and ad hoc committees. They demanded city, state and federal money to help rebuild the place they called home. They did get some money, cleaned up some of the streets, fixed some of the sidewalks and houses and put in small parks and gardens.

They even had a shopping center built in the heart of the neighborhood.

But the vast majority of the people in Strawberry Mansion in 1979, the year I arrived, were hanging on by a thread. Forty percent of the neighborhood's families were living below the federal poverty level. Most of the others were barely above it.

People from the outside look at neighborhoods like this, neighborhoods that they or their parents knew in the old days, and they talk about how different the place is today, how dilapidated it has become. They blame it on the African-Americans. These outsiders say that the "blacks" brought it down. They talk about how nice things were until the "blacks" moved in. But what they don't admit is that failing neighborhoods have multidimensional causes. They don't acknowledge that the forces that bring neighborhoods like this to their knees must share in the responsibility for rebuilding them. All Americans have a stake in somehow finding a way to help revitalize these neighborhoods.

Beyond that, what few outsiders realize is that even amid the wreckage and the ruins of a place like Strawberry Mansion there burns the same spirited pride and determination that anyone who has ever had hope for themselves and their children can recognize. I knew that there were many people in this area who had given up, who had yielded to drugs and desperation. But I also knew there were just as many who were full of the force that keeps every one of us from surrendering, from giving in and giving up when the nights seem so long and the days so hard.

As I first drove down those narrow, potholed Strawberry Mansion streets on that March morning in 1979, steering my brand-new navy-blue Coupe de Ville past those puzzled faces, I was filled with that force.

And I was determined to find it behind every one of those doors.

CHAPTER
2

AS DEPRESSING AS STRAWBERRY MANSION MAY HAVE AP-
peared to an outsider, it harbored decent, hardworking
residents. My own upbringing, though far from ideal,
had prepared me for the kind of longing I was to see in the faces
of the Strawberry Mansion kids. My own childhood taught me
that a child instilled with hope, curiosity, opportunity and the
values of hard work can achieve anything.

For as long as I can remember, I wanted to be a schoolteacher. I spent my tenth and eleventh summers running a mock
classroom in the basement of our house in Coatesville, Pennsylvania. Eight or nine neighborhood children came every day. Of
course, I was always the teacher and I insisted on the most orderly
of classrooms. My father would say, "You must make your school
so enjoyable and interesting that the children will want to attend.
Make sure that everyone learns something and their parents will
encourage them to come every day." I followed that advice,
though a few times I had to go to Daddy for teaching ideas. I had
to restrain myself from rapping my students' palms with my ruler
as I had seen some of my teachers do when a child was not on

task. Daddy often came down to watch me and my students. He regularly said, "You're a natural teacher, you remind me so much of my mother."

Momma and Daddy divorced when I was six. All eleven of us children had seen it coming for a long time, so their separation was no big surprise to us. But it must have surprised someone, because the Coatesville newspaper gave it a headline: *THE BERGERS DIVORCE AFTER 25 YEARS AND 13 CHILDREN.*

I was the youngest of what had been thirteen children. Margaret died at the age of six months in 1923, and Betty, the eldest, who had suffered from epilepsy, died at eighteen—one month after I was born in October 1937.

My family did not have an easy life, but how many poor people born at the turn of the century had? Both of my parents came from Virginia. Daddy's father, Grandfather Berger, had been a slave near Lynchburg, in the center of the state. He was seven years old when the Emancipation Proclamation was signed. Like many freed slaves, John Berger took the surname of his slave master. He and Elizabeth Powell, a white woman, became life mates and had three children, but they never married. A black man and a white woman weren't allowed to marry in Virginia in those days. It was not until 1967 that the U.S. Supreme Court struck down laws in sixteen states that made interracial marriage a crime. Virginia was one of those states. Until 1967, a Virginia couple could be imprisoned for five years for violating that state's "racial integrity" law. Elizabeth Powell came from a well-respected family, and as unhappy as they might have been about her choice of a mate, her parents made sure that no harm came to her, her husband or their three children: Mary, John and Sarah.

Elizabeth was a schoolteacher, but since there was no school for African-American children in Lynchburg (and separate educations were mandatory), she taught her children at home. They were as educated as the whites in her school, though they never sat in a formal classroom.

Elizabeth died at age fifty-one in 1914, when my father was twenty years old. Soon after the funeral, he followed the advice that she had given him. "If anything happens to me," she had said, "you take Sarah and go right away to stay with your Aunt Lou." Daddy took his younger sister, Sarah, to live with his father's sister and her daughter Mary in Coatesville, an industrial town forty miles west of Philadelphia. There he went to work in Luken's Steel Mill.

Two years later, on a Sunday afternoon, Daddy met his future wife, Homesell Goodall. Her family was from Orange County, in the foothills of Virginia's Shenandoah Mountains, north of Charlottesville.

Mother had come to Philadelphia to live with a cousin when she was three years old, and attended Philadelphia Public School until the fifth grade, when she went to work as a chambermaid for wealthy families in the string of suburbs called the Main Line: Berwyn, Paoli, St. Davids, Villanova and Bryn Mawr. As she got older and became more experienced, Mother learned how to get the most for her efforts. She preferred to work for the very wealthy. "Rich folks treat you differently from half-rich ones," she would tell me. "Half-rich ones want everything their neighbors have. They want you to do everything their neighbors' maids are doing. But their neighbors have two or three maids doing it, and the half-rich family has only one, and that's you!"

My mother worked hard. She did as much work in one day as the average maid did in two. She had a great reputation among her employers, and it gave her the freedom to select where she worked. She did not tolerate flirtatious male bosses or disrespectful children, a fact she made clear before she accepted any job. If she was treated disrespectfully or unfairly, she quit. There were always prospective employers waiting to offer her more money or increased benefits.

My parents met during World War I when Momma was sixteen and Daddy was twenty-three. They were married three weeks later. The next year the Army drafted Daddy and sent him to France, where his well-spoken manner and impressive good looks earned him a job as the officers' "office boy."

After the war, Momma and Daddy rented a farm from "Old

Man Ruth," as we all called him, in Erceldoun, a small borough outside of Coatesville. I was born in the house on that farm, which once had been a stop on the Underground Railroad for runaway slaves during the nineteenth century. Three years later we moved to a farm in Downingtown.

When my parents began farming full-time, Daddy quit his job in the mill and Momma went back to work as a live-in maid on the Main Line to ensure some regular, dependable income. She came home on Thursdays and alternate Sundays. There was very little other work available to an African-American woman.

Mother was a skilled worker. She knew how to remove stains from and care for all fabrics. She could press and iron. She knew how to maintain all furniture surfaces, whether wood, shellac, varnish or paint. She recognized the quality of furniture, what was solid and what was veneer. She learned to identify and name fine china and crystal. She knew the correct setting of a table and how to plan, prepare and serve a full-course meal from soup to nuts and demitasse.

We didn't have much during the Depression and post-Depression years. We eagerly awaited Momma's return home from work to see what used clothing her employers and their friends had given her. All too often the clothing was not suitable for children. Mother would say, "They bring cleanliness and warmth. Style is not important."

My oldest sister, Marie, did not share Momma's sentiment and refused to wear her fur coat to school after that awful first day when the children made fun of her. Each day, she hid the fur coat under the cornstalks and changed into a cloth one before catching the school bus. My brother Buck, however, agreed with Momma: he wore ladies' silk stockings to school when he couldn't find socks. He kept his hands in his pockets to keep the stockings from falling down. During one recess, he went chasing classmate Fatty Arbuckle to retrieve his lunch, and the stockings fell down his legs and right over his shoes, forming two long trails behind him. The children howled with laughter as they watched Buck desperately trying to pull his shoes from far inside the stockings.

One afternoon Momma brought home a burlap bag filled with high-heeled women's shoes. My brothers Buck and Johnny saw the high-heeled shoes and began snickering. They could picture my sisters tripping around in the high-heels at school as everyone laughed at them.

But my brothers stopped laughing when Daddy took that bag of shoes out back, dumped them by a tree stump and began chopping the heels off of every one of them. As he finished each pair, he called out a name.

"Johnny!" He handed Johnny a pair of shoes.

"Buck!" He handed Buck another.

"George!"

"Ethel!"

"Ruth!"

And on down the line until every child had a pair of those shoes, boys and girls alike.

When they went to school the next morning, not much learning got done. The Berger children were walking around in chopped-off, wooden-heeled shoes, going clickety-clack, clickety-clack, and their classmates were on the floor, laughing hysterically.

When the teacher saw every child in the room howling except the straight-faced little Bergers, she scanned the class and thought, "What is it this time?" Soon she noticed the shoes and left the room, closing the door behind her. She, too, could not resist the urge to laugh.

We had no electricity or running water in our home. The outdoor toilet was stocked with old telephone books and dated Sears, Roebuck mail-order catalogues. We'd crumple the pages, rub them together to make them soft and use them for toilet paper. We used kerosene lamps and lanterns and slept on the floor, with straw to relieve the hardness, since only Momma and Daddy had a bed. Like most children, we waited for Daddy's final call before running out to milk the cows and then to catch the school bus. We sometimes went to school smelly and poorly groomed.

We attended school in a one-room schoolhouse. At one time

there were eight Bergers in one classroom. Buck joked, "When we moved, they closed the school and waited to see where we were moving, to decide where to open the next school." Our lunch was a biscuit cut in two and spread with pan gravy to make it appear there was meat in the middle. The deception worked until one day ornery Fatty Arbuckle took Buck's lunch to examine it more carefully and told everyone of his findings.

Often children shared their lunches with us, but others stepped on their leftovers to make sure that "them Bergers ain't getting this."

My father applied for and received a $10,000 grant from the federal government in 1941. This event spelled monumental change in our lives. Each year on New Year's Day all of our family sat around the table to plan together. I remember us gathering that New Year's to make plans for the year to come, when the money would arrive. Daddy said that Momma would stop working and stay home with us; Sarah would be able to go to college to be a doctor when she graduated from high school; my oldest brother, Howard, could train in a real gym to be a boxer; and overall conditions for everyone would improve. Daddy led the family in prayer as he did every New Year's Day. This year was different! We held hands a little tighter as if to assure each other that this was really going to be the best year of all.

Momma continued working and waiting, but when the check finally came, Daddy said nothing about her quitting her job and staying home. Finally, she lost faith. After twenty-five years of marriage and taking care of other people's children while hers fended for themselves, she gave up her wait and left Daddy. She settled in Pittsburgh, where she had relatives, and returned to Downingtown only to kidnap us one or two at a time and take us to Pittsburgh.

First Momma took Ethel and Ruth from the school bus. By then, we had a big dairy farm to run—thirty-seven milk cows, four horses and other livestock. With this responsibility, Daddy could not immediately pursue Momma. He wrote to her and to her relatives in Pittsburgh imploring their assistance to encourage Momma to come home, to preserve the family and their farm, for which they had worked so hard and waited so long to come to fruition. Nothing worked with Momma. She had made up her mind.

She next came back and took Johnny, on whom Daddy depended the most. The three oldest children—Howard, Sarah and Marie—were already out on their own, so Johnny shouldered a big part of the responsibility. When he lost Johnny, Daddy went to Pittsburgh and tried to talk my mother into coming back, but to no avail.

With the help of her employer, my mother got an apartment in Pittsburgh's Hill District projects, a community called Elmore Square, Terrace Village One. Once she had secured a three-bedroom apartment, she came back for more of her children.

When George left, Daddy was forced to sell the farm. I shall never forget the day of the big auction, people bidding on everything that could be pushed or picked up, including my pig. I didn't want to part with that pig, but I had no choice. When it was sold, Daddy told Buck and me to catch it, deliver it to its new owner and collect my five dollars. I ran through a barbed-wire fence trying to grab it and ripped a gash in my leg. The scar lingers as a lasting reminder of my pig, our farm and a dream dismantled.

AFTER HE SOLD THE FARM, DADDY WENT BACK TO COATES-ville, rented a room and applied for federal housing. The size of the house depended on the number of people in the family. Daddy listed all of his children on the application. He had a birth certificate for each one, so he qualified for a brand-new, three-bedroom house and decorated it beautifully with Chippendale furniture.

By the time Daddy moved in, the only child still living with him was my youngest brother, Sylvester. At the urging of the others, Momma didn't take Sylvester. He was always Daddy's favorite and was very spoiled. "They deserve each other," she whispered, as if to shield the fact that she had left Sylvester.

I stayed with Momma my first three years of school. Learning presented frustrations. I was good in math. I could speak and reason well. But I could not read. I had no word-attack skills, no sense of linking sounds to letters. I probably had a learning disability, which today, at a good school, would be diagnosed and transformed with an appropriate prescriptive program. But back then all they could see was a little girl who mixed up letters, seeing the word "name" and pronouncing it "mane." I was assigned to the mentally handicapped section of first grade, but my sister Sarah, who was attending the University of Pittsburgh, objected so strenuously that I was returned to the regular class.

I learned to deal with this reading problem on my own. A child with a deficiency in one area often learns to build strengths in others. It was my compensatory skills that got me through those early years of school without being able to read.

In November 1946, Daddy and Buck came to Pittsburgh and kidnapped me in front of the A. Leo Wilde School, and so I returned to Coatesville in the same manner in which I left the area three years before.

In order to hide me from Momma, Daddy took me to live in Lancaster with one of his friends. Even though I had spent September and October in the fourth grade in Pittsburgh, the Lancaster school staff assigned me to the third. This return to the third grade was both disappointing and rewarding. My classmates didn't know I was repeating a grade, so for the first time in my life I was not in the lowest reading group and I received the award for the best mathematics student in the class.

To add to that success, the following summer I learned to read. The way it happened was almost magical. My father sent me South that summer to live with his girlfriend, Minnie, who had gone to North Carolina to visit her mother. Daddy felt that her activities would be curtailed if I was along; he wanted me to keep an eye on his girlfriend for him. I saw a lot more of Minnie's mother that summer than I did of Minnie; my presence did not thwart Minnie's activities at all. I, however, was under house arrest, held in by the extremely hot weather. I had never been in a place as hot as Wilmington, North Carolina. I stayed inside all summer long with Minnie's mother, who was in her seventies. After breakfast we'd clean up, move to the living room and talk. Both of us were happy for the company. She soon learned that I could not read.

"Child, what do you mean you can't read?" she asked.

"I don't know how. I just can't do it."

"Why, sure you can."

We talked about my problem and she began to explain the reading process to me as she understood it. She talked and I listened. The process began to make more sense to me. She used pictures, letters, songs and candy wrappers. Daily, I was building confidence and skill.

Then one morning it happened. Maybe the time had come, maybe I had just reached the stage in my life where I was ready to understand. But I looked at the word "sand" and I saw the word "sand." I saw the word "bet," put an *m* in place of the *b* and made "met." I put an *s* there and got "set." Suddenly I could see sound and letter relationships, the most primary reading skill. I was boiling over with excitement, I felt as if the clouds had parted, as if heaven had just opened. It was so simple! It made so much sense! I came running down the steps screaming.

"I can read! I can read! Listen to this, I can read!"

From then on I was always in the top sections and in the top of the class. There was no stopping me.

THE FOLLOWING SEPTEMBER I WENT BACK TO LIVE IN COATESville and enrolled in the James Adams Community School, a combined elementary and junior high school that served the African-American population in Coatesville and surrounding areas. Even though we actually lived in a neighboring township, we went to the Coatesville school because the township refused to have integrated elementary and junior high schools and lacked the funds to provide segregated secondary schools.

At James Adams, all our books and instructional aids came from the white schools. When those schools received new supplies and equipment, we inherited their used materials. When our stage curtains caught fire, we were sent the old curtains from the white Gordon Junior High School and they got new ones. During the first assembly after that incident, our principal, Mr. Anderson, said, "These curtains are not new. They are Gordon's used handovers, as usual. Thank God they haven't yet figured out a way to give us their paper and pencils after they have used them." We all laughed.

Our band uniforms came from the white high school by way of Gordon, along with our used track shoes. Often the track shoes were so worn the cleats stuck up into the shoes. The James Adams boys put cardboard in those shoes and still beat Gordon's track team.

The basketball team was an integrated unit, composed of players from both James Adams and Gordon. The team was a perennial powerhouse, with many of its players going on to become starters on several of Coatesville High's state championship teams. I remember what a struggle it was for Mr. Funk, the Coatesville coach, to keep his best players in the game. I'll never forget one night when the Coatesville High principal noticed that all five players on the floor for our team were black. He jumped up, frantically signaling to Coach Funk.

"Look!" he yelled. "Our entire team is *Negro!* We can't have this! You must keep some whites on the floor at all times!"

The message Coach Funk later shared with his black athletes could just as well have been shared with any of us: "If you are not twice as good as the whites," he said, "you won't get a chance to play."

Mr. Anderson delivered that message in assembly after assembly. He continually emphasized that we would never be first if we did not study hard and go on to college. I remember him standing on that stage bellowing his demands for perfection and commitment from us.

"Yes," he would begin, "right now we get the used curtains, shoes, uniforms, books and supplies. But one day it's all going to be different."

Then his tone would rise.

"When the laws are changed," he would say, moving toward a shout, "I want you to be ready to go down to City Hall and take over the mayor's used office; go to the city councilmen's offices and take their used seats. Walk over to the First National Bank with a brand-new nameplate in your hand, take down the used one there, throw it in the trash and put your name on that door, the door marked 'President's Office.' "

By then Mr. Anderson would be roaring, pounding his hands on his used podium.

Mr. Anderson and his staff at James Adams were determined to inspire their students to achieve—to *over*achieve—and to go to college. "Negro history" and racial pride were taught daily, reminding us of the struggles of the Negro race and how our situations were much better than the Negroes who had risen to international stature under much worse conditions.

We were so driven to be prepared to compete with the white children at the high school, we were warned so often of the competition and challenges we would face there and we were reminded so often that each of our performances would reflect on all of us that none of us even dreamed of making an excuse for poor performance, a poor attitude or poor attendance. Our school was accountable for us, and we were accountable for ourselves. There was no excuse. Our standards were incredibly high, because we truly believed our lives and our futures were at stake.

Madeline Jones, who attended James Adams with me, once told me, "I didn't believe there was any such thing as a dumb white kid."

That's the attitude with which we students at James Adams prepared for high school.

❖

BUT BEFORE I GOT TO COATESVILLE HIGH, I HAD MORE TIME to spend in Pittsburgh. Momma came in March 1950, during my seventh-grade year, and convinced me to come to Pittsburgh to live with her again. As much as I did not want to hurt Daddy by leaving, I knew Momma was right when she told me it was time to be with her and to learn the skills a girl needed to know about grooming, housekeeping and growing up.

After settling in with her, I went to register in the neighborhood school's seventh grade. The staff attempted to exercise the option of putting me back a grade, as was the tradition when African-American children transferred from another school system. This practice was widely used and came to be accepted, even by the African-American community. This had happened to me in Lancaster, but there Daddy's objection was overridden because of my reading limitation. This time, I refused to be "put back." This was the sort of challenge for which Mr. Anderson and the staff at James Adams had been preparing us. I had worked hard for three years readying myself for a day like this. Now it had come.

When the counselor, Mr. Tom, told me that he was assigning me to repeat the sixth grade, I told him, "No, mister. I have been put back once, and I'm not doing it again. I am not going backwards anymore."

I sat down in a chair and refused to leave. I sat in that office all day. At the end of that day, I went home. The next morning I came back and was told again that I would be in the sixth grade. Again I took a seat.

"I've been through the sixth grade and half of the seventh," I repeated. "I'm not going through it again."

By now Mr. Tom was furious.

"You are a *hard*headed little girl, aren't you?" he said.

So there I sat for another day. When I returned the next morning, Mr. Tom called the principal to end our deadlock. The principal telephoned James Adams, was told I had made top grades there both in the sixth grade and at the beginning of that seventh-grade year, then hung up and assigned me to the best seventh-grade class in his school.

I could just as well have been held back if I had not persisted. Think about how many hundreds of children over the years didn't. Think about how their young lives were affected, even changed forever, because of that often unchallenged practice. Judgments like that, based on racism, sexism or just plain stupidity, should not be allowed to affect the lives of children.

BY THE TIME I ENTERED HIGH SCHOOL, I HAD ESTABLISHED myself as an honor student. School was going well, but my situation at home was becoming a struggle. Mother began picking and fussing at me in a way she never had before. She began appearing at the school unexpectedly just to check on me. She walked me to and from church, not allowing me to go anywhere else. I was a teenager now, and all my mother saw was a girl ripe to get pregnant.

"If you get pregnant," she'd tell me, "I'm going to put you into a home."

She was so worried I was going to fall through the cracks. She couldn't see there was no chance in this universe that I was going to let that happen. I knew by then exactly what I wanted—or what I *didn't* want.

I did not want to be poor, and I did not want to be pregnant.

All I had to do was look around at the girls I knew who had babies. Theirs was no life for me, and I knew that. Being pregnant at that age was the end of life, as far as I could see, just the absolute end.

My mother's constant threats regarding my getting pregnant, her shadowing me, fussing and picking at me all the time, became unbearable. I was in high school now, sixteen years old and quite capable of caring for myself.

My brother Buck tried to smooth things out. I'd ask, "Buck, why do you suppose she acts as if she hates me all the time?"

"Madeline," he'd say, "Momma has had a hard life, and

there are a lot of things catching up to her now. She's gotten as round as she is tall. She's getting old. She sees her own falling-down body and compares it to your growing-up body. She's looking at you, your life just beginning, and she feels cheated."

Buck was right. So I tried being more patient at home. I already had things mapped out in terms of what I was going to do when I finished high school. College was a given. There was no maybe about it; I was *going* to college. I was going to be a teacher. I was going to have my own place. I was going to drive a Cadillac. I was going to have a maid. I was going to have all these things, and nobody was going to tell me differently.

When I heard my mother telling a friend one afternoon how she would be finished raising kids and finished sending kids to school once I graduated, I realized she had no college in her plans for me, that she would not be supporting me any longer. I knew I had to leave if I was to fulfill my dreams.

That was August 1954, a month before the start of my senior year. I packed everything I owned, went back to my father and finished my last year at Coatesville High.

Wouldn't you know, they tried to hold me back there as well. I made their honor roll the first semester, then in the winter a counselor called me in and told me I didn't have enough "Carnegie Units" to graduate. I had never heard of a Carnegie Unit. No one had ever mentioned it to me. Then the counselor began going down a list of credits I was missing.

"You have a half year of chemistry," she said. "You need a whole year.

"You have a half year of American history.

"You have a half year of health."

I asked her why no one had told me this back in the fall. I asked her why I had been given six extra study halls a week—forty-five minutes apiece—for this last semester instead of the classes I needed. Then I asked her to wait while I called my father.

Daddy came to the school and wasted no time getting to the point.

"I don't know who made my daughter's schedule," he said,

"but I strongly suggest that you get her records together so that she can graduate, or you will find yourselves facing a lawsuit."

The principal was in that office in a minute. He looked over my schedule, then said, "If she needs a half year of chemistry, put her in the chemistry class *now*. If she needs a half year of history, put her there."

They did the same with health, and I had no problems in any of those classes. I just went about the business of making my grades, and when I graduated in the spring of 1955, I was in the top 10 percent of my class.

I was going to college.

WEST CHESTER STATE TEACHERS COLLEGE WAS TWENTY-TWO miles west of Philadelphia, about fifteen miles from Coatesville. It was a pleasant place to get an education, a comfortable campus with good teachers. More importantly, I could afford it. I had been working hard, saving hundreds of dollars, which I thought I would need for college. Then I discovered that the tuition at West Chester was ninety dollars a year. Ninety dollars! I could kick a lamppost and get ninety dollars, I thought to myself.

I registered at West Chester the day before school was to open. At first, I was told my application was too late and that I would have to wait until the next semester to begin. When I explained to the dean that I simply had to begin that semester, that I had read that students who took time off frequently did not complete their education and that the last thing I needed was another statistic not in my favor, he was struck by my enthusiasm and waived the admission deadline. He registered me in Elementary Education and I was on my way.

I was living with my father while going to school, and at the end of my freshman year, I began looking for summer employment. There were no such jobs for African-American college students in Coatesville. All summer jobs traditionally held by college students there were reserved for whites. So when my girlfriend Barbara asked if I would come with her to work for the summer at a restaurant in New York, where the salary was thirty-five dollars a week plus room and board, I said that sounded good to me.

As soon as school ended, we drove to Riverhead, Long Island, eighty miles from New York. We parked our car in front of a building under a neon sign reading "Riverside Bar and Grill." I was shocked. My mother had always made the bars and grills in Pittsburgh sound like the very gates of hell, and now here I was going through these gates to work and to live. Mother could not ever know this. I explained to the proprietor that I knew nothing about liquor or beer. There was never any alcohol in either my mother's or my father's home. I could name only two whiskeys; Four Roses and Three Feathers, or was it Three Roses and Four Feathers? I was never really sure. Mother used these names when she was castigating someone for using alcohol. She made it sound as if they were drinking the devil's own brew.

The Fitzgeralds, the restaurant's owners, assigned me to work at the fast-food counter. I had never in my life fried a hamburger on a grill, nor had I ever thought of working in such a place. George, the cook, readily recognized that my skills, if I had any, did not lie in fast food. He told me to just serve sodas and keep the dishes washed.

After one week, I was assigned to the bar. I could not imagine how I could fill that tiny shot glass from a full bottle and not spill a drop. I had to learn the names and prices of the drinks and then mix them with speed and accuracy. I was reminded of my eleventh-grade typing class: I never had learned the necessary speed and accuracy. But in a few days I learned this job as if I were going to make it my life's career.

When I was given a short uniform from the rental company's weekly delivery, despite my protests about wanting a longer one, I ripped out the hem and wore it frayed, hanging loose and unironed. No one nor any job was going to make me look like a floozy, a point the Fitzgeralds finally conceded. According to them, I became the fastest barmaid who ever worked at Riverside. They really liked me and I was good for business, that summer and the next.

At the end of my junior year, I looked for employment in Nantucket, Massachusetts, a small island thirty miles off the coast. There were many housekeeping jobs there since most of the regular maids would not go to Nantucket, but for me and plenty of other college kids, it was a last resort; room and board, thirty-five to fifty dollars a week, Thursdays and Sundays off and use of the car after dinner. I hated housekeeping more than any job I could have imagined. Mother had always told us to study hard and finish school so that we wouldn't have to be a domestic as she had been all her life. Yet here I was, a third-year college student and a domestic. If there was any circumstance in my life that clinched my drive to finish college, it was those two summers that I worked in Nantucket.

Mrs. Ashbury, one of my employers, insisted on ringing a bell when she wanted something during dinner. I hated that bell more than anything in my life. I asked her not to use the bell since the dining room with its hardwood floors was situated next to the kitchen and I could almost hear her and her husband chew their food. Surely I would have heard her whisper to summon me. But she continued to use the bell, to remind me that I was the maid, I believe. I surely did not act like her maid. I would not buy a uniform and she refused to buy one also. We did not like each other. She tolerated me because no one would work out in the country where she lived and I stayed because I needed the job.

"You are the first nigra that I ever met that come near my intellectual level," she said to me during one of our conversations. She was a Southerner whose verbal ability made me wonder if she had finished the fifth grade. She was about six or seven years older than my mother, but far beneath my mother's intellect. The fact that my mother spent much of her life working for people who considered her their inferior was more than unjust; for me it was almost unbearable. The only way I withstood those two summers in Nantucket was knowing that they would help get me through college and on to my career.

When I graduated from West Chester in the spring of 1959, I was among 343 graduates certified to teach in five departments:

Elementary Education, Secondary Education, Health and Physical Education, Music Education and Nursing Education. There were twenty-one African-Americans in my class. Fourteen of them—two-thirds—were in Elementary Education. This leads me to believe that my elementary assignment was not coincidental. Minority, female and less academically talented students were encouraged to take the Elementary Education course. This probably is one of the reasons why there are few African-American teachers in the secondary schools today and explains the low caliber of elementary teachers in general.

I had taken the required National Teacher's Examination, and when I applied for a job in Philadelphia's inner-city schools in the fall of 1959, they not only hired me immediately but told me I could name my school.

"Whichever one you select will be fine with me," I told them. "I don't know a thing about Philadelphia."

But I was about to learn.

C H A P T E R
3

WHEN I ARRIVED AT THE MORTON MCMICHAEL ELEMEN-
tary school in 1959, it was soon to become the largest
elementary school on the East Coast, with an enrollment
of 2,300 students. It was located in the section of Philadelphia
called Mantua, about ten blocks west of Strawberry Mansion on
the other side of the Schuylkill River. The two neighborhoods
shared the same background, but desperation was not yet in the
eyes of the families living there. These were families of the 1950s,
very different from the families of the subsequent decades. Their
homes had not yet been subjected to twenty years and more of
neglect. Their streets had not yet become war zones. Civil unrest,
gang combat and drug violence were still in the future. These
families' struggle was to improve their station in life, not merely
to survive.

I began my teaching career that fall in a fifth-grade classroom
filled with forty-two stationary wrought-iron-and-wood desks. I
carried a folder for each student, with five years of accumulative
records showing the rate of progress, the number and names of all

schools attended, yearly attendance and past behavior and subject grades for each year. The reading consultant advised me to look at the records and get to know my class. I thought to myself, "I'll get to know my class by interviewing them, their parents and the teachers from the previous years. I will really get to know these little children who will be depending on me to help them learn the curriculum of the fifth grade. I will not disappoint them."

I decorated the room and sat behind my desk thinking back to the basement classroom I had created eleven years before. Daddy had been right. We had made it fun and kids did come every day. I would follow his advice with this, my first real class.

Two days later, the children lined up in the yard, anxiously waiting to meet their new teacher and to end a summer of "nothing to do," as they said later. I was even more eager to meet them and to end my own long summer of waiting.

I allowed the children to select their own seats—an extra desk was brought in to accommodate the forty-third child assigned to my class—and then told them about my family's farm and our thirty-seven cows. Once a cow was assigned a place in the barn, no matter how many cows were in the barn, each cow went each day to her own place. "I'm sure that each of you is brighter than any one of my father's cows," I told them, "so I won't have to remind you to always take the same seat, will I?"

"Nooooo, Miss Berger," they replied in the classic elementary school singsong manner.

I loved those children and they loved me. I was going to teach and they were going to learn. I was going to show them I loved what I was doing and I loved them. There would be trust in my classroom, and respect. We were in this together, I told them. My goals were their goals. My rewards were theirs. My successes and my failures were inseparable from theirs.

Defining our mutual needs endeared us to one another. I have heard teachers say to a misbehaving class, "I have mine, and you have yours to get," or "I get paid on Friday whether you learn or not," or "It's your time you're wasting." These are attitudes that do not belong in a classroom. They demonstrate low expectation, a lack of clear mission and the absence of commitment.

I explained to my class, "You do the best that you can and I will grade you according to your progress. I am going to teach the best that I can and Mr. Davidoff is going to grade me according to your progress. Can I depend on you?"

"Yesssssss, Miss Berger."

The children were so good that Philip Davidoff, the principal, began to watch us closely. He couldn't understand why my class was so responsive and well behaved. "Why are those children so quiet in the halls, in lines and in your classroom?" he asked. "Do you threaten them?"

"No, Mr. Davidoff, they just *like* me," I told him.

When my students' scores on an early standardized test—the Philadelphia Map Skills test—were higher than the rest of the school's, Mr. Davidoff was back with more questions. He wondered if I had coached them during the test. So he tested them himself. They did even better.

"How did you do this?" he asked.

I explained my method, a game I had devised to motivate the children toward a true sense of geography. I had drawn an outline map of the United States on the chalkboard, and each day we drew in the states, rivers, lakes or borders that we were studying. On Friday afternoons we erased the chalk, divided into teams and had a contest that required placing the items back on the outline map.

It was a simple setup, based on the principles of competition and fun. Children love competition, as long as they each have a chance to share in success. One point I always made clear in my classroom was that there were no losers. One team might have scored more than another in our Friday-afternoon game, but *everyone* was a winner when it was time to take the standardized test. We were all on the same team then.

Beyond behavior and performance, another priority with

that first class of mine, and with all the classes that followed, was attendance. I couldn't do a thing with the children if they weren't there. If a child was absent, I didn't just mark it in my book and go on about my business, because this was *our* business. I wanted to know *why* he or she had not come to school that day. When children returned after an absence, I grilled them sternly, checking to see if they had a legitimate excuse. My standards were strict and specific. A temperature over 101, a communicable disease, a funeral among friends or family—these were legitimate reasons for a child to miss school.

If the reason was questionable, or if the child did not have a reason, I didn't leave it at that. Even if the child *had* a good reason, I would find a way to visit his or her home. If there had been a funeral, for example, I would come by to offer my condolences—and to urge the parents to have the child in bed by the normal hour that night and to send him or her to school the next day. For some families, the grieving process went on for several days, out of respect for the dead. But children, I told them, do not need to be around so much sorrow. They should observe the ritual, and then return to school.

The point of getting out into the neighborhood was to connect with the families, to see them in their own environment, to understand better what the lives of my children were like beyond the classroom. I wanted the families to get to know me, to see me as a human being truly involved in their children's lives, and not just a figure behind a desk in a classroom. I needed the families' involvement and trust just as much as I needed the children's.

Going out to my students' homes that first year opened my eyes like nothing I had ever seen before. There were not too many teachers who went out into the neighborhood as I did, and what I saw gave me my own education of sorts. I had grown up poor, but I had not seen what *city* poor was before this.

I walked into homes with no glass in the windows, with fabric tacked over the frames to hold back the wind. Some homes had only boxes and blankets for furniture. One home had no floor

—just dirt. Many of the homes had no heat or water. Some had little or no food.

I needed to see these things, to truly understand the circumstances that affected and shaped my children, physically, emotionally and behaviorally. I did what I could to improve the conditions for some of them. At school, I inspected my children in the morning and helped them look their best if I could. Small things like combing hair and cleaning ears can make a world of difference in how a child looks and feels about himself.

As for the problems these families had at home, I did what I could there as well. I learned from my brother-in-law, who worked in real estate, what a landlord's legal responsibilities were. I could see that many of the apartments I visited did not meet inspection standards. I learned that many landlords bribed city inspectors to ignore building code violations and to issue licenses illegally.

I obtained brochures from the city and reviewed them thoroughly with the children, telling them what landlords are required to supply to tenants. The children, ten to thirteen years old, were old enough to encourage their parents to complain.

The first report card conference night I had twenty-seven parents in attendance—far above average. Again, Mr. Davidoff was at my classroom door.

"What's going on here?" he asked. Then he asked for my grade book, expecting to see half my students failing. Generally, parents only came to these conferences when their children were failing. When Mr. Davidoff saw the good grades filling my book, he was at a loss.

"They like me, Mr. Davidoff," I said again. "They *want* their parents to know me."

I had already met many of the parents during my visits to their homes. Others had come to see the teacher they had heard so much about from their children. Early on, they all let me know how I had become a part of not only their children's lives but their own.

"Dinner," one parent told me the year after I had had her child in my class, "has not been the same for us since my son left your room."

OF COURSE, EVERY CHILD DOES NOT FALL IN LOVE WITH HIS teacher. Some wind up in direct competition. Boys and girls who are accustomed to being leaders among their peers sometimes find it hard to give up their position of authority, even to a teacher —*especially* to a teacher. Eddie was such a boy.

Eddie was one of my fifth-graders that first year. He was an angry, tough little boy. He did not wear poverty well. It was deprivation that made him resentful and disillusioned. He had a reputation as the toughest guy among his peers and was eager to protect it. When I arrived, it was clear we were headed for a showdown. I needed to build a reputation of my own. I needed to be the undisputed head of my class.

Eddie's turf was physical. He was constantly picking fights with other children, and he never lost. At first I simply chastised him for hurting the other children. He only clenched his teeth and fists and glared at me in anger.

When he continued to fight, it became clear I had to do more than talk to Eddie. I did not want to have him suspended. His records showed that he had been suspended many times the previous year, indicating that suspension did not work with him. All Eddie understood were challenges, so one morning, after I pulled him off a boy he was pummeling on the playground, I said, "Eddie, you must *stop* hurting other children."

As always, he just glared. Then I said something more.

"If you hit another child," I told him, "I will hit *you*."

He did.

I did.

I hit him on the arm. Not with anger, but with firmness. Not hard enough to hurt him, but hard enough to show him I was serious.

Eddie cried. The next morning he was not in the line on the

yard. I moved through the early minutes of that day mechanically, waiting for Eddie to arrive—without his parents and the principal, I prayed.

My prayers were heard. Eddie entered the room alone a few minutes late, put his coat in the coatroom, went to his seat and began the day as usual. No mention was ever made of the incident. Eddie's behavior markedly changed. He didn't turn into an angel, but from that point on Eddie was a much better-behaved boy than he had ever been before.

Later in my career, I encountered a similar situation with Tammy, a ten-year-old girl, who was much more subtle and cunning than Eddie. Maturity helped me realize that student leadership must be encouraged and directed so that it presents no threat to the authority of the person in charge. I used that wisdom with Tammy.

I made her my helper. I assigned her the responsibility of passing out the paper for assignments and checking to see if students had their homework while I checked the roll and took care of routine morning duties. When I finished, I would say, "Tammy, how many rows can you report a hundred percent homework finished?" She encouraged the children to do their homework so that I would be satisfied with her reports to me. Often, mimicking one of my pet phrases, she would say to a child whose homework was not finished, "Who died in your house last night?"

After three weeks of school, Tammy's mother came onto the yard on her way to work. She said, "I came to see who this teacher was who kept Tammy in her room three weeks without sending for me. This is the longest that Tammy has ever been in any classroom without someone calling me to come."

Tammy stood there wide-eyed, proudly waiting for my answer. She knew that I liked her and that the report would be good.

There is no manual that can show a teacher how to deal with a power struggle with a student. Some children can be coaxed into cooperation, others respond to threats. Some can be soothed, others must be confronted. Each situation is different, but the imperative remains the same: There can be only one person in charge of the classroom, and that is the teacher.

SOMETHING ELSE I DID TO FORGE A BOND WITH MY STUDENTS during my early years of teaching was to meet them outside of school—on Saturday afternoons at the park and sometimes on weekday evenings when I would bring three or four of them home with me.

Beginning with my first year, I often joined anywhere from eight to a dozen of my students on Saturday mornings at a park near the school. I was young, I had strong legs and I would race with them.

"Come on, Miss Berger," they'd chant, "see if you can beat us."

I would. I'd beat them all, and they loved it. Even Eddie, who until then had been the champ with his feet as well as his fists, was left in my dust. He respected that. Some of the kids came and went, but Eddie was there every Saturday, first in line to meet me when I got to the park.

I'd buy Popsicles, and we'd break them in half and pass them all around. Spending days together like that helped me establish a bond with the children, a basis to build on in the classroom. This was my pleasure as well. I loved the kids. I loved being around them. I still had some of that child in myself, and that's something I think has helped me throughout my years as both a teacher and an administrator—I have always kept a part of that child within me. It's in there now, and it's something kids can always connect to.

The students I brought home with me connected to it. I got married in 1961 to Lewis Smith, the brother of one of the teachers, and that's when I began bringing some of the children home with me. Lewis was gone during the week, working for the federal government in Baltimore. We only had weekends together, so I used my weekday afternoons and evenings to play with the kids.

Almost every day I would bring to my house as many kids as my car could carry.

We would play together, and sometimes they'd help me clean. We would do the wash, or some ironing, or maybe scrub the floors. I'd pay each of them a dollar, and then I'd fix dinner for all of us. The menu was generally simple—fried chicken, mashed potatoes, green beans—but it was tasty, it was filling and it was fun. Once we were all seated around the table, I'd ask the children, "Now tell me, if you went to a restaurant and you had this meal, how much do you think it would cost?"

"Two dollars," one of them would say.

"Three!" another would answer.

"Four!" someone else would shout.

"Well," I would tell them, "if you went to a restaurant and they said you could have this dinner for a dollar, would you be satisfied?"

"There's no way you could get this dinner for a dollar, Mrs. Smith."

"Oh yes, there is," I would say. Then I would ask for my dollar back from each of them, to "pay" for the cost of the food.

"Mrs. Smith, that's not fair."

But they were grinning when they gave up those dollars. We would play the same game the next time they came back. And they always came back.

I LEARNED AS MANY LESSONS DURING MY FIRST YEAR AT McMichael as my students. My eyes were opened in many ways, mostly in terms of understanding the conditions and circumstances of my students' home lives. The more I learned, the more I realized how essential it was to get the parents involved in their children's experience at school. I became even more convinced of the importance of parental involvement after I saw what happened to a little boy named Conrad.

There were only two children identified as white at McMichael. One was a quiet little boy named Francis, who lived in a group home supported by the Department of Human Services. The other was Conrad, who was the antithesis of Francis. Conrad strutted about the building wearing an arrogance that should never adorn a child. Behavior that would earn his classmates instant punishment went virtually ignored when Conrad was the culprit. The administrative assistant did not chastise Conrad when he was sent to him for disciplinary action.

Every large school with a predominantly African-American population had an African-American disciplinarian—"black buffers," I called them. Businesses have them also. They are there to deal with minority problems. "They can relate better to their own," has always been the explanation.

The administrative assistant at McMichael aspired to be principal and wasn't taking any chances fooling with a white student or his mother, so he just ignored Conrad's transgressions or tried to gently coax him into better behavior. Minority children, on the other hand, were suspended or punished in some way. If an African-American parent complained about suspension or treatment of a child, the assistant felt sure that they could be appeased, pleased, outtalked or placated in some way at the school level. He had no such confidence with a white parent.

This dual standard regarding the treatment of Conrad came to an abrupt end when Conrad acted up one day and disregarded the direction of the principal. Mr. Davidoff, who was white, was not intimidated by the threat of a confrontation with a white parent. He suspended Conrad. Everyone was delighted that somebody was finally willing to discipline this eleven-year-old boy who had been allowed to act in such an obnoxious fashion.

The shock came two days later, when Conrad returned to school from the suspension. The administrative assistant, knowing that it was the policy that a child returning from suspension had to be accompanied by his parent, referred Conrad and his escort, a black woman, to the principal's office. Mr. Davidoff was irate that Conrad dared to return from a suspension without his mother.

"Conrad will not be reinstated without his parent," he said, in his most authoritative voice. "I will only discuss Conrad's behavior with his mother."

"I *am* his mother," said the woman. "You got some kind of a problem with that?"

Mr. Davidoff nearly fell out of his chair.

"No," he said, trying to compose himself.

The word swept through the school like wildfire.

"Did you hear about Conrad?"

"Yes! His mother is as black as coal!"

"The buffer must feel like a fool," I said to my girlfriend. "There he's been all this time, taking all that foolishness from Conrad when he could have suspended him at the drop of a hat like he does the others who get on his nerves." I laughed and laughed.

The attitudes around that school toward Conrad changed drastically and immediately. There was no more special treatment for that little boy. Neither Conrad nor the children knew what caused the change, but the entire staff and I did: "It was old man prejudice poking up his ugly head again in the life of another child."

Whenever an African-American or other minority parent complained at the district office level, the problem was most often remanded to the school. Whites, however, were always granted an audience downtown. The perception was that white parents knew how to access the system and pose a threat but the minority parents did not.

This scenario is not peculiar to McMichael or Philadelphia. There are more minority children retained in grades, suspended, expelled, denied admission to special programs, hit and otherwise mistreated in schools than their white counterparts. That is the way it was in 1959 in Philadelphia and that is still the way it is today. Informed parental involvement in school is the answer to correcting these ills.

All parents need equal access to school policy, information and avenues to address their concerns. If they are not given that access, they must *get* it, by informing and involving themselves in the affairs of their children and their school—*their* school.

DURING MY EARLY YEARS AT MCMICHAEL, ONE OF MY pleasures, and the source of much of my early knowledge, was the lunch period I shared with my colleagues. School started at 8:45, with lunch from noon to 1:15. That hour and fifteen minutes was an invigorating and extremely fruitful break in the middle of the day, for students and teachers alike.

The school virtually shut down during that period. All the children went home. As for the teachers, it took most of us perhaps fifteen minutes, at most a half hour, to eat our lunch. That left an hour to simply sit and talk with one another—to talk about the children, about our classes, about *teaching*.

There are so many ways teachers learn how to teach. They are taught formally, in colleges and universities. They are taught through books, through the literature which all professionals must stay abreast of to keep current in their fields. They teach themselves, through constantly keeping their minds, as well as their eyes, ears and hearts wide open to all that is happening around them.

And they teach one another, which has become increasingly difficult with the limited time teachers have to interact and share their experiences.

Every day at McMichael was an informal in-service session, with teachers discussing in detail their textbooks (which ones seemed to work and which didn't), their students (which kids seemed to respond to which methods) and their knowledge of the children's lives outside the school (which families might be having particular problems). Every day we had teachers telling one another about a lesson that worked particularly well that morning —or one that *didn't*. We had old teachers talking to young teachers, sharing information and borrowing ideas.

This was something natural. It was not on anyone's daily schedule. It just happened organically, and it worked. But like so many other practices, it was swept up and swallowed in the swirl of the 1960s. Of the many changes that affected education during that decade, one was the federal lunch program, which brought food into the schools. It was a noble program, a *needed* program. But it had its side effects.

The most glaring was that it erased this enriching midday break. The children were now eating in the school, and no child takes an hour and fifteen minutes to eat lunch. Naturally the schools began shortening the lunch period, until they finally cut it to the half-hour lunch we still have today.

That was fine for the children, but it effectively killed much of the communication among the teachers. That ripe, fertile break in the middle of the day was lost, and so was the rejuvenation we all had felt. Besides being a time for sharing, that seventy-five-minute break was a time to refuel, to gather energy the way athletes do at halftime during basketball or football games. With no break, we had teachers running to get their lunch, rushing to eat it, then running to get their children back to class for the afternoon, where the same kind of output was expected as in the morning.

In many cases the energy was simply no longer there. The result was that many teachers prioritized their days, spending their mornings teaching their most essential lessons, usually reading and math, and their afternoons winding down with less rigorous activities, such as art and even games. When that happens, everyone loses—teacher and student alike.

Where is the consistency in the thinking that says we need a two-month break in the year but not a one-hour break in the middle of the day?

The midday break of yesteryear needs to be returned to both the teachers and the students in our schools.

SCHOOLS NEED TO BE RESTRUCTURED AS WELL SO THAT CHILdren and teachers become our primary sources of discovering what methods work best. A question that should be asked of students is: "Under what conditions did you learn most and best?" Successful teachers should be asked the same question as they relate to teaching.

Students can tell us so much if we are willing to listen to them. When an optometrist is diagnosing a sight problem, he asks the patient, "At what distance do you see best? Can you see at night?" We must be willing to work with children and their teachers to answer our own questions.

Some of my best strategies and practices came at the suggestion and direction of children. I learned from the students. One morning Rebecca, a seventh-grader, snatched her paper from her desk as I approached. She held it in the air so that I could not make any notations on it with my red pencil.

"Just tell me where there is something wrong and I will change it," she said. "I don't want any red marks on my paper. Why do teachers use red pencils anyway?"

Later I thought, "Often the only marks on a child's paper are the red corrections or X's noting something incorrect."

I began to put C's on examples that were correctly done. Then I switched to blue pencils, and I never ordered red pencils again.

AS A STUDENT AT WEST CHESTER STATE, I COMPLAINED along with fellow students that there were too many methods courses on how to teach: science in the elementary grades, reading in the elementary grades, and social studies . . . , art . . . , music . . . , physical education . . . , arithmetic . . . Unfortunately, the college listened to us. Today, I am sorry that they did. A teacher needs to learn how to teach each elementary discipline, and each one is different from the others. Just because I know how to change a tire doesn't mean I know how to bake a cake. How to teach the short-*a* sound has nothing to do with how to regroup or borrow in a subtraction lesson or how to demonstrate in a science experiment that air occupies space.

Today's inner-city teachers not only need to come into the

community with knowledge and understanding about the culture, they need to come with many strategies for teaching and holding the attention of children who grew up watching professional entertainers perform on television. Teachers need to recognize early that most of their lectures cannot compare with TV entertainment with its special sound effects and backdrops.

Teachers must turn their classrooms into productions, of a sort, with everyone—students and the teacher alike—involved in the performance. The children should be approached as performers, with the teachers acting as directors of the activities, much like the directors on a TV set. They need to describe to the children the goals of a lesson and then set about reaching that end in a creative, entertaining, *involving* way. The classroom or set decoration needs to be that of the children. Planning must allow for the children to be the stars and the supporting cast. It is a necessary and very difficult task of the teacher to make sure that each child gets his turn in the major as well as the supporting roles.

School boards must be more discerning in their selection of teachers and principals. Often more time is taken to cast a person to be a game show contestant than we use to cast a teacher or principal for an educational position.

IF EDUCATORS WERE ASKED TO IDENTIFY THE GREATEST PROBlem facing schools today, discipline would probably be ranked number one, number two and number three. Their complaints are heard so often today:

"The behavior of the children today is deplorable."

"They have no respect."

"They don't come to school to learn."

"They don't try to follow directions."

My response is yet another question: What happened to so drastically change schools that many educators fault children rather than our own inability to deliver quality education?

Judging from what happened to the Philadelphia School District, it appears that many of the problems in education today began in the 1960s. Much of what happened here at that time occurred in schools across the country in varying degrees. Few major cities escaped being over-"ized" during this period. Education was unionized by employees seeking job protection; politicized and criticized by candidates seeking a platform that would be popular; wrongly utilized by temporary employment seekers; polarized by issues such as curriculum, integration or desegregation; centralized or decentralized as fashion dictated . . . and the list goes on. In the end, education was victimized.

Monumental changes began in education in Philadelphia in the sixties, and essentially the same changes occurred in every major city in the country. A dizzying assortment of lines were drawn on the education battlefield, beginning toward the middle of the decade, when the city hired a new school superintendent named Mark Shedd. He came from a rural school district in New Jersey, where his program and philosophies had been implemented successfully. But his ideas, policies, and procedures were not acceptable to the big-city power brokers in Philadelphia. An example was the situation of substitute teachers in our system.

Our schools had come to depend on capable, well-trained substitute teachers who had assumed full-time teaching positions but had not passed the required National Teacher's Examination, a qualification to be a regularly appointed, full-time teacher in the city of Philadelphia. The school system saved money by using these substitutes, to whom no benefits had to be provided. This was one way for the school system to help balance its budget. I've seen a recent rise in the number of substitutes used in the city of Philadelphia, and I wonder if the same reasons might not be behind it. I also wonder if the school board is aware that this might be the case.

There were approximately 2,000 substitute teachers in our system in the early 1960s, and the vast majority of them were African-American. When Shedd took the superintendent's job, one of the first issues he faced was the demands of African-American leaders who were adamant about having teachers in our schools with the same qualifications and certification as those in the largely white suburban schools.

Shedd responded to those demands by dismissing almost all 2,000 of the city's long-term African-American substitutes. To fill these positions, he organized a massive recruitment effort. He imported and hired young teachers from across the country who met the entrance requirements. Most of these new teachers were white and had little experience with inner-city children. Soon the children began to get out of hand. Since these newcomers had displaced the friends of the regularly appointed African-American teachers, many of the veteran teachers just stood back and let their new colleagues fail in order to prove that they should not have been there in the first place.

With these recruits came men who could escape being drafted into the Vietnam War if they were schoolteachers. Many of these newly appointed teachers did not have one day's teaching experience and sometimes hadn't taken one course in education. They came at a time when many in the civil rights movement were saying to our children that whites were not to be held in high esteem or trusted. These were the days of the inner-city riots. The children showed little respect for these new teachers and no respect for their authority. The Stokely Carmichaels, Rap Browns and Malcolm X's of the world were seriously questioning and denouncing the motivations and actions of white society.

The children and their parents literally dared these newcomers to the community to say a cross word to them. I helped some of these new teachers; but I, too, became vexed when they complained about the children or blamed them for their ineptness.

I remember stepping out of my classroom one afternoon because the commotion next door had become just too much. The teacher in charge of that class was a young man who had gotten a teacher's deferment to avoid Vietnam. The class on the other side of me had another young man who had done the same thing. He wasn't even *trying* to be a good teacher. He was simply surviving, simply hiding out until the war was over.

But the first man was truly trying. He wasn't getting anywhere, but he was trying. So this particular day I walked over and
he came to his door, almost frantic, desperate to control his kids.

"I want *respect!*" he said to me. "They don't give me *respect!*
What the hell am I supposed to do?"

"Just go back in your classroom and *teach*," I told him. "They
don't have any guns in there. In Vietnam they've got guns. Isn't
that what you came here for, to dodge those guns? Well, you're
here. You got what you wanted. So stop complaining, go back in
there and deal with what you've got."

It was a mean thing to say, but that was how I felt. It simply
broke my heart to see our school, which had been so efficient and
so effective only a few years before, coming apart before my very
eyes.

It continued to come apart as more pressures pushed in from
other places. The teachers' union, for example, was organized at
this same time, during the mid-sixties. Salaries escalated fast, encouraging some of these draft dodgers to stay around. They found
that they could pass the test for administration, and many became
principals. Now we had principals as well as teachers who were
not professional educators. Many of them had as few as thirty
credits in education and no methods courses. They did not know
how to teach.

The strength of the newly organized teachers' union empow-
ered and protected both good and unsatisfactory teachers alike.
The union hired organizers who presented themselves as strong
union men and women. They went about literally pushing administrators around, threatening the new superintendent and his staff
with various petitions and threats of strikes.

Shedd, the "new man on the block," did not want to start his
tenure with a teacher walkout, so he gave in to most of the demands, and the union quickly acquired a great deal of clout, strik-
ing fear into the heart of almost every principal in the city. The
principals became unwilling to challenge the teachers' union, lest
they fall into the bad graces of the new superintendent.

The principals themselves underwent radical restructuring

as the new superintendent, recognizing that an overwhelming majority of principals in the city were white Jewish men, exercised his right to hire 5 percent of the school administrators without going through personnel testing. He began using this "5 percent" clause to promote African-Americans to the position of principal.

The principals themselves, both white and African-American, began to take the course of least resistance with the unions, making school-level deals with the union representatives and giving in where they could in order to avoid confrontation. Principals began to collude with the union to get repairs done in their buildings by having the building or district union representatives plead their cases with the school district. This avenue of help, while serving an immediate need, lessened the stature of principals in the perception of teachers, parents and students.

At the same time all this was happening, federal programs were increased in the school district, mandating many components and activities, including parental involvement. Parental membership on committees, task forces and boards was an unconditional requirement. Many parents began to flex muscles they didn't know they had. They sat on boards with the district superintendent and other school district officials along with occasional union representatives and school board members. They began to make demands on principals. They took their demands and complaints to fellow committee and board members at the district offices and the administration building.

Suddenly, the district offices, which had always remanded the problems of minorities, were now granting them an audience. All too often, in an effort to appease the parents, the district offices did not support the principals. This caused many principals to assume the "turtle syndrome"—they shut themselves in their offices and hid.

Changes bring controversy. Controversy creates enemies. By the late sixties, Mark Shedd had made enough enemies so that Frank Rizzo, a campaigning mayoral candidate, made firing Shedd a plank in his platform. The teachers' union also supported Shedd's removal. Rizzo was elected and he appointed a new school board, along with a new superintendent, and Mark Shedd became history.

But much damage had already been done. During all this time, the teachers who simply kept their classes quiet and brought no attention to their classrooms were often the most rewarded. Many did not teach at all. They gave their students busywork: duplicated work sheets and directives; spelling word lists to be written ten times; rote memorization to be copied endlessly from the chalkboard. They showed movies and film strips. When children were not quiet they would be ordered to write: "I must do my work and follow directions" hundreds of times. This was all too common.

I watched a fellow teacher who was not even sure of his students' names. He would read the roll from a blank mark book and grade each child according to his or her appearance and manner.

No one was watching the teaching process. Only the test scores and report card grades were monitored. District superintendents, principals and teachers began to make sure that test scores looked good, doing whatever it took to push those numbers up, no matter how meaningless they might be. I found out just how meaningless they were when I eventually became a principal myself.

But in the late 1960s, I was not yet dreaming of becoming a principal. I was still totally involved in teaching. I was heartbroken to see what was happening around me, although it all made perfect sense. The cascade of events and changes had created a perfect recipe for chaos. Buildings were full of African-American children being told to hate the white man. Classes were headed by white teachers, many of whom were hiding from the war and many of whom had never before seen a black child in their lives. Principals were backpedaling from the newly unionized teachers. Teachers were flexing their newfound muscles and pushing demands on the principals, as were parents and students, who had found new muscles of their own.

There were good intentions behind almost all the changes

happening at that time. I could see the value in each of them. *I wanted to see the best possible teachers in the classrooms. I wanted to see more African-American administrators. I wanted* teachers to have their rights, to be able to demand fair and supportive treatment. *I* believe children have their rights as well. I *believe* the African-American community—parents and other residents—are not obliged to just sit back and take what's given to them, that we need to push and show our strength when fairness and decency are not forthcoming. *Anyone,* of any race or gender or age, must do the same.

But the piling up of all these issues, everything happening at once, was too much for the system to take. Too much energy and emotion was unleashed in too many directions. I think that's what the 1960s was all about for society in general.

I know that is what it was about for the schools in Philadelphia.

CHAPTER

4

 BY THE END OF THE 1960S, MY CAREER WAS BEGINNING to shift from teaching toward administration. I had come to understand how fundamentally important the principal's role is in determining the quality of education and services a school delivers to its students and to its community.

There are many forces that determine how well a particular school fulfills its educational and social responsibilities. The capabilities and morale of its staff is one. The involvement of its parents and community is another. The support of district, city and state officials is vital. Yet no single factor is more important than the principal. The success of any school depends on teamwork among its teachers, students and parents, but the person who must bring that team together, give it direction, guide it and constantly keep it fueled with energy and incentive, is the principal.

I understood that by the end of the 1960s, but before I made my move toward becoming a principal, I had some lessons to learn about the politics of education—lessons that would serve me well when I eventually moved from teaching to administration. I was taught some of those lessons during my time in the teachers' union.

I joined the Philadelphia Federation of Teachers in 1965 because I saw a need for teachers to have strength at the bargaining table. Teachers needed a contract that spelled out clearly our rights and responsibilities. We needed strength to see to it that those rights were enforced. The school district needed the strength to see to it that we carried out our responsibility as well.

I felt that unions would improve teaching conditions, raise salaries, secure equal job opportunity for all teachers and thereby improve education. I was committed to that cause, but acting on that commitment was not as clear-cut as it might have seemed. When the city's teachers went on strike in 1970, black teachers who supported the strike were accused of supporting the "white" union against African-American children, who comprised more than 65 percent of the public schools' students. I had just joined the Heston Elementary School staff and encouraged the teachers there to support the strike. I was able to convince my colleagues to stay out of the school, but I could not persuade them to picket. When I arrived at Heston at seven o'clock on the first morning of the strike, with my placard hanging around my neck, I was alone.

It was not long before I was harassed. At nine that morning, I was approached by two very vocal African-American community activists.

"You ought to be ashamed of yourself, depriving little black children of an education," they said to me. "There you are, joining that white union to put your foot on the necks of your own kind. You are a disgrace to your race."

I tried explaining that we had attempted to settle our dispute at the bargaining table, that the board's refusal to discuss our contract in good faith had forced us to strike. But this pair would have none of it.

"Bargain in good faith?" one of them answered. "Good faith is not the problem. The union is not interested in education. Their interest is money, and you are just another white folks' nigger.

"You want to get paid for preparation time?" he added. "Prepare at home like all the teachers before you did."

"What do you do for a living, sir, if I might ask?" I quietly replied.

"I'm a fireman," he answered proudly. There were very few African-American firemen in Philadelphia at that time.

"A fireman," I said. "How many fires did you put out this month?"

He didn't respond.

I turned to the small crowd that had assembled. "I'd say that he gets paid for far more preparation time than we are asking for," I said. "What do you think? He's out here picking on me because I'm all by myself!"

The crowd laughed and urged the man and his friend to leave me alone as they themselves dispersed and left.

The next issue of the American Federation of Teachers publication featured a photograph of me picketing alone that morning in front of the Heston School.

By the end of 1970 I was very involved in the union. That summer I attended the American Federation convention in Pittsburgh, where I heard Al Shanker, the president of the New York chapter, speak of the threats facing public education in America and of the need for teachers to come together and respond to those challenges. I wanted to be part of this new movement. When I came back from that convention and was offered full-time employment as a union staff representative, I accepted.

MY PERSONAL COMMITMENTS NEVER STRAYED FAR FROM THE ideology I brought to my career. My first husband had died in an auto accident, and by the time I became a representative I had married Earl Cartwright, a fellow teacher at the McMichael School. Soon after Earl and I married in 1965, an endless trek of live-ins began with my eldest niece, who was sixteen when she came to live with us. She stayed for a little over six months.

Earl and I wanted to have children but I did not want to stay at home. So we agreed that we would hire a housekeeper to take care of our daughter, Jill, so that she wouldn't have to get up early in the morning to go to a day-care center or a sitter. Luckily we found a very competent housekeeper. She cleaned house and watched the baby. Since I was able to teach Jill to read by age three, we enrolled her early in kindergarten.

Another niece and her twenty-month-old son came to live with us in 1975 while she commuted to Cheyney State University. She stayed three years. In 1979, Tyrone, the rather incorrigible son of another niece, came to stay with us while his young mother of nineteen cared for her other two children. The "little while" was extended to eight years.

My father lived with us from 1972 to 1975.

Karen, a weekend visitor one Fourth of July, stayed until December because her mother went to California and made no other plans for her daughter.

Jill and Earl watched as our boarders came and went. They rarely commented except to keep each other informed as to who was coming and where the last had gone.

I explained to Jill that we were more fortunate than many children in the world and that we must be willing to share our good fortune with others. We had a responsibility, I told her, to make the world a little better. Jill willingly shared Earl's and my attention as well as her toys. The exception was her bed. Whenever the number of children exceeded the capacity of the guest room, Jill pulled out the sleeping bags for them.

Earl and Jill knew what I wanted for the children in the classes and schools where I taught. They began to see how small deeds made such big changes in the lives of children. Helping children grow up happily was a part of me, and they allowed me to be myself.

When I told Earl I was going to be a full-time staff representative for the Philadelphia Federation of Teachers, he was stunned. He couldn't imagine my leaving the classroom. He thought I would never leave working directly with children. But I didn't see the move as leaving the children. I saw it as taking part in the process that determines the resources available for most of society's needs, including its educational needs. That process, of course, is political.

In the summer of 1971 I went to Harrisburg to work for three weeks as a lobbyist for our federation. By the time I left, I had learned a lot about behind-the-scenes legislation—more than I wanted to know. After three short weeks, I understood why education so often was at the bottom of the budgetary pile in Pennsylvania. It would not surprise me if what I saw in the back rooms of the Pennsylvania statehouse was also true in other places around our country.

I saw bribery and corruption. The deal cutting that went on among elected officials shocked me. Back then I was a little more innocent, a little more naive than I am now. This was just before Watergate and its aftermath, before the public distrust and disgust with government began growing to the point where it is today.

Among the wide variety of lobbyists I saw when I arrived in Harrisburg, I met only one other woman and no other minorities. There was no one to direct me or give me advice, no one even to introduce me. I was on my own. The first day I walked into the capitol building, I had to ask someone to show me to the booth where lobbyists sat during the sessions.

I didn't know a soul in that room. My only resource was a capitol directory giving the names, photographs and legislation sponsored by each elected official. I needed more help than that. When I saw a young African-American page being escorted up an aisle and out of the room, I followed him into the hallway.

"What happened?" I asked.

"Aw, I fell asleep. You're not supposed to fall asleep in there."

"I see. So, do you know a lot of these people?"

"I know all of them."

"Whom do you know the best?"

"My uncle."

"Your *uncle?* Who is your uncle?"

"James Barber."

I couldn't have been luckier. James Barber was a state representative from Philadelphia and chairman of the Black Caucus, a very influential man. I asked the page to introduce me to him, and I was on my way.

Representative Barber had not seen an African-American lobbyist for a union before, and he had seen only one woman. He took an interest in me and made a point during that first day to introduce me to other African-American legislators. Soon I learned that every one of them was from either Pittsburgh or Philadelphia—both places where I had lived. This made all of them my "homies," giving us an immediate bond. Among the legislators who became my friends was a state representative from Philadelphia named Earl Vann.

I sat beside Vann my second night in Harrisburg, when I accompanied Barber and some of his colleagues to dinner. Toward the end of the evening, Vann patted his chest pocket and commented to the gentleman next to him that he had left his wallet at home. I quietly eased fifty dollars under the table and into his hand.

He returned the money at lunch the next day. Mr. Vann was a politician in the truest sense of the word. He told me that he had never worked at anything in his life except politics, and he proceeded to teach me the inner workings of the legislature in Harrisburg.

As we were walking down a corridor in the capitol building one afternoon, another representative stopped Vann and said, "We need you on the floor this afternoon. The vote on HB 27 is 'Yes.' "

"How much?" said Vann. That's all he said: "How much?"

"Two-fifty."

"You haven't said anything yet," said Vann, smiling his true politician's smile. "You haven't said nothing."

"Three," answered the man.

"I'll get back to you," said Vann, and we moved on.

"Madeline," he told me as we walked down the hall, "when

I first came here, they were giving me fifty dollars for my vote, until I found out some of them were getting thousands to deliver the Philadelphia vote. I make them pay up now.

"Sometimes," he said, laughing, "I make them make payments on that back money as well, the money they kept when I didn't know any better."

I was shocked and outraged. This was the cold truth hitting me in the face. They were selling votes. Their votes were up for sale to the highest bidder, and I realized our union didn't have the money to compete with all the other lobbyists bidding for their own interests there in the capitol.

It became clear to me exactly why education suffered and continues to suffer as monies are appropriated across the country. We didn't have the means to buy our way in. We didn't have the savvy or the clout that counted. We didn't have cash.

Who is putting up the money for legislation for our children today, for quality education?

Who can sponsor legislation that links salaries to accountability and still be in their legislative seat for the next elected term?

Who is putting up the money for the "choice in education" legislation?

Who stands to gain? Children? *Which* children? *Some* children? Urban children? Suburban children?

Are there lurking out there somewhere big businessmen who want to make education big business? Who will be their clients? Will they look at the achievement of children or will their bottom line be how much profit they can make? Will their questions be: "What is the best book?" and "What are the best materials?" Or will they simply ask, "What is most cost-efficient?"

Will the school year be shortened on the basis of the question of cost? Are school codes already being changed to meet the needs of a cost-efficient business rather than the needs of students and teachers?

Who will fight for the education tax dollar and who will determine how it is spent?

And who will recognize that the losers in this fight, the casualties in this ongoing war, are the children?

These are questions I was forced to face during my term in Harrisburg. I couldn't answer them, but I could see where I now belonged on the battlefield of education. I understood that the place where I could most truly make a difference in education was not deep behind the lines, there in Harrisburg, but back at the front, in the schools.

Only this time I wasn't content to stay in a single classroom. I was ready to learn how to make myself into an effective principal.

I HAVE SEEN TOO MANY TEACHERS LEAVE THE CLASSROOM and go into administration for the wrong reasons. Many of them are careerists, simply looking to climb the ladder from teacher to principal, then from principal to a job with the district office downtown. Their incentives are more money and more prestige.

Others want to avoid the headaches that come with dealing directly with children in the classroom. I have seen plenty of teachers become principals to get *away* from the children. During my time with the union, I went into schools all over the city, and I saw many principals whose method of operation was basically to hide out in their office while a teacher or an administrative assistant ran the school.

When I came back from Harrisburg, I talked to Dick Hanusey, my district superintendent, about the situation I saw with the principals in some of our schools. Dick and I had butted heads many times in the past, as I represented the union while he represented the administration. We had been on opposite sides of the table, but we respected and liked each other.

"Dick," I said, "the problem with these schools is the principals. There are just too many incompetent or unmotivated principals out there."

"Well, Madeline," he said, "if you feel that way, why don't *you* be a principal and run things your way."

"I think I could," I said.

"Then do it, Madeline," he said. "I really think you ought to do it. The schools could *use* a Madeline Cartwright on the right side of the table."

I couldn't stop thinking about it. I called Ed Simpkins, who was the chief negotiator for the school district of Philadelphia. He had been the chief negotiator for the Detroit Federation of Teachers before moving to the other side of the table. We met, and I told Ed I was considering switching sides, so to speak.

"*You* did it, Ed," I said. "How did you do it?"

"Yes, I did it, Madeline," he said. "But what you're talking about doing is totally different from what I did.

"I switched sides," he continued, "but I also switched *cities.* You're talking about switching sides in the same city. That's bold, Madeline. That's as bold as brass."

We talked some more, and I told him how tired I had gotten of the union itself. I relished defending teachers when they were wronged, but I would not support a teacher who deserved the punishment or treatment he or she was getting from the administration. The inner politics of the union itself had begun to wear on me as well. The time had come for me to make a move.

"Well," Ed Simpkins said at the end of our talk, "you've got to do what you've got to do."

I did. In the summer of 1972 I left my position on the union staff, and that fall I went back to teaching, at the Belmont Elementary School. I also went back to school, beginning the graduate work necessary to get a principal's certificate. In the fall of 1977, after being certified and then passing a citywide examination, I began my career as a principal.

That is not to say that I stepped right into my own school. First I went through a baptism of fire in the spring of 1978 as a temporary principal at the Henry H. Houston Elementary School.

This was a school in a relatively affluent area. The parents were *very* involved in their children's school—so involved that they had driven out the principal who had begun that school year, as well as the one sent to replace him. These were people with influence. If they didn't like something, they went straight to the school board, and the school board *listened*. When I went downtown to pick up some paperwork before heading out to Houston, one of the people in the office used the term "hotbed" to describe the situation there.

When I got to the school, I learned what he meant. Before I was into my office, I lost my secretary. I said, "Good morning," and she greeted me back. Then I said, "I am Madeline Cartwright, the new principal." She said, "What?" I repeated myself. She took a second, then she began gathering up her belongings.

"Well," she said, "I certainly won't be staying."

In ten minutes, she was gone.

Word of the school's new principal, its female principal, its *black* female principal, spread quickly. The parents who formed Houston's Home and School Association called a meeting. They invited me to come, and when I showed up it was apparent from the outset that this was closer to a kangaroo court than a meeting.

The meeting was held at the home of one of the parents, with about thirty men and women poised to rake me over the coals. They began by asking me about my background and my credentials. Soon they were asking me about my husband and my family, questions I refused to answer. They then told me they had done some research on me and had some concerns about my work with the union.

"Well," I said, "as you did your research on me, I have done some research of my own on you. I understand that you were dissatisfied with Mr. Fine, the previous principal, and I understand you were dissatisfied with his replacement, Mr. Ionelli.

"I understand that the main problem some of you had with Mr. Ionelli was that you wanted to write his teachers' lesson plans and he would not allow that.

"Reverend Olson," I said, turning to one of the parents, "I understand you demanded to sit in on your child's classroom.

"Mrs. McGregor," I said, turning to another, "I understand

you wanted to take your child in and out of classes as you pleased."

You could feel the shock settling over that room.

"Yes, I have done my research just as you have. And I can assure you that I have come into this school to be the very best principal that I can be, and that I will do all I can to ensure that each of your children receives the best possible education while he or she is at this school."

With that I left. Some of those parents remained adversarial until the end of that school year, but their children loved me. I went to every recess and every lunch. I was in every classroom. I was in the halls during the day and out on the yard when the buses arrived in the morning and when they left in the afternoon. The children had never seen anything like it before. I was theirs.

They pitched in, helping me when I needed it. Some of the children in that school smoked marijuana. They snuck around the building before school, between classes, doing it wherever and whenever they could. One morning a little boy, a first-grader, came to me and said, "Mrs. Cartwright, there's some boys smoking grass in the basement."

"How do you know that?" I asked him.

"Because I could smell it," he said.

"How do you know what marijuana smells like?" I asked him.

This six-year-old boy did not blink an eye.

"I smell it all the time at home," he told me. "My dad smokes grass."

I COMPLETED THAT SCHOOL YEAR AT HOUSTON, THEN SPENT the fall in another temporary position, as principal at the E. Spencer Miller Vocational School, where I had worked as an administrative assistant during the time I was studying to be certified.

Miller was a school for mildly retarded children. There were three hundred students enrolled, ranging in age from fourteen to twenty-one. They were predominantly African-American, and almost all of them were bused from other sections of the city.

The school had been in disarray when I had first been there as an administrative assistant before taking the principal's position at Houston. Students stood outside the front of the building smoking marijuana in broad daylight. Children ran up and down the halls. Some teachers were not even in class. They often could be found down in the lunchroom, having a cup of coffee while their students hung out in their classroom doorways.

There was absolutely no respect in that building: no respect for the principal, no respect for the school. The students had no respect for themselves, so the first thing I did when I stepped in as principal was call an assembly to address that issue.

"Children," I said, "do you know what everyone in the city calls this school? They don't call it E. S. Miller. They call it *Easy* Miller. They have no respect for this school. They have no respect for *you*."

Then I said, "Boys and girls, we must change the impression people have of this school and of you, and we must begin by changing our behavior, by changing what people *see* us doing."

I began not by simply forbidding the children to act in certain ways but by convincing them that their behaviors truly reflected poorly on themselves. In other words, I used the principle of cooperation rather than coercion.

I went into the classrooms to determine exactly what the problems might be there. I did not wait in my office to sort out the signals. I went straight to the sources.

The building maintenance room, where students were trained to clean windows and floors, was a case in point. They had sample windows of every kind in that room, each set up on a small stand for the students to work on. They had floor samples as well, made of concrete, wood, tile. This was a state-of-the-art classroom—the entire building was extremely well equipped. But all I was getting from the teacher in that particular classroom were pink slips—discipline referrals. A steady stream of pink slips was coming out of that classroom. The teacher apparently could not control his kids.

So I went down to the room, I gathered the children together and I said, "What is the problem here?"

One of the boys said, "Mrs. Cartwright, we work on these windows. We work on 'em *hard.*

"And *he,*" the boy said, referring to the teacher, who was out of the room, "he messes them up again as soon as we're finished."

I observed the next class, and indeed the teacher went around at the end of class smearing grease on every one of those sample windows, preparing them for the next class to clean. Meanwhile, the class that had just finished had to watch their efforts of the past hour be completely undone.

I took the instructor aside at the end of that afternoon.

"Mr. Wilson," I said, "there is no point in having these children wash those sample windows when this school is filled with *actual* windows that are filthy. Why don't you take your students out and let them clean *those* windows. Take them out to the front porch and let them clean *that* concrete. Take them down to the cafeteria and let them clean *that* tile."

"But, Mrs. Cartwright, this room is equipped . . ."

"Mr. *Wilson,* please listen to me. I do *not* want you to do anything else in this room. I want you to take your students and their work outside."

The instructor was teaching ninety children each day. When their efforts were turned toward the building itself, that school was spotless within a week. It stayed that way, and we had no more problems with the children in those classes.

I will never forget the pride those kids felt. They would grab me by the hand and pull me with them. "Come see my *windows,* Mrs. Cartwright!" "Come see my *floor!*" "Come see my *kitchen!*"

There was nothing complex about what I had done. It was a simple idea. But it made all the difference in the world to those children. Having a sense of ownership, of connection, of seeing the rewards of their work, of feeling proud about themselves, of understanding and believing that there was something in that school for them—these became the fundamentals of all that I had learned both as a teacher and as a beginning principal.

In the spring of 1979, I was finally set to apply my education to a school of my own.

That is when I was assigned to Blaine.

5

 LIKE THE STRAWBERRY MANSION NEIGHBORHOOD ITSELF, aine Elementary School had its own long history. It too had gone through a century of changes that left it with only its name to link it to its past.

The school was built in 1895, to accommodate the sons and daughters of the Italian, Irish and African-American families flooding into Strawberry Mansion at that time. The building was named after James G. Blaine, a Pennsylvania-born politician who had made a serious run for the United States presidency in 1884. Blaine, a Republican, was actually ahead in that race before his political career was thwarted by the now infamous phrase condemning Democrats as the party of "rum, Romanism and rebellion." Blaine didn't actually utter those words—they were part of a speech by a Protestant clergyman. But Blaine was in the audience that night, and the next day his name was connected to the phrase in newspapers across the country. Outraged Catholics flocked to the Democratic side of the ticket, and as a result, Grover Cleveland won the election in November. Blaine, a beaten man, went on to serve a term as Secretary of State under Benjamin Harrison before dying in 1893, two years before the school named after him was opened.

The shifts that took place in Strawberry Mansion over the next half century were mirrored in the Blaine School. By the 1950s the school's population had become predominantly African-American as white children moved out of the neighborhood with their parents. By the end of that decade, the school's student body was almost entirely African-American and the building was falling apart from age and disrepair, just like the homes around it. In 1959, when the city drew up a list of overcrowded, antiquated public schools targeted to be torn down, Blaine was at the top of the list.

In 1966 the original Blaine building came down and ground was broken for a new school, a $1.6 million facility equipped with thirty-two classrooms to handle about a thousand students. That building, a three-story, L-shaped, brick-and-cinder-block structure on the corner of Thirtieth and Berks streets, opened in the fall of 1967.

Fewer than ten years later, in 1975, that building appeared on a list of twelve Philadelphia public schools scheduled to be closed, this time because of underenrollment. The abandonment of the neighborhood around it was reflected directly in the school. The seven hundred students attending Blaine at that time were not seen as sufficient reason to keep the school open. The plan called for a newly constructed junior high school just three blocks away to siphon off Blaine's seventh and eighth grades, with the rest of Blaine's students sent to other elementary schools.

But this time the building was saved, as the now politically active neighborhood that had worked so hard to have the school built fought to save it. City politicians had begun to recognize the advantage of using schools to influence votes as well as serve as polling places. Although the building was showing wear and tear from neglect and inferior building materials, it was still relatively new. The decision was made to remove it from the list.

This was the building I drove up to on a Monday morning in March 1979.

Beginning a new job at a new school in March was an advantage not available to most principals, teachers and students. Most assignments were in September, when everything is unsettled, too much change occurring at one time.

I was fortunate. The only new face in Blaine that day and many days thereafter was mine. Everything else was in place. If only it could be that way for all new teachers and principals! Thanks to Christine Lindsey and the staff of Blaine, I was greeted with complete order. If new teachers could be brought into the schools during the year, when school is operating, and be assimilated into the structure of an operating class with a daily routine in place, a lot of stress could be eliminated for everybody.

The Boston Symphony Orchestra, with all its talent and skill, would not do well on opening night if 30 percent of the musicians were new, as well as the conductor. This would be unheard of, ridiculous. Yet this is the scenario in the inner-city schools in September.

AS I PARKED ON THE ONE-WAY STREET OUTSIDE THE FRONT doors of Blaine—it seemed that every street in that neighborhood was one-way—a few old fellows sitting by a little pile of tires and hubcaps in front of a small dark structure no bigger than a shack smiled and waved. This was Jack's repair shop. It was not hard to identify, because there was an enormous pile of tires two stories high across the street. That mountain of rubber served as an apartment complex for the breeding of rats, stray cats and dogs.

Down the street, a blue-and-white cinder-block warehouse was the headquarters of one of the largest "chop shops" in the city of Philadelphia, a place where car thieves could bring their stolen automobiles to be broken down and sold for parts. Jack's business was nowhere near as large as the chop shop's, but it was legitimate. Jack and I would become good friends in the coming years—I still call him my "boyfriend" when I see him—and he was always there to keep an eye on the teachers' cars, to see that they didn't get vandalized or end up in a chop shop themselves.

Across the street from where I parked, living in one of the row houses there, were the only souls I already knew in that neighborhood: the family of Kitty Morris, a woman who had helped take care of my house back when I was teaching at E. S. Miller. Kitty's son Laverne, whom everyone called Peewee, was sitting on the front steps as I unpacked my car that morning. He was twenty-one years old, and had been correctly classified TMR —trainable mentally retarded. Peewee worked as a volunteer at a nearby hospital.

"Hi, M' Carwrigh!" he hollered with a big grin. "How you doin'?"

"I'm fine, Peewee. How are you?"

"M' doin' au righ, M' Carwrigh."

" 'I am doing all right,' Peewee," I corrected him. "It's 'I am doing all right.' "

"Me . . ." he began again.

"I, Peewee, I."

"I goin' to work, M' Carwrigh," Peewee enunciated carefully and with pride.

"I am, too, Peewee." I laughed. "I am going to work, too."

FROM THE OUTSIDE, THE BLAINE BUILDING LOOKED SOLID, IF nondescript, its red-brick walls painted a uniform gray and scrawled with graffiti. Trash was strewn across the blacktop playground, from fence to fence, ankle deep in some places. A slight breeze stirred the refuse and rustled the leaves of the trees along the sidewalk behind the school. Out front, where I stood, there were no trees. Just the street and the row houses, Peewee and I.

As I stepped inside the front vestibule, with its attractive marble steps and wall of glass doors, I was greeted by a message spray-painted on the south wall in foot-high letters: "F—— You."

I was not discouraged. As I stood in that entrance hallway, in front of the auditorium, I said to myself, "Here you are with an opportunity to put into operation the years of getting ready to 'principal' this inner-city school, a chance you so much wanted. It's all here, made to order: a population that needs something more, an educational program in place and a building not so old that a facelift would not make a difference. Everything you wanted is here. You believed that a school can make a difference, and now it's up to you to convince others." I remembered the argument I had with a professor in graduate school who said teachers and school personnel don't make a difference. I was ready to make a believer out of him, to show him.

A woman walked up, greeted me and introduced herself as Liz McCain. It could not have been a more propitious introduction. If there was one person I would need to rely on more than anyone else, that would be Liz. She was the school community coordinator, whose job entailed, among other things: visiting homes, attending community meetings, conferring with students and keeping parents aware of school activities. One of her major responsibilities was to keep parents and community informed about federally subsidized programs available to provide materials and services to qualified children.

Liz knew the houses and apartments in the neighborhood better than the mailman. She was just as friendly and as folksy as could be. I know I was beaming that first morning, smiling so hard my lips looked about to split. Just being there took me back to my first year at McMichael in Mantua. McMichael had been a low-income school with much defeat hanging in the air, but it was a place where big gains could be made. I had made great strides as a teacher at McMichael, and I had once asked the principal, Philip Davidoff, why good things weren't going on in all that school's classrooms.

He said, "It's not as simple as that."

I said to myself, "But it *is* as simple as that. It is just as simple as *wanting* to do it."

When I decided to work in school administration, that's what I intended to do, to make a difference in a school given up as hopeless. I wanted to show that it could be done, that the children would learn if my teachers and I let everyone know that we expected children to elevate their minds and that we expected parents to be involved in the process.

Everything I wanted was right there at Blaine. That's what I told Liz McCain that first morning, and she listened. Transforming Blaine was like religion for the both of us, and neither of us was ashamed to show it. I could see right then that she was going to be on board with me.

Another ally was Raymond Brooks. Raymond was forty-four —four years older than I. He had spent his entire teaching career —twenty years—at Blaine. He had taught many of the children's parents and was shop steward for the teachers' union as well. Raymond Brooks was invaluable. He could help both with the community and with teachers who might be resistant to change.

Like Liz, Raymond enthusiastically bought into my philosophy. He welcomed fresh ideas, and he was ready for a principal with whom he could be friendly rather than cold and formal. Raymond would become an important part in my plan for this school, a vital part.

On paper, I knew what the school presented to me: roughly five hundred students, grades kindergarten through sixth, and thirty-two teachers, ranging from veterans with decades of experience to first-year teachers fresh out of college. I had seen and studied records of the students' past performance on the city's standardized tests. The records showed outstanding scores, far above average.

But I knew there was more to this school—more to any school—than just numbers. There is an essence, a mood, a spirit, an attitude among the students and staff in a school that define it and make it distinct from any other school. It can be found in the faces of the children and their teachers as they walk through the halls, it can be heard in the sounds they make as they move about the building, it can be felt in the very air. Anyone who has spent as much time in schools as I have can sense the spirit of a school almost immediately. I got a good sense of Blaine that very first day, and I was puzzled by what I felt.

After I put my things in my office, I walked out front to greet the students as they began arriving. I could see right away that the children were orderly. They made noise, they roughhoused, they did the silly little things all children do, but they were not out of hand. Christine Lindsey, the principal before me, had put a premium on decorum, on order both in the classroom and out. She wanted teachers to teach and students to behave. She wanted classrooms to look like classrooms, teachers to look like teachers and students to look like students ready for school, not for a sports event. She wanted a seriousness about teaching and learning.

There was nothing wrong with that, nothing at all. In fact, I was impressed. But something felt unbalanced about this whole picture. I couldn't put my finger on it at first, but it came to me as I moved throughout the building that day.

There was no *joy* in the air. There was little happiness on the faces of the teachers or the students. This just was not a happy place, and to me, that's vitally important. To me, school should be a happy place, a pretty place. It should look and sound like children. This is the essence of a successful school. An atmosphere of joy is the first thing I look for in a school building. And I did not find it at Blaine.

When happiness, eagerness and enthusiasm are absent in a school, it becomes apparent that other things are missing as well. As I watched the children going home that afternoon, I noticed that many of them were not carrying books. Now how in the world, I asked myself, can they do homework if they're not taking anything home with them?

I made a note of that, as well as of the answer I got from May Wilson, one of the teachers I stopped in the hall that first afternoon. She looked mighty grim. I said, "Mrs. Wilson, how come you're not smiling?"

"Mrs. Cartwright," she said, "there is *nothing* around here to smile about."

◈

AS I MOVED ABOUT THE SCHOOL, I SOON SAW ONE MAJOR reason why there was a cloud over the children. His name was James Lowe.

James Lowe was the school's NTA—non-teaching assistant—a position created by the school district to take care of essential non-teaching duties, such as ordering, distributing and keeping an inventory of supplies, supervising children in the hallways, helping handle the thousand and one little things that could keep teachers entirely away from teaching if they had to take care of them by themselves.

But Mr. Lowe had taken his duties and responsibilities far beyond those of an NTA. With time, and with the previous principal's blessing, Mr. Lowe had turned the entire school into his little fiefdom. He told the teachers when they could and could not have their supplies, and he used that power to put himself in control. This might sound insignificant, but when a teacher is sitting with thirty-three children in a classroom and the paper supply runs out, that's no small problem.

Beyond his ordinary duties, Mr. Lowe had been given a free hand with discipline, a responsibility that did not come with his job. He had been given the authority to suspend students, and he exercised his authority with relish. He wore his power well—he was a short, stout man, built along the lines of singer Barry White, and he dressed just as well, always wearing a three-piece suit. The children cowered whenever he came in sight. They simply shrank, scared to death of Mr. Lowe. He would walk out on the yard in the morning, say "Freeze!" and five hundred children would stop dead in their tracks.

I thought that was all right when I first saw it. Again, this was order, everybody minding. I thought this might be an asset, a man who could control children with such authority. Mr. Lowe could take the entire student body into the auditorium and have all of them sitting perfectly still and silent. Which is exactly what bothered me. It was *eerie.* I said to myself, "This is not normal.

This is not natural for little children to be perfectly still like this, not moving, not giggling or smiling, not making any noise at all."

When I was a teacher, I often used the analogy of a washrag to illustrate how to get children ready to learn. Take a washrag, twist it up tight, put it into a pail of water, and it will soak up very little of the liquid. Take that same washrag, loosen it, shake it out, then dip it back into that pail, and it will come up soaking wet, just full of water.

The children in Blaine were tight. It is hard for children to learn when they are wound up tight. It is hard for children to absorb their lessons when they're apprehensive, afraid of making the wrong move, of doing the wrong thing.

Some people would say the alternative to control is chaos. I say the alternative is to have children be children, to let them act like children, play like children, run and jump and laugh like children.

I couldn't tell immediately how much actual learning was going on at Blaine. The test scores I had studied looked good—too good. It wasn't until later that I would learn how meaningless those scores were. But one thing I did realize right away was that Mr. Lowe could no longer be permitted to rule this school. The first thing that was going to stop immediately was his authority to suspend students.

My second day at the school, I saw Mr. Lowe taking two boys aside and telling them they were out of school, suspended.

"Mr. Lowe," I said, "may I speak to you?"

Mr. Lowe saw me, a new principal, as a challenge to his authority, to his power. He walked with me to my office defensively.

"Mr. Lowe," I said, once we were alone, "you may not suspend children. Nobody in this school has the authority to suspend children except the principal, and I don't approve of suspension unless a child presents a clear and present danger to the safety of himself, or other children, or the staff. I have never suspended a child in my career, Mr. Lowe, and I don't intend to begin now.

"If you have a problem with a student that you cannot

solve," I continued, "you may send him to me. But there will be no more suspending."

The man left my office as hot as a box of matches.

I knew I had made an enemy, but that's the way it was going to have to be. Things were going to change, even if it meant some battle lines would have to be drawn.

FROM THAT FIRST MORNING IN MARCH, I SPENT THE SPRING getting the lay of the land. Not only was I gauging the attitudes and needs of the staff and the students; I also took a close look at the building itself. The actual physical structure of a school, its condition and appearance, has much to say about the condition and attitudes of the students and staff who inhabit it.

What Blaine's physical structure had to say was not encouraging. When I first entered the front doors, I was struck by the utter filth of the place. Roaches were everywhere. I opened a closet door in a kindergarten classroom and its inside looked as if it had been painted with mud and bugs.

I said, "God, what in the world is this?"

The teacher said to me, "The roaches feed on the glue in the binding of the books."

I said, "Empty the closet immediately and save what you want. Everything else must go."

Each kindergarten room had a sink and a faucet. The cabinet under each sink was infested with roaches, free-living insects multiplying as they pleased, nobody disturbing them.

But I didn't have to go into the classrooms to find roaches. My own desk, the principal's desk, had roaches in it. My telephone had roaches. I laid the receiver down hard on its cradle one morning, and two roaches came scampering right out of the phone base.

There were mice as well; droppings were everywhere. The building's cinder-block walls were caked with dirt. The window shades were twelve years old, and they had never been cleaned. Unless it was torn or broken, there was no such thing as replacing a window shade in the Philadelphia schools, and there was certainly no such thing as washing them. The custodians did not have time to wash window shades, and besides, no one asked them to do it.

There were five part-time women working in the school for five hours each day, but the bulk of the building's maintenance and cleaning was done by Mr. Bailey, our custodian, and his assistant, Mr. Brazille. They seemed to spend most of each day changing light bulbs. In fact, changing light bulbs was their priority. Whenever Mr. Bailey and Mr. Brazille finished a break, they would come down the hall with those fluorescent tubes in their hands, going to replace a light. That was the most viable part of their day, changing bulbs.

Meanwhile, the rest of the building was going to seed. The toilets seemed eternally clogged and inoperable. In the boys' rest room, where there were typically six toilets and eight urinals, half the toilets would be stopped up with fruit from lunch or pencils jammed in the pipes and wrapped with toilet paper. The children would continue to use all the toilets, including the clogged ones. The stench was unbearable.

Although Mr. Bailey cleared and cleaned some of the toilets, the place still stank. The odor permeated the hallway. At first I didn't know where all of that stench was coming from, but I told Mr. Bailey that there was no way I would abide this condition. The smell had to go.

"Mr. Bailey," I said, "there is no way children can be expected to go to the bathroom in this place. These little boys and girls have to use the toilet and hold their breath at the same time. It's just too difficult. Try it sometime."

He said, "Mrs. Cartwright, I cleaned this bathroom. The smell is coming from the floor, from that cement there. There's urine in the cement. Ten years of urine. It won't come out."

I was blessed by the fact that Mr. Bailey was also new at Blaine, having been assigned there a month before I arrived. It wasn't as if this was his mess, so he didn't feel personally attacked when I said, "Let's do something about it." When I asked him to get a bucket of hot water and some scrub brushes, he looked puzzled, but he quickly got them.

Meanwhile, I took off my shoes and stockings, set them on a sink, pulled up the front of my dress and got down to some serious scrubbing. Mr. Bailey ran back and forth refilling the bucket while I scrubbed the floor. He didn't make any gesture toward helping. I think he was in shock. Occasionally a little boy wandered in, gave us a glance, used the bathroom and left.

After about an hour I lifted my head and sniffed the air.

"Mr. Bailey," I said, "do you smell anything?"

"No."

"That's right, Mr. Bailey. The stench is gone. It does come up out of the cement, doesn't it? Now, it's not my job to scrub bathrooms, and I don't intend to scrub another one. I want you to scrub the remaining toilets so we have clean facilities for the children. Can you take care of that for me right away?"

"Yes indeed," he said.

WORD SPREAD QUICKLY ABOUT THE PRINCIPAL'S GOING BARE- foot in the boys' room, scrubbing the floor and the toilets. Raymond Brooks laughed so hard he almost fell over. "I don't believe she scrubbed that toilet!" he said.

The parents didn't believe it either. Talk went through the neighborhood about the new principal at the school. Parents began popping in just to look at me! I had no idea at the time how this incident—and others like it—would serve the school and the children in the years to come. But the parents were buzzing about this.

"Those bathrooms don't stink over there anymore."

"That lady cleaned it up, I'm telling you she cleaned the toilets. My Monroe saw her."

They figured if I was up there in that bathroom scrubbing that cement, I must not feel that I was too good to associate with them. So they began talking to me. They came on the schoolyard in the morning just to chat, to be friendly. We talked about the children, about what was going on in the school, in their house, in my house, and about what we were going to do next in the school.

We talked, and we touched. I touched them, and they touched me. And I touched the children. I went around the school daily touching children, giving them pats, squeezes and hugs and kisses. For some of the children, the only touching they experienced daily was being pushed, shoved or hit. I let them all know, children and parents alike, that there would be absolutely no hitting on school property without a consequence. I would be the only person allowed to exercise the option of corporal punishment.

By playing to each child's strengths, instead of concentrating on their misbehavior, teachers can almost eliminate the need for severe punishment. We set up structured guidelines—rules for when students should be lined up outside, or seated silently within the classroom—but we didn't expect perfect behavior all the time. We allowed the children to be children within those guidelines. Then, when a serious infraction occurred, punishment was taken seriously. Threats are meaningless if they aren't carried out. Conversely, a child should be allowed to whisper and squirm occasionally without being scolded constantly.

I was the only person allowed to spank a child, and that was only when the teachers had exhausted all their disciplinary resources. I had a paddle I called Bertha and the kids knew that if all else failed, I'd use it. Of course, I'd call the parent and discuss it first, but by the time a child wound up in my office, Bertha wasn't merely an idle threat, and the children responded accordingly.

But Bertha did not become a tool for me until I was in charge of an entire school. I encouraged teachers to control their classes through constant communication and caring.

I didn't allow *anyone* to hit the children on school property, including the parents. For a parent to hit a child at school, in front of his classmates, is embarrassing for a child. Of course, what happened off school grounds was another matter. What the children found at home was going to be harder and take longer to deal with than any problem we had at the school. I had a general sense of what the children went home to, although my actual experience of some of their horrors was yet to come.

I knew that most of the children went into their homes, dropped off whatever they brought from school, which in most cases was nothing, then went out onto the street and stayed there until dark, or even later. They were basically street children after school and before bedtime. Some of them were more at home on the streets than they were in the places where they slept.

These children were hard-core survivors. They looked after one another. Some of them had no one else to take care of them. Many of them had learned how to change their little baby sister's or brother's diapers before they knew how to tie their own shoes. Most were either on the street or watching television for hours at a time.

Mindless people would say, "Look at that, these families are on welfare but they have television. Where are their priorities? They don't have enough money for suitable clothes or quality foods, but they've got a TV. Why don't they buy books, build personal libraries and encourage their children to read?"

My response is: "Don't speak to me about priorities. A family living on welfare in rented rooms and apartments can afford very few other luxuries for the children. There is no encouragement to build a library or any other collection for that matter. The repeated, 'in the nick of time' relocating that many of these families experience provides no space and often no time to take anything except essentials. Often the only eviction notice afforded the poorer than the poor is: 'Get out of my house (room, apartment) this minute.' "

Most of this moving was done on the poor man's moving van—a shopping cart from the nearest grocery chain store.

Television provides some sanity for the parent. No matter who or what the circumstance, there has to be provision for some entertainment, some diversion, some relief . . . or emotion will give way to madness. During the settling of the West in the early days of our country, the wagon masters made sure that there was a fiddle or an organ somewhere in the precious space of the covered wagons to provide the entertainment that was so necessary for the perilous journey. The long, day-in-day-out journey through life in America's poverty-stricken ghettos is far more nerve-wracking and perilous than what those wagon trains went through.

To a family in suburbia, television is just one of many activities from which to select. To people with alternatives, television can even be seen as a sin. But when there is nothing else, television can be a salvation.

It's the same with sneakers and jackets. People criticize these items' importance in city children's lives, saying that the parent gets maybe a couple of hundred dollars bimonthly and she spends half of that on a pair of sneakers for her child. What people don't realize is that a pair of sneakers may be the greatest wish that that parent can grant the child. She can't give a nice, or even acceptable, house. She can't provide a vacation, a summer camp, piano lessons, a trip to grandparents' home, farm or estate for the summer.

But she can give her child a pair of sneakers or a jacket. When I would see one of our children walk into the schoolyard wearing a new pair of sneakers, staring down at his feet so everyone else would look, I would be the first to say, "Oh, I really like your new sneakers." If I passed a boy wearing a new shirt, I'd say, "Mmmmm, I *like* that shirt." I always tried to make the little things count; there were so few pleasant big things.

It's important for a child to feel good about himself, especially children who don't have much. But they must be helped to put the sneakers and jackets that serve a need for today in the proper perspective. They must realize that there is much beyond the world in which they are living right now, they must retain the ability to dream, and they must be convinced and reminded that the most certain avenue to fulfilling their dreams is education.

◈

TOO MANY PARENTS, TEACHERS AND CHILDREN FELT THAT the situation in Strawberry Mansion was hopeless. They could not imagine the children of the Blaine School performing as well as the rest of the world, let alone better. I saw and heard evidence of this attitude at all levels: "These children are accustomed to little or nothing and cannot be raised above this attitude." Clearly, there had to be a change in attitude across the spectrum. But attitude is intangible, I thought. What must be done to affect attitude change? I decided to make some tangible improvements right away, changes everyone could see, changes that would tell them, "Yes, it can get better around here."

Scrubbing the bathrooms was a tangible change.

Keeping the trash off the schoolyard was another. The asphalt on the yard was hidden under food wrappers, soda cans and broken bottles. It was especially abominable on Monday mornings.

Once again I called for Mr. Bailey.

"Mr. Bailey," I said, "is this normal and natural, or does something happen over the weekends around here that I don't know about?"

"Oh no," he said. "That's the way it is on Mondays always."

"Oh no, no, *no*," I wailed. "This has to be cleaned up now."

So Mr. Bailey and I went digging into another mess. But this time we involved the children as well. Even Mr. Lowe joined us with a broom in his hand as we pulled every trash can in that building out onto the yard and filled it with trash. When we finished, there was nothing left but tiny scraps of paper covering the asphalt like confetti. Then I made an announcement.

"Boys and girls," I said, "no one can come back into the building without a ticket."

"Ticket?" they said. "What's she talkin' about, a ticket?"

"Everybody has to have a ticket," I repeated. "Your ticket to get into this building this morning is a piece of trash."

With that, there were five hundred children scrambling for one of those pieces of paper. The playground was spotless in a matter of minutes. Some of the younger children couldn't even find a piece, so they asked a friend to tear off part of their piece to share.

That became our regular Monday-morning routine, and other days also if the playground looked like it needed it. I didn't force anyone to join in, but if I saw a child not helping, I went to him and said, "Is Blaine your school? Do you want to be a part of our Blaine family? Being a part of the family means helping to keep our school home clean."

Occasionally I would announce that we would all go in late, because we were going to take a walk around the school block. We were going to make all sides of our school look better, I told the children. I had Mr. Bailey and Mr. Lowe put trash cans at each corner and off we would go, picking up trash on the sidewalks. The children were directed to deposit a piece of trash in each can as he or she passed. Mr. Bailey would just stand there shaking his head. He could not believe what he was seeing.

I had Mr. Bailey on my mind with all of this. This was part of his job, keeping that playground clean. But he had a lot to do as it was. Sweeping a schoolyard nearly a block large would take too much time away from chores that only he was capable of doing. There were problems around that building that needed the attention of a skilled mechanic.

In relieving Mr. Bailey of some of this time-consuming un-skilled labor, I didn't ask only the children to pitch in. I went to the root of this trash problem as well. I said we needed to put cans out on the yard for the weekend people and anyone else to deposit their trash in.

Mr. Bailey was skeptical.

"How long do you think a trash can is going to last out there?" he said.

"Put the trash cans out there, Mr. Bailey, and we'll see how long they last."

Then I went to visit the young men who played basketball at the far end of the schoolyard. I passed these young men daily, on my way to and from the school parking lot. I always stopped and greeted them. They always greeted me by name, as did nearly everyone in the neighborhood. I told them that most of the broken glass that we found on Monday mornings came from bottles that they left there on weekends. I asked them if they would put their empty bottles in the cans we had supplied. This would discourage the children from picking up the bottles, throwing them onto the roof and climbing up to throw them back down, breaking them all over the yard.

"No problem," the ballplayers said. They began using the cans for trash and bottles, and our glass problem was erased. It was as simple as that.

Those same trash cans we put out on that yard in 1979 were still there twelve years later.

ANOTHER BUILDING BLOCK I PUT INTO PLACE THAT FIRST spring was my assemblies. I called assemblies anytime I saw a need to talk to my children. These assemblies were a cross between gathering around the campfire, having a town meeting and going to church. Actually, they were a lot like going to church.

And I was the preacher.

I had grown up going to church regularly. Our family began each Sunday with Sunday school, followed by the morning service, then the afternoon youth program union and finally the night service. That was a full Sunday of people teaching what is right, what is proper and acceptable, over and over and over again. What to do, what not to do. A moral framework, I guess it could be called.

Very few of our children at Blaine went to church, as I discovered at one of our first assemblies when I said, "Raise your hand if you went to church last Sunday." Maybe ten or twelve hands went up among five hundred children.

The children were not getting instruction on what was and what was not acceptable behavior. The teaching I received in church or in my family about love, trust, charity and the like was not given to our children at Blaine. Too many of the children were not getting the benefits of religious or other value training. Those unacceptable tributaries that can branch out from rivers of character if there is no individual or institution providing for character building can take over and become the main streams. Someone or something must provide for character building. As we at school recognized the need to develop the mind in one way, I took it upon myself to expose the children to sessions of character development, citizenship strengthening, community living or whatever title is acceptable. This is what some people might call "values."

I could use assemblies as a values-teaching tool with my children at Blaine because they were still at an age where they would listen and respond at such gatherings. From my experience, by the time children reached middle, junior high and high school, assemblies were almost impossible to conduct with order and attention. The students at that age who had never been taught how to behave in a large group were unable to do so and were unwilling at that point to learn.

Our children at Blaine learned. On any issue needing clarification or discussion that arose in the school—from neighborhood matters to world affairs—I called for an assembly. The issues didn't have to be earthshaking. I passed a boy in the hall one morning, complimented him on the new shirt he was wearing and he just grunted. "I don't like this shirt," he said, scowling. "My mother bought me this old shirt. This isn't what I wanted."

I called an assembly. I brought the children together and I told them what the child had said.

"Now, if your mother buys you a shirt or blouse," I began, "if your mother buys you anything at all—you must understand that nobody gave that item to your mother. She had to do without something that she could have bought for herself to get something for you. She could have taken that five dollars and bought herself some lipstick, some fingernail polish, or a hoagie or a steak sandwich, or a pair of stockings. But instead she bought you something, because she wanted to make you feel good. She wants you to have the best of everything. Your parents or whoever takes care of you want the best for you. They may not be able to provide the best, but they do want the best for you. When your mother buys you something and you say, 'I don't like this stuff. This is not what I wanted,' that hurts.

"You should not hurt your mother like that," I told them. "You must show appreciation for your mother. Don't hurt her. She is doing the best that she can. She must get some acceptance from someone. Often you are the only one that she can go to for a hug or a 'thank you.' Give it to her, boys and girls. She needs it as much as you do. Don't hurt each other, and don't hurt your parents or whoever keeps you. Go home today and put your arms around your parents and say, 'I love you.' 'I love you,' children. Say, 'I love you.' Now practice all day so that when you get home you can say it with real meaning. 'I *love* you. I love *you*. I love you.' Put the emphasis wherever you are most comfortable putting it, but say it. And *feel* it."

They listened. They listened when I called an assembly about painting graffiti on the schoolyard walls. And they listened when I talked about the most universal of elementary school pranks—pulling the fire alarms.

I came down the center aisle of the auditorium one morning banging rapidly on a chromatic bar with a mallet. When I arrived at the microphone, through which I rarely spoke, I hit that mike about ten times with the mallet. As I did this, Mr. Brooks turned the volume up as loud as it would go. The children put their hands over their ears. I said, "Boys and girls, there is one among us who likes to hear bells. I want him or her to get his or her fill right here and now."

Then I took out a baby rattle. "Or is it simply noise that he or she needs? Whatever it is, I want to answer that need, so that that person will not interrupt our learning to provide the entertainment that he or she needs for his or her baby mind.

"No, no, no! Don't point him or her out to me," I said as I turned my back to them. "You know that person is sorry and does not want anyone to know that it was he or she who mimicked a ridiculous prank that they heard someone had done somewhere else. That person knows who he or she is and doesn't need anyone pointing any fingers."

We rarely had an alarm pulled after that assembly. Occasionally a new kid who had missed our "good-living sessions" broke our rules. But the children would quickly tell that new student how we lived at Blaine. If he or she didn't get the message, or if the message wasn't given, I knew it was time for a session to be repeated.

I regularly discussed child abuse with our children in our assembly program. I would present a case and ask the children how the child in the situation could have helped himself. We decided together that children must learn acceptable responses to angry or frustrated parents; that they must go home and share with their parents what they learned in our assembly program on child abuse.

Many children said that their parents got angry when they didn't answer a question. I could readily identify with this scenario, as my own daughter, Jill, would, from the earliest age, immediately turn into a mute when questioned about any rule or infraction.

We identified questions for which there are just no acceptable answers. Such as: Why did you not leave play and come home on time? Why did you steal a quarter? Why did you play in my makeup? Why did you eat something you were told not to eat? Why did you take your mother's jewelry or Daddy's tools to school?

These questions have no answers. My grandnephew Tyrone would answer, "I don't know. I'm just crazy, I guess." This response reminded me that there was no answer to why he poured out my best perfume, other than the fact that children commit many mindless acts. This "crazy" answer further reminded me that the question was a vent for my own frustration.

Punishments should be decided on together with the child. Maybe no television or video games or going outside to play for a set period of time was the solution. The children and I agreed that any punishment which would cause a child to lie was an unfair punishment. Some angry parents seem hell-bent on making the child change his story. In each of our assemblies, I begged children to give the parent the sought-after truth. I reminded them that holding out could cause them to be hurt. We would "playact" or use creative dramatics to show children situations that could result in child abuse.

Sharing what was learned in school, we hoped, would give both parents and their children an opportunity to discuss child abuse together during calm times.

Each of our child-abuse assemblies ended with the children being advised to report any and all cases of abuse in which they were involved, or just heard about, to their parents or to our school personnel.

In other assemblies, we identified situations to be suspicious of, such as adults asking, "Can you keep a secret?" We advised children that they must have no secret that they could not share with their parents or trusted friends. We advised them to tell such a person that they were not allowed to keep secrets from their parents or friends. Then children were encouraged to tell of any and all situations that appeared suspicious to them. To borrow an old saying, "Better to tell it and risk shame than to keep it and be in pain."

In these assemblies, we taught the children ways to take care of themselves and their siblings. I advised the children not to cook without supervision, to eat ready-cooked food only. We talked about fire and some of the causes of house fires. We emphasized the obvious: not playing with matches, candles or any other flames. I told them of my little niece who started a fire by reading under the covers with her electric lamp after her mother said, "Lights out." I explained that a bulb against a curtain or any flammable material could easily start a fire.

"If a fire starts," I told them, "never try to put it out. Yell for your brothers and sisters and evacuate the premises. Talk with your family and practice evacuation just as we have fire drills at school. Tell your parents to be sure to keep a light on at night. Many children and adults alike become disoriented or lost in the dark. Practice moving around your room in the dark so that it is not unfamiliar to you. Have a fire drill in the night when everyone must be awakened. Set the alarm clock to ring for a night fire drill. Make sure that there is a smoke detector on every floor. Remind your parents daily until they get a smoke detector. If you have a problem convincing your parents, tell me so that I might help you. Plan to stay alive."

One session that needed repeating more often than I wished was an assembly I called when three of our children, three six-year-old boys, were coaxed into a house and raped by a man with gonorrhea. As a result, the children were hospitalized with the same disease.

"Children," I told the assembled student body, "we are so busy warning little girls not to go into houses or not to talk to strangers, we forget to tell the boys they're in the same danger. Well, they are. It happened to these boys. They went into somebody's house when they should not have."

The children needed to understand that it wasn't just the girls who were vulnerable out on the streets. That's the kind of thing every one of my assemblies was about—understanding.

OF COURSE, THERE WERE SOME SITUATIONS NO ASSEMBLY could resolve. Like the situation I faced with Frank.

Frank was a fourth-grader who would occasionally arrive at school behind the wheel of a stolen car. The other children would be out on the playground waiting for the day to begin, and here would come an automobile with a little nine-year-old boy at the wheel, his head barely high enough to peek out the windshield. He would cruise slowly around the block, making a big show of it so all the children could see him. Then he would park the car someplace and come into school.

I talked to him and notified the police the first time it happened, but that didn't help. The police did not even investigate. It happened again and again. Finally I pulled that little rascal into my office when the police were there on another matter. I said, "This little boy has stolen so many cars that I can't even count them all."

"No, Mrs. Cartwright," said Frank, sticking his chin out and shaking his head, "I only stole *three*."

The policemen merely shook their heads and went on with the business at hand. If the police or the insurance companies had stolen-car hot lines, at least someone could have notified the car owners. I learned from Frank that most of the cars came from around the hospitals, where doctors and nurses worked the night shift.

I had to laugh and cry at the same time with a boy like Frank. I knew his background; I knew his mother had eight children and she was not yet thirty-three years old. She couldn't read. She had gone to a special school and was EMR (educable mentally retarded). Her children had more intelligence than she had, but they had no one to guide them.

None of my assemblies could possibly have supplied the kind of help that Frank and his brothers and sisters needed. I wish there could be assemblies of welfare staffers and health and social agencies to give a woman like Frank's mother the guidance and support that she needs. She had been identified in elementary school as mentally limited, needing special attention to continue in the school program. Yet no agency recognized and followed through with continued special help in parenting skills. Until society recognizes that special-needs children grow up and become special-needs adults heading special-needs families, there will be more and more children like Frank and Tyrone (the boy nicknamed "Ethiopia") living in homes with parents whose mental ages may be six, seven or eight.

Frank eventually was incarcerated for stealing cars, joining his two older brothers who lived in government facilities where their addresses were on their shirts rather than on their doors. If the money being spent to house Frank's brothers had gone into guiding his mother when she was a young woman with no children or later when she, with special needs, was the head of a household, what might have been? What could have been? Right now we can only see what is.

Maybe Frank could have been saved if someone had done a little more. Maybe we can still save his sisters from taking their places in welfare lines as young mothers heading households. Maybe we can keep *their* children from being infant mortality statistics if we plan programs to provide guidance centers in communities that need them. Should little Tyrone have had to wait until morning to have his third-degree burns treated, or should there be a twenty-four-hour hot line for special-needs families?

Now that we have lifted teachers salaries to a level where some can afford to retire, maybe we can call on these retired teachers to help organize assistance for our special-needs families. Teachers know who and where these families are; they deal with them daily. They know their needs.

Frank and Tyrone lived in homes whose problems were easily traced to mentally limited parents. Robin—the only white girl in our school—had a different problem. She was one of only two white children in our school. The other was her brother Leonard.

I couldn't help but notice Robin and Leonard the first day I arrived at Blaine. Leonard was a ten-year-old fifth-grader who seemed to have adjusted to the Blaine School environment. He ran and played as the other little boys did at recess time. When he had a problem, he went to Mr. Brooks or Mr. Lowe, or he came to my office.

But Robin was another matter. The first day I saw her and her brother, I could see how he looked after her. He was there with Robin in the morning, watching over her on the playground, and he waited for her after school, taking her hand and walking her home with him. But when she was without him, Robin had problems.

She was white in every sense of the word. She was *white* white, with bouncy, curly red hair. There was no black in her whatsoever. She was white from every angle. A person could tell looking at her from *behind* that she was white. There was absolutely no chance for her to even begin to blend in or fade back. Among that sea of children, Robin was completely out of her element. She even wore white folks' clothes: little cotton dresses with short, puffy sleeves and anklets and shoes, not sneakers as almost all of the Blaine children wore.

During recess, she kept to herself and always stood close to the wall of the building; that way there were only three sides to watch. Once in a while a little girl would approach Robin, take her by the hand and try to gently pull her along to befriend her. Robin would not allow herself to be pulled away from that wall, though she did not yank her hand away from the child. In the way that children communicate with each other, Robin made her feelings known without words. She did not want to play. She didn't jump rope. The children could not understand that at all. *Everyone* jumped rope.

Robin never smiled, and smiling was very important with me. If I saw a child not smiling, I'd go over, tickle him, give him a hug, say, "Why aren't you happy?" and I'd always be able to coax some kind of smile out of him.

But I couldn't do it with Robin.

I wondered from the beginning what Robin and her brother were doing in the heart of North Philadelphia, attending Blaine. I knew of no other whites in that neighborhood. The only whites I saw were our school's teachers and business people, none of whom lived in Strawberry Mansion. There weren't even the usual insurance men or door-to-door salespeople I had seen as a child growing up in Pittsburgh and Coatesville. Whites were afraid to come into that area—adults were afraid. But Robin and her brother were forced into this neighborhood, a place where uninformed outsiders assume everyone carries knives and will cut, rape, fight or mug any white for the fun of it. Is it any wonder that Robin wouldn't leave that wall?

Compelled to respond to the misery of such a fragile little

child petrified with fear, I sent for Robin's mother. She came immediately. I invited her into my office.

"There is no problem," I said, sensing her puzzlement and concern. "I only want to talk to you about your children."

Then I asked her point-blank, "Why do you and your children live here in this neighborhood?"

She told me that she had grown up in South Coatesville, where the mills were, the poorest end of town. It was there, she said, that Robin and Leonard had been born in an earlier marriage and it was there that she met her present husband, who was African-American.

"Mrs. Cartwright," she said, "when I was a kid, it was hard. The black children called us poor white trash. The whites didn't call us anything. They just acted like we didn't exist. I think the whites made up the 'poor white trash' name so that we would not be thought of as white like them. So you see, Mrs. Cartwright, I was not white and I was not black. I was just poor white trash.

"Then, a couple of years ago, I met my present husband. Mrs. Cartwright, he treated me like I was somebody; somebody worth loving and caring for. This is the first time in my life that I felt loved. When I moved here I knew that it would be hard for the children, but here was love that had never been a part of any of our other relationships. Mrs. Cartwright, this is so much better than where we came from. Here, at least, we are safe in our house; my husband loves me and the children. He wouldn't let anything happen to us. He treats all of the children the same—mine and the one we had together."

She wiped tears away from her eyes as she spoke. I tried to hide the tears collecting in the corners of my own eyes. I had been called "colored," "Negro" and now "African-American," but I always belonged. I was always a member of the black race and I was always taught to be proud of my race. This woman didn't even have a race that was willing to accept her and her children.

I could sympathize with how she felt. I could see how she had come to be living black. But I told her that I felt that she should not have brought her children into it. I said it didn't seem fair to them, that this was just too hard a situation for them to have to handle. I asked her why she didn't give the children to her mother, or to a sister—to somebody—to raise them in an environment that would be easier on them.

"Because they're my children," she said, "and I want them with me."

I could understand some of how she felt. But I compared it to the decision that a woman must make when she is considering giving up her child for adoption or removing children from a war zone. There are questions that must be answered. Is it love or selfish love that makes a woman keep a child that she knows she cannot care for properly or who is in danger? Was it fair that Robin was forced to live black because her mother had decided that she wanted to live black? For eight years Robin had lived in a world where African-Americans had been pictured on television as bad. When a crime was committed by an African-American, there he was, in handcuffs on the screen. White criminals were more often than not spoken of in absentia. Robin lived for eight years where chocolate cake was devil's food cake, where people were blackballed, blacklisted or blackmailed, and the black sheep in the family was the bad one, where even the villain among Saturday-morning cartoon characters was black or wore black clothing. She lived for eight years in a world where "black" and "evil" were treated as synonyms.

Neither Robin nor any other child needs to be thrust alone without orientation into such a situation. From eight in the morning until three in the afternoon, and maybe on into the night, Robin had no one with whom to share her frustration. How could she be expected to learn at a normal rate and under normal conditions?

I had many times been the only African-American in my class. However, I was never afraid. I had not been programmed to fear white folks. I knew that the cowards hiding under the white sheets and hoods were bad, but none of the children in the schools where I went wore sheets and hoods. It's different for white children. Black children perceive white people differently than white children are taught to perceive black people. It is not as simple as what is or what is not. It is the *perception* of the individual that counts.

So Robin and her brother stayed at Blaine. And poor little Robin just became more and more unhappy. Her class wrote theme papers that spring, and the teacher posted them on a bulletin board in the hall. I read some of the papers so that I could comment to the children on their good work, as I often did. When I came to Robin's paper, I thought, "Now I'll have something pleasant to share with her." But then I read it:

"BLACK," it was titled.

"I hate black," it began.

"I hate collard greens. I hate pigs' feet. I hate corn bread. I hate black. I hate everything black.

"I even hate black crayons."

I reached up, pulled that paper down, folded it and put it into my pocket. Robin already had enough problems. If the children, or the staff for that matter, had seen that paper, life would have been even harder for Robin. I wondered why the teacher had posted it. Did she want Robin's row to be harder to hoe, as the old saying goes? Was she angry with Robin for hating "black"? Was she putting Robin in the bag with prejudiced whites? I never knew the answers to any of those questions nor did I ever discuss Robin's paper with any of the staff. I was too afraid that she would be held responsible for her feelings.

Things never got better for Robin. When her brother finished the sixth grade and moved on to junior high school, Robin moved on also. I never saw her again. I don't know what became of her.

All too often children are held responsible for responses and attitudes that circumstances force on their little minds—minds too young to adequately process such hardships and prejudices. As eight years of her life had programmed Robin to hate, so are African-American children exposed to those same nomenclatures, television newscasts, productions and cartoons that rip away at their racial pride and self-esteem. Consequently, they, like Robin, have trouble learning.

PROBABLY THE BIGGEST SINGLE MOVE I MADE THAT SPRING was my first parents' meeting. This was the big test, as far as I was concerned. The children were a captive audience. The teachers were also. But the parents could come or not come as they pleased. Prior to my arrival at the school, almost nobody came to parents' meetings. Those who might have wanted to be part of the school just didn't feel welcome, and there were those who could not have cared less.

But I cared. I wanted them. I needed them. Without the involvement of parents, none of this was going to work. No matter how much we might do in those eight or so hours that the children were at school, their parents had the power to undo it all, by intent or by sheer lack of support and reinforcement. I desperately needed the parents' help, I needed their interest and involvement, I needed their trust and their blessing.

Most of the staff scoffed, some because they were cynical, others because they had a vested interest in my failure. When I put out the call for the first parents' meeting, I knew there was a lot on the line, maybe everything.

So I didn't just send home a flyer with the children. Half of those notices would never find their way home, and if they did, they probably wouldn't be read. I made the children my messengers. If I could get them excited about this meeting, then they would take care of the rest. They would make sure that their parents attended.

I have seen, too often in too many schools, principals and teachers trying to deal directly with parents, in essence going over the heads of the children, thus leaving the children out of the process. The result is two parallel tracks—principal-to-parent and principal-to-children—and a lot less parental participation. If children are brought onto the team and involved in the process of getting parents involved, parents will come. Enlist the aid of the children to reach the parents and pull them on the team with the school, and the team then will be unconquerable.

My first step was to get the children to care about the school and about their principal, to want to have their parents know me. By the time I announced that first parents' meeting at Blaine, I'd gotten the children's attention. They wanted their parents to see who I was. I seized that small bit of momentum and steered it toward the meeting. I called an assembly and told the children they had to bring their mothers to this meeting. "Your mother has to know Mrs. Cartwright," I told them. "She must know me. It's important."

I said, "Every day between now and that meeting, I want you to go home and tell your mother the meeting is coming up, and I want you to tell her something about Mrs. Cartwright. Tell her something I said on the public announcement system that morning. Tell her something I did that day. If you can't think of anything that I did or said that day, then you tell her what I was wearing. Say, 'Mrs. Cartwright had on a green dress today, Mommy.' "

The next day I was sitting in my office, with the door wide open, as I always kept it, and I could see the children passing by in the hallway, stopping and peering in to see the color of my dress.

"What does she have on? What color is it?"

"Blue! It's blue!"

No one believed I could deliver these parents. Raymond Brooks said, "They're not going to come, Madeline. They just don't come. Never have. Never will."

There were plenty of teachers who didn't want the parents to come. Many of them were simply frightened by my energy. They said, "This woman does not stop. First thing you know, she's going to expect us to go like that. All of that energy she's unleashing right now on this building, unleashing right now on the children, unleashing on the community, well, the day is going to come when she starts unleashing it on us. What we've got to do is beat some of that energy out of her, beat that enthusiasm down before she starts directing it our way."

All I heard from the teachers was: "It's not going to work, it's not going to work." And all I kept saying was: "It *must* work, it simply *must* work."

The week of the meeting, I began driving slowly up and down those streets, all four windows down, blowing the horn and yelling at the children out on the curbs, "Go get your mother! Go get your mother!"

As their mothers came, I said, "We're having the meeting Thursday night, and you gotta come. Are you coming?"

"Yeah, I'm coming. If I don't, Sheila will die, I believe."

I went on down the street a little farther, blowing the horn again, and the children brought their parents. I saw adults waiting for a bus, I pulled over and told them about the meeting. I made them promise me they would be there. When I saw some others standing outside a store, I did the same thing. I spent many afternoons going up and down the streets with people looking at me as if I were absolutely insane.

When Thursday came, I was hyped. I called an assembly just before school let out and asked the children how many of their parents were coming. I asked them, "When I get on the PA tomorrow morning and ask you to raise your hand if your parent was at the meeting last night, will your hand be raised?"

"Yes!" they shouted.

"I can't hear you," I said, walking up the middle of that auditorium aisle.

"Yes!"

"I *still* can't hear you."

"Yessssssss!" they sang in their loudest voices.

The entire neighborhood could hear those children screaming inside that school building. It sounded like cheers after the game-winning point in a championship basketball game.

Earlier that day I had asked Mr. Lowe and Mr. Davis—the administrative assistant—to put some folding chairs down in the orchestra part of the auditorium for the staff to sit so they wouldn't take up seats that I would need for the parents. I also asked them to put my microphone down on the floor, not up on the stage. I always liked to be down with the audience when I spoke. I heard both of them chuckling as they went down the hall to the auditorium.

At four o'clock I walked down to the auditorium to see how things looked. The microphone was set up, but there were no chairs. Now, I didn't mind these men laughing at me, but not doing what I asked them to do was another matter.

I tracked down Mr. Davis.

"Where," I said, "are the chairs I asked you to set up?"

"Mrs. Cartwright," he said, "I hate to burst your bubble or rain on your parade, but you don't need any chairs. Those parents aren't coming."

I was so angry at that moment, I could have just bitten that man. But I bit my tongue instead.

"Mr. Davis," I said, mustering more patience than I could have imagined I had, "no matter what you do or do not actually believe, I want you to *act* like you believe in this and any program that we launch here. Convince me, the staff and anyone involved that you believe. You're supposed to be my assistant, and if you don't believe you belong in that role, then pretend you do until the time comes when you can arrange a transfer out.

"As for right now," I said, "go put up the chairs like I asked you, please."

The chairs went up.

The meeting was at seven o'clock. At six, I looked in the auditorium and saw about fifty people. Liz McCain came over to me and said, "Mrs. Cartwright, if don't another one come, this is more than we ever had."

I said to myself, "That's fine," but nothing less than a full auditorium was going to make me happy. I had read the riot act to Mr. Davis about getting those chairs set up. I'd thrown down the gauntlet with him and said, "I'm the boss here and I am willing to pay the cost." A mere fifty parents was not worth the cost.

I needed those chairs to be filled.

At six-thirty, parents began pouring through the doors as if they were coming to a free Michael Jackson concert. Many of their children were with them, pulling their parents over to me, saying, "Come on, Mommy. I want you to meet Mrs. Cartwright. This is my principal, Mommy."

I stood shaking hands, and by seven o'clock the place was packed. Every seat was filled and they were still coming in, lining the walls, standing up, spilling into the outside hallway, packed twenty deep.

It was time, and as I went walking down toward the front of that room, looking at those faces in that room, those hundreds of faces, seeing my teachers packed into those chairs up in the front —those extra chairs—I said to myself, "God, I knew it, I just *knew* it. I knew they were coming."

That's what I told them, turning around and facing them with a grin bigger than Jimmy Carter's.

"I am so happy to be here with you," I began. "I knew you were going to come so we could show our children that we are together, so you could know their principal and you could know their teachers.

"Now I'm going to introduce every teacher," I said. "You listen for your child's teacher's name so you'll know what that teacher looks like, so you'll know who that teacher is."

I began calling the teachers' names, and I noted the parents' reactions. I called Mary Freeman's name, and the house came down. They just clapped and clapped and clapped. So I knew Mary had a power. I went a little further, came to Raymond Brooks, and again the room exploded with cheers. Mary and Raymond, they'd both been at Blaine a long time, and they were popular. The people loved them; the same with May Wilson, Verdie Brown and Florence Musgrave. These would become the linchpins for me—Raymond and Mary and Verdie and Mrs. Musgrave—not just with my staff and with the children but with the community.

Then it was time for me to speak.

"I am here to make this school serve the children," I said.

"Children are going to enjoy coming to this school. Children are going to learn here. They're going to come every day, and they are going to learn.

"Now, I came from the same place as you," I said.

I then told them about my childhood, about being the thirteenth of thirteen children, about living in a house with no beds, about sleeping on the floor, about moving into the projects when we left the country, about how we didn't have any shoes. I told them about my daddy chopping off those high heels. They laughed so loud at that story that I had to stop for a minute.

Then I said, "I'm not from the Main Line. I *live* on the Main Line, but I've come up through the ranks. I have survived and beaten the odds to be standing up here tonight.

"Now, you must give me credit," I said. "I must have more sense than some of you, because I made it out and some of you are still here."

They loved that. They were laughing and nudging each other and having a good time, a comfortable time. I was dressed up, looking like new money, everything matching.

"See these clothes?" I said. "I bought this outfit yesterday for the show tonight. I'm not going to say to you that I'm ashamed I have this fancy outfit. I have ten more just like it at home. I am sorry that you don't have one. I wish you had one, too. But I have mine, and it looks *gooood*, doesn't it?"

The room went wild, just bursting with laughter and cheers.

"I'm going to help you," I said. "I'm going to make sure that your child gets the best education that we can deliver. He is going to get a fair shake and a fair share. For one thing, there will be no suspensions from this building unless your child presents a clear and present danger to himself, other children and the staff. And I have yet to meet an eleven- or twelve-year-old child that I cannot handle."

That stopped them right there. They started cheering again.

"I have never suspended a child in my life," I said, "and I'm not going to start here. But your children have got to treat us with respect. We're going to treat them with respect, and we expect the same. They must come to school to learn and they must learn. The only choice that they have in the matter of learning is whether they will do it with a sore butt or a well butt."

Oh, the parents liked that. They clapped and clapped. Then I went down into the crowd like a country preacher at a revival, pacing up and down that aisle, really putting on a show.

"Our teachers need to be respected," I said. "They must feel good about themselves. Children, if you see how pretty your teacher looks in school, go on home and tell your mother how good she looked. Our parents out here tonight, see how nice these teachers look? Give them a cheer, too. Go home and tell your child his teacher looked good tonight. Don't they look good? They may not look as good as I do, but they look good, don't they?"

By this time the teachers were laughing and clapping right along with the parents.

"I want to be successful," I said. "But in order for me to be successful, the children must be successful, and the teachers must be successful. Success for any of us is success for all of us. The same with failure.

"If your children come to school, that's going to help us. If your children learn, that's going to help us. If your children don't do those things, ladies and gentlemen, I will not be keeping this job. And I need this job.

"I love children, I really love children. But I need my paycheck, too. I get paid every two weeks if I keep this job, and the only way I will keep this job is if your children—our children—do well.

"That Cadillac you saw parked out front, that belongs to me. It costs me two hundred and sixty-five dollars a month to keep it, and I can't pay for it without you. Will you help me pay for that car?"

The room burst into an ovation.

"Are you telling me that I will be able to keep it?"

The cheers and applause got even louder.

And that was it.

Amidst cheering and applause, I walked down the center

aisle and into the foyer to personally greet my new congregation, who assured me that we were together—parents, teachers and I— to serve the children.

The folks came streaming out of the auditorium bent over laughing, everyone chattering a mile a minute. They told me how happy they were that I was their new principal. One tiny, elderly lady made her way over and took me aside.

"Honey," she said, patting me on the arm, "now don't you worry about a thing. We're going to help you to *pay* for that Cadillac."

CHAPTER

6

 THERE WERE MANY PARENTS WHO DIDN'T KNOW WHAT to make of me after that first spring meeting. They could see I was good at smiling, shaking hands and telling stories, but only time would tell what actual good I could do for their children.

Meanwhile the teachers sweated out that semester wondering if their fears about my shaking up their lives were well founded.

I wasn't about to walk into that building and alienate the staff by turning their world upside down overnight. Most of the big changes would come later, after we had time to identify specific problems and come up with a long-term plan together. But there were some areas that needed to be addressed immediately.

Teacher attendance, for example, was an issue that could not wait. I had once read a dissertation by a principal in Glassboro, New Jersey, indicating that in schools where the principal answered the phone, attendance improved by 15 percent. I remembered thinking, "My God, if attendance can be affected that much just by picking up the phone in the mornings, why doesn't everybody do it?"

So, my second day at Blaine, I began answering the telephone myself. This caused a commotion second to none. School policy required teachers to call the school before eight-thirty if they were going to be absent. Some teachers called early, before the secretary arrived, hoping to reach the cleaning lady, who took down names without asking questions.

Now I was there at seven-thirty to answer the phone.

"Good morning. Blaine School. This is Madeline Cartwright."

Click. Dead line.

Another ring.

"Good morning. Blaine School. This is Madeline Cartwright."

Click.

A couple of minutes later, another ring.

"Good morning. This is *still* Madeline Cartwright. If you're not going to come to school today, you're going to have to tell me."

On Monday mornings when the weather was bad, the phone would ring, and I'd answer, "Good morning. It's Monday, it's raining and I'm here."

Click. They'd hang up, give up and come in.

Even after my careful plan to create no enemies, a few teachers complained to district superintendent Jeanette Brewer's office. They reported that I was intimidating the staff into coming to work when they were ill. They told her some teachers were too afraid to take a day off sick. So Dr. Brewer called me.

"Madeline," she said, "what is this business of your telling people they can't take off sick?"

"Jeanette," I said, "I've done no such thing."

"Well, tell me exactly what you say to these people when they call to tell you they're sick."

"I ask them what they're sick *of.* I say, 'Are you sick of the children? Sick of the school? Sick of me?' I want to know exactly what sort of sick they're talking about. If they're so sick or hurt that they're truly unable to teach that day, that's fine. Otherwise I expect to see them.''

Dr. Brewer advised me to discontinue any questioning beyond that which was required by the school district. The morning following that conversation, she called again—at 7:55.

"Good morning," I said. "Blaine School. Madeline Cartwright."

"Good morning, Madeline. Jeanette Brewer. How are you this morning?"

"Oh, fine, Dr. Brewer, and on my best behavior."

We made small talk about my new assignment. I again thanked her for allowing me to come to Blaine. She looked for the first opportunity to hang up, and did. She called back a few more times over the next several days, and I was always polite and friendly. Then it happened.

One rainy Monday morning, the phone rang about 7:40. Jeanette had never called that early, so I felt safe.

"Good morning. It's cold, it's rainy, it's Monday morning and I'm here."

"Yes, Madeline, and I'm here *also!*" replied Dr. Brewer in a most annoyed voice. "I *told* you I was not going to have you answering the phone in that fashion."

"Oh, Dr. Brewer, I felt sure that it was you on the other end. I was only injecting a little levity."

"Um-hum, I bet you were."

I answered the phone as I had been instructed from then on. But the point remained, *I* answered the phone. And it had the intended effect. I began having perfect attendance among my teachers more days than not.

OF COURSE, THE ESSENTIAL PART OF GETTING TEACHERS, AS well as children, to come to school is to make it a pleasure being there. From the beginning, I did my best to provide whatever I could to show my staff I cared about them. Sometimes the smallest things can reap enormous benefits in terms of morale.

On mornings when it snowed, for example, I always stopped at a restaurant and bought some doughnuts. When my staff arrived, hot coffee and doughnuts would be waiting for them. I wanted them to know that I thoroughly appreciated their coming and coming on time when the weather was bad.

A fellow principal told me that when she was a teacher, she always stopped for breakfast on snow days because the principal would be glad to see any staff *whenever* they arrived.

I shared this story with my staff and told them I didn't feel that way, that I expected professionals to come to school on time no matter what the weather.

"Come to school and I will never make you cover the class of anyone who is absent," I told them. "You will not miss your preparation periods if I can prevent it. If you wake up late, come in anyway. If you have to leave a little early, all right, but come. I would much rather give an hour to you than to a substitute whom I do not know. If you need an hour in the middle of the day, we can probably work it out. When I am given a choice of doing without you for an hour or for a day, I will always opt for the hour."

I told the staff that many schools in Philadelphia had four, five and six substitutes a day. Often there were not enough substitutes to cover all the vacancies—substitutes chose the school to which they would go. Some principals divided the children of uncovered classes among the teachers present. These children often disrupted their temporarily assigned classrooms and caused not only one class to alter its routine but four or five classes. I promised that this would not happen at Blaine. When we were short a teacher, we kept the class together and covered it with our support staff. It was not unusual for me or the administrative assistant to teach classes.

After about a month, my teachers were in the habit of coming every day. Probably the best example of teacher dedication occurred when Marie Winters broke her leg.

Marie was a first-grade teacher, one of the best I had. She was a natural. Marie could teach like Johnny Mathis could sing. She had graduated from State Teachers College, where excellent board writing was demanded, and she always wrote her daily plan on the board in perfectly formed letters. She knew the children. She was crystal-clear in what she said and how she said it. She demonstrated and involved her students in the learning process. She facilitated learning. She rarely sat, except when she joined her students in learning groups. Other than that she was always on her feet, up and around the classroom. She was firm but gentle and caring. The children loved her.

One morning that first spring, Marie called and told me she had broken her leg. She said that the doctors told her she'd have to be out of school for a while.

"How long, Marie?" I asked.

"They say they'll be taking the cast off in about six weeks."

"Six weeks! Marie, you're not planning to stay out six weeks, are you?"

"Mrs. Cartwright, my leg is broken."

"Marie," I said, "a broken leg is no reason to stay out of school six weeks."

"You must be kidding," she said. "You can't be serious."

"Marie," I said, "there are boys who came back from Vietnam with no legs at all, with no hope of being able to walk ever again, and they found a way of getting themselves up and able to work."

"But, Mrs. Cartwright . . ."

"Marie, I'll get you a wheelchair. I'll give you a classroom assistant every day, all day, to help push you around. But, Marie, you gotta come. I can't do without you for six weeks. You *gotta* come."

When she reminded me she couldn't drive with that leg, I went over and picked her up. I brought her in that day, then arranged for her to have a ride every day for the next six weeks. The first morning Marie came through those doors in that wheelchair, the entire school was in the hallway to watch. All eyes wanted to see this teacher in a wheelchair. The other teachers could not believe it. If Marie was making this kind of commitment, where did that leave everyone else? Where did that leave the parents of the children? Where did that leave me?

Marie's appearance in that wheelchair with an assistant pushing her was an inspiring sight, the sort of thing that builds morale, and morale was the bottom line of attendance, among staff as well as students. So we worked to improve morale by beginning to clean the building and the teachers' lunchroom.

The teachers' lunchroom was as dirty as the rest of the building. No one bothered to clean the stove. The cleaning ladies somehow felt that they shouldn't have to clean up after the teachers. So I hired a day worker to clean the stove and the refrigerator for the teachers and then advised the cleaning ladies that they had to keep it clean from then on.

Day after day I did everything I could to boost morale. Stress and frustration will grind away at morale more than any other factors, and I recognized that. So even as I began shifting assignments and responsibilities within the school, making the changes I felt necessary to facilitate more efficiency and effectiveness, I was careful not to put too much stress on my staff.

Gathering the children after recess and getting emergency supplies ranked about the same on the stress scale, and I made changes in both areas. I began requiring the administrative staff to go onto the yard before school and at recess to form the children into quiet lines for the teachers' arrival.

This was an important task. Often when the bell rang signaling the end of recess, many children did not stop playing. Teachers who had problems controlling their children in the classroom often found the same problems extending onto the playground. Getting their students out from among the sea of children running around a yard the size of a city block was a monumental task, and the problem was not just theirs alone. One or two classes out of control on the yard would mean thirty to sixty children running, pushing and playing among other classes' lines, disrupting them as well.

At the same time as I focused on reducing stress by increasing order on the schoolyard, I changed the past practice of distributing supplies only on the first day of the month. I allowed teachers to get emergency supplies any time they needed them, simply by sending a note to the office. Of course, this change did not sit well with Mr. Lowe, who guarded the supplies as if they belonged to him. But teacher morale was far more important than Mr. Lowe's protection of his turf.

Another change I made to relieve stress was to make allowances for unscheduled breaks. If a teacher needed a momentary break away from the students, we were there to offer relief. Better to have an unscheduled break than a teacher or student hurt emotionally or physically.

Another underestimated stress reliever is a sense of humor. We injected levity wherever and whenever we found it, to ease the hard job of teaching and learning in the middle of what so often seemed like a war zone outside. Laughter can do wonders when the heat is on.

I read a study which found that teachers assigned to classes with low-achieving students had the poorest attendance. This was no surprise. Low-achieving students, as rewarding as they are to work with, can take a lot more energy to teach. So I changed to heterogeneous groupings, distributing the lower and slower achievers equally among our teachers. We found that the attendance of both the teachers and the children in these classes improved immediately after the shift.

None of these changes were revolutionary in themselves, but each had a great effect in boosting morale and setting the stage for other, more sweeping changes yet to come.

I SPENT THE REMAINDER OF THAT SPRING PUTTING STOPGAP measures into place, correcting situations that needed immediate attention.

The constant consumption of junk food was one such item. Junk food was so commonplace in the Philadelphia schools that the term for the time that the children were given to go outside, to use the toilet, to stretch and to play games—the time called recess —meant something else to most of the children. When I first came to teach in the city, a little boy came to me one day in tears and said, pointing to another little boy, "Miss Berger, he took my *recess!* He took my *recess!*"

I thought to myself, "Now, how could that child have taken this boy's recess?" I had no idea what the boy was talking about. Then it came to me. Some kids ate so much during this break that they didn't think of recess as a time to play; they thought of it as a time to snack. The word had become synonymous with whatever snack they had. A bag of chips became "recess." A box of cookies was "recess." "Give me a minute," a child would say, "I've got to get my recess."

Persuading the children that the elimination of "recess," as they knew it, was in their best interest proved to be a huge endeavor. I called for an assembly to tell them about my new "no junk food" rule. I said, "Boys and girls, I really need you today. I need you to help me convince the child next to you that what I am about to say is best for everybody. Will you help me?"

"Yessssss," they replied, as usual.

"We have made a new rule that will help us to learn better and to be healthier. Do you want to learn better?"

"Yesssssss," they sang.

"Do you want to be healthier?"

"Yessssss."

"Well, so much candy is not good for your teeth or good for you. Chewing gum sticks on our clothing and floors and wastes the cleaning people's time. Potato-chip and other junk-food wrappers litter our yard and our school. Roaches and mice feed on crumbs and particles from junk food. So I have made a rule that you may not bring any more junk food to school or any more money to buy junk food outside. We will allow only fruit for recess or for a lunch treat. The test for what is allowed is this: If it didn't grow on a tree or bush or it is not in its natural state, then it is not allowed in our building or on our schoolyard."

An announcement that we would now have school on Saturdays could not have caused more of an uproar among the children than this one.

I began counting from one to five, as I often did when I wanted the children's attention. They knew there must be complete silence when I reached five or I would be unhappy with them. This always worked.

"One . . . two . . . three . . .

"Excuse me. I am not going to be happy if I have to count all the way to five. Then there may not even be fruit."

The children quieted themselves. Only a few continued.

"I hear voices," I said, using yet another method of getting their attention. They repeated after me: "I hear voices." Then the auditorium was silent.

"Did you tell me that you wanted to help me?" I said. "Well, I need you to help me now by convincing anyone who does not want to help Mrs. Cartwright to cooperate with our new rule. Raise your hand if I cannot depend on you, as you know that you can depend on me."

No hands went up.

"Well, that's settled. Now everyone is going to help to keep our school clean and neat. Everyone is going to learn more and be healthier by not bringing any more junk food. If anyone forgets and brings junk food or money for anything except school supplies from the office, Mrs. Cartwright will take it and keep it. Any junk food that comes into this building will not be returned to the child or his or her parents.

"You must go home today and discuss this rule with your parents so that they will know about it," I said. "If you know any child who is absent today, you try to get the word to him."

The word went everywhere. Junk food at Blaine became almost nonexistent, and not only were the building and grounds cleaner but the afternoon energy level of the children, normally sapped by the sugar and sweets they were putting in their systems, increased greatly.

It was easy to understand how the students' habit of snacking began. For many of the children, the only real meals they saw were the ones fixed in the school lunchroom, which almost every child at Blaine received free or at a reduced price through the federal breakfast and lunch programs. Many of the children ate no breakfast at home and arrived at school too late to eat the federally funded breakfast. Their parents often gave them money to buy something to eat, and since they were not allowed to eat in the classroom, they saved the breakfast they had bought until the morning recess.

Some of the children ate two lunches. There was one little boy who ate *three* each day. That was fine with me. I was never able to discover whether that child truly had no food at home or whether he was just a particularly hungry little boy. In any event, anytime there were lunches left over, I allowed them to be eaten. There was to be no waste, I warned the children, but I encouraged them to help themselves.

I also encouraged the teachers to eat the school lunch in the lunchroom with the children. If the students saw their teachers eating the same food they had, they would be more encouraged to eat it, too.

My teacher's eating it, figured the children. *Mrs. Cartwright's eating it. So it must be good.*

Most of our staff ate the school lunch daily, including me. In fact, I made a habit of taking a fork and walking around the room, sampling bites from the children's plates. That was another way of telling the children this was good food. It was good for them and it was good for me.

AT THAT JUNE'S GRADUATION CEREMONY, I ISSUED A CALL to arms. This was one of the three most important days of the year in the community, along with Easter and Christmas. These were days when families truly came together and almost all parents fully supported their children. This was an ideal time to bring the community in on a project that would boost morale both in Blaine and in the surrounding neighborhood like nothing else we had done that spring: This was the time to take that tired building into our hands and turn it into something truly new, something in which we could all take pride.

Usually about a hundred students graduated from the sixth grade and another ninety from kindergarten. Every seat in the auditorium was traditionally filled for the event. This was the first spring that all special education students participated fully in the graduation ceremony. Before then, because the decision whether they advanced or not was made at the district office and not at the school, they were often left out of the graduation ceremonies.

I said I didn't care how or for what reason a child was leaving Blaine, whether it was to move into another level of special education or to go into a magnet school for academically talented or musically talented students, I still wanted them to participate in our ceremonies. I wanted all of our children to be a part of our celebration.

So that spring, and from then on, our special education students took their places in the boys' line or the girls' line, according to height along with everyone else. As the double line marched in to "Pomp and Circumstance," the child walking beside a special-needs child proudly took the arm of his partner and guided him down the aisle, up the steps to the stage and to his chair before going to his own place.

Parents with jobs always took time off to be in the audience. Grandparents came. Everyone came to graduation, and they all came on time. I made sure of that by spreading the word that the doors would be closed at ten, when the children marched in, and no one would be admitted while a child was speaking.

This was a special and meaningful day for every child and his family. The staff made sure that each boy and girl walking across that stage came away with something to show, whether it was a certificate for attendance, for good behavior, for improvement, for being on the safety patrol, for being in the choir or for participating in gymnastics.

After all the awards were issued, I spoke. I thanked the parents for their overwhelming support during my first months there. I went over our school rules and plans for the next year. Most of the parents had younger children still in the school, and as always I seized the opportunity to encourage parental understanding of the school program and parental participation. I then spoke about the condition of the building.

I said we were going to be starting a new chapter in the history of this school in the fall, and we needed to have the building clean for our children. I told them that there was a lot to be done between graduation and the start of the new school year and that Mr. Bailey and Mr. Brazille and the part-time cleaning ladies could not do it all.

I needed the parents' help.

"I am going to come in my jeans, with my scrub bucket," I said. "I need *you* to come in *your* jeans, with *your* scrub buckets. If you don't have buckets, we'll find some for you. But we need you. Now raise your hand if you care about your children and their school building and you can help us make it clean."

The hands went up by the dozen. I had Mr. Davis get every name, and I wouldn't let them drop their hands until each name was on his list.

ON THE FIRST OF JULY, I DROVE UP IN MY CADILLAC, dressed in jeans and sneakers, my hair done in cornrows, ready to dig in for a month of making the building sanitary and aesthetically pleasing to children. When I stepped out of my car there were eighteen parents waiting by the front door, ready to help me.

It was unbelievably hot outside those front doors—summer in the city. People in the neighborhood were hiding indoors with the shades drawn to hold in the cool left over from the night. Heat waves were doing a dance off the streets; dogs were hiding under parked cars, panting in their little pieces of shade. When Mr. Bailey opened the school doors to let us in, it was even hotter inside.

I said, "Mr. Bailey, what is this? There is heat coming from the heaters. What are you trying to do, burn us out?"

"No, ma'am," he said. "But you need hot water to do your cleaning, and I can't heat the water in here without turning on the building's heating system."

"You're kidding."

"No, ma'am, that's the way it is."

That's the way it was. So we opened every window we could and began our project. We felt as if we were working in a sauna, but we persevered. We took down the shades and spread floor stripper on them, then scrubbed and hosed them down. We went into every classroom, into every closet, into every sink and every bathroom, cleaning corners that hadn't been touched in twelve years. We washed, wiped, scraped and scoured.

And we talked. Day after day, for a month, we shared stories as we worked. We talked about our pasts, about our childhoods. I told them stories about mine to show that I had come up through poverty and conditions similar to theirs. But as I listened to them tell their stories, I could see that my childhood experiences were nowhere near as difficult as theirs. The stories I told were like child's play compared to the lives of some of these women.

Eva was an example. She was about five foot three, an attractive woman, with scars around her face and hands. I could see she had been through some rugged experiences. Her expression, her whole countenance, suggested she was not a happy person, that she had had a difficult life. Eva had six children and was twenty-seven years old. She had had her first child when she was twelve.

She told us about the winter when she was nine years old and how her mother took her and her three sisters to a city park on a snowy day. Eva's mother stopped at a bench, sat the four girls in a row and told them to stay put, not to move. She told them that she was leaving and that somebody would come by and get them. She was not coming back, she said, and they were not to get up or to try to go back to their home. Then Eva's mother walked away. That was the last Eva ever saw of her.

Eva said she and her sisters sat on that bench for a long time, huddling together for warmth as the wind bit at their solemn little faces. Eventually a policeman noticed them and took them to the police station. Later they were placed in foster homes. Eva spent time in several homes, and they worked her hard in each one. She said she was raped more than once before she was twelve.

Now she was here, living on Thirtieth Street, just across from the school, with six children of her own—well-behaved children, very well-mannered, clean and neatly dressed.

As I listened to Eva's story, I knew that I would never do anything at Blaine to add to the anguish of these struggling young parents or their children. I was going to make their lives better in every way that I could. Blaine was going to be a pleasant memory.

Every morning that crew of parents arrived by nine. We worked through to lunch, then took a break. I borrowed a thousand dollars from my husband, Earl, at the beginning of the month to buy supplies that we would need, such as paint, rubber gloves, food and beverages. But feeding lunch to eighteen adults every day was becoming too expensive. So I searched for help with the food.

Fortunately, the city ran a summer recreation program in the Blaine gymnasium. The program provided a free lunch for the participating children. Naturally they had some extra sandwiches left over at the end of each lunch period. When I discovered that, I asked if we could have the extras. The woman in charge objected, telling me that the lunches were for the children. After explaining to her what I wanted them for, I counted out eighteen sandwiches. The woman objected vociferously.

"You've done your duty," I told her. "Your bosses expect you to put up a reasonable objection, and you've done that. It would be above and beyond the call of duty for you to block that doorway or try to wrestle me down. No one expects you to do that. If you feel that you should do more, call your boss and tell him Mrs. Cartwright, the school principal, took eighteen lunches."

It was as simple as that. From then on, the woman was friendly. She even had the eighteen lunches waiting for me each day, counted out in a box.

After about a week, a television crew came from the local CBS affiliate. They had heard about the parents and me spending our summer cleaning our school, so they came out to take a look. They talked to us and taped some footage for that evening's news.

"While some Philadelphians were cooling themselves in the shade this morning," announced Channel 10 reporter Sheila Allen to that evening's viewers, *"a crew of parents and the principal at the James G. Blaine School were cleaning the shades and windows in their school."*

The next morning, those parents were buzzing. They were excited about seeing themselves and me on TV. A dozen new parents showed up to help. Even a couple of teachers came. They were all talking about that TV spot. It seemed the only time anyone ever saw television crews in Strawberry Mansion was after a murder or a fire. This was something new, and all the parents were happy about it.

"They were not reporting who cut who," said one.

"They were not reporting who got shot," said another. "Nobody's house burned down. This was *good* news on that television. This was all good."

"Did you see me?" said another. "*I* was on there."

This *was* good. This was good news.

BY THE END OF THAT MONTH, WE WERE JUST ABOUT FIN-ished. The windows and walls were washed, the floors scraped and scrubbed, the shades cleaned and hung back on the windows, the toilets spotless and odor-free.

But the place still looked dull and dingy. What it needed was paint.

Like so much else that involved going through the school system, getting a building painted took next to forever. When I called downtown, I was told that Blaine was number seventeen on the list. I was also told that it had been six years since the last school had been painted. At that rate, I would be dead and buried by the time we made it to the top of the list.

So I hung up the phone and dialed Earl Vann.

Vann was a city councilman now, with an office downtown. He was delighted that I was asking for something. Politicians are favor granters. That's their lifeblood. I had never asked for anything before, but here I was now, acknowledging Vann's talent and power.

He told me to come see him, and I was there within an hour. He had seen me and the parents on television. He knew what we'd been doing for the past month. When I told him we needed to have our school painted, he smiled his usual politician's smile, showing "all thirty-two." Then he picked up the phone and motioned to me to have a seat. I listened as Vann chatted with the mayor, Frank Rizzo.

"Hello, Frank! Earl Vann here. How are you?"

They had a little exchange of pleasantries, then Vann got to our business.

"Frank," he said, "I'm sitting here with a school principal. Now listen to this. She's been down there at her building with some parents, washing windows and scrubbing floors."

There was a pause.

"Yeah, that's right, the ones who were on television."

Another pause.

"Well, they need to get her school painted and she's having trouble getting the school district to help her."

Another pause, then Earl thanked the mayor and hung up.

"Madeline," he said, "the mayor told me he's got eight more months in office, and he figures that's certainly time enough to get a school painted."

Within fifteen minutes, someone from the school district called Earl to ask him which school needed painting.

The next day a man met me at Blaine to show me the choice of colors: eggshell white, bone white, oyster white, or antique white. I told him it seemed as if he was listing the ingredients for a fish stew rather than colors for an elementary school. I wanted our classrooms and halls to look bright and cheerful, just right for children. I wanted the office to rival the neighborhood McDonald's restaurant, to look clean, bright and inviting, to set a mood, to support a healthy climate.

With the mayor behind us, there was no way this man was going to quibble over colors. We wound up with pineapple yellow for our hallways and the auditorium, pastel greens and blues for the classrooms and yellow and green—our school colors—for the office . . . with matching mini-blinds, which I bought with my own money. We put decals on the front of the counter and hung ornaments and plants from the ceiling. I had the cinder-block walls of my office plastered and painted—at my own expense. "No cinder blocks in the executive suite," I thought to myself. It just wouldn't do to have parents, school hierarchy and salespeople see the principal sitting in a room that looked like a garage.

Even my brothers Buck and George pitched in to help improve the office. Buck brought in his rug shampooer and cleaned the carpet while George hung the mini-blinds. They were both so proud that I was a principal.

As a final touch, and while I still had the ear of the school district downtown, I asked them for some surplus paint and I bought a case of rollers. Then I called in Mr. Bailey and explained my battle plan for dealing with graffiti.

"As soon as it goes up," I said, "let's get out there and paint over it. As soon as they hit, *we'll* hit. We've got all this paint and even more where it came from. They're buying or stealing theirs, so there's no way they can keep up with us. We'll outlast them, and eventually they'll just give up."

Sure enough, they did. Graffiti became rare on our school building. If it did go up, I knew there was something going on in the community, something they were feeling. For example, the invasion of Grenada brought a burst of graffiti all across Strawberry Mansion. People were worried, worried our country was going to go to war, which in a neighborhood like this meant the best young men would be going to fight in the armed services and perhaps be killed. Our best young men traditionally joined the armed services for employment or to build a college fund. If they were in harm's way, there was tension in the neighborhood air, as if everyone was high. One outlet for that anxiety was graffiti.

The frantic, free-form scrawling was like a barometer, a way to measure the mood of the neighborhood. That is the kind of thing I came to learn in Strawberry Mansion. I learned to look beyond what I was seeing on the surface, to pay attention, to understand what the symptoms and signals really meant.

When the children arrived for the first day of school that fall, for the beginning of my first full year as principal, they entered a sparkling building. It was as if a new school had opened.

In more ways than one, it had.

CHAPTER
7

NUMBERS AND STATISTICS, IMAGES AND ANECDOTES, ALL those glimpses an outsider gets when he takes a peek at a place like Strawberry Mansion are nothing more than snapshots. But real life is not frozen in a frame. Real life is not a snapshot. It's ongoing, it's alive, it flows, it shifts, it's always in motion and it can only be experienced and understood over time.

Who has the time to climb into the life of a place like Strawberry Mansion—who besides the people actually living that life? I had the time. I had to have it. How could I address problems if I did not thoroughly understand the needs?

The children attending the Blaine School lived within a sixty-four-square-block area—four blocks in each direction from the school. There were no school buses, except for the special education students brought in from other parts of the city. Everyone else walked from his or her home to the school.

There was no way to comprehend quickly the lives our children were living in the hours when they weren't at school. I got a sense of it just by looking at the neighborhood and at the children, but there was no way to truly understand life in that community without watching it over time, without seeing those lives play themselves out.

I had spent my first spring and summer addressing the immediate needs of the staff, the students and the school building. Now, as my first full year began, it was time for me to meet the students and their families on their own turf, to understand where and how they lived.

There was much to understand.

The homes in Strawberry Mansion were largely decrepit leftovers from the last century, chopped up inside by slumlords who would nail up a couple of walls of plywood, screw a sink to one wall, run some water into it, nail a board next to it, set a hot plate on that and call the room a kitchen.

The slumlords sectioned small houses into "apartments," with one bathroom in each building for three families to share. There were better homes than these, and there were many that were worse.

City records showed that the average family income in Strawberry Mansion was $450 a month, and that 95 percent of those households were on welfare. Our school records showed that fewer than ten of the nearly six hundred children attending Blaine by my second year there did not qualify for the free or reduced-price lunch program.

Our records also showed that fewer than twenty of our children went home to both a mother and a father. The others lived with a single parent, foster parents, grandparents or relatives.

A check of lunch applications revealed that the average age at which the mothers of our students had their first child was sixteen. Many were barely thirty when they became grandparents.

Children in homes like these learn early to be caretakers. It is not strange for them to see their mother and their sister each having a baby at the same time. The mother might be only thirty and the sister thirteen, and both might have a year-old infant who needs care. The mother in such a situation sees her thirteen-year-old daughter with a child and says, "For God's sake, I have my *own* baby. I can't take care of another one." The daughter, who has been helping raise the other children until now, is suddenly occupied with her own baby.

So the other household duties fall into the laps of the little siblings, the children from ages six through twelve whom I greeted as students every morning at Blaine.

Sometimes we had children who didn't come to school because they were home caring for their brothers and sisters. Regularly I would have several third- and fourth-graders absent because they were home watching babies. That was very, very common, a fact of life.

A child grows up fast when he is changing diapers and putting food on the table before he has even begun the first grade. A child sees the world a certain way when his house is wall to wall with babies and children and mothers, and there's no man living there because the father is living with his own mother or is off in prison. Many of our children were familiar with the names of Graterford and Holmesburg—the two largest prisons in the Philadelphia area.

So many of our children had family members incarcerated that I felt I had to address the problem in an assembly. Children felt the shame of their imprisoned loved ones. I wanted them to know that they didn't have to feel shame.

"The fact that your mother, father, sister or brother is in prison has nothing to do with you," I told them. "You are not responsible for your family. Your family is responsible for *you*.

"I'm certainly sorry your mother, father, sister or brother is locked up. But that has *nothing* to do with you, with who you are or with your aspirations. We are here to help you reach your goals and to realize your dreams. We must learn here how to obey laws and how to survive and live in our school, our community and our country. We are not always treated fairly, but we must learn to endure hardships as our ancestors did and make the world a better place for ourselves and *our* children.

"You must help your family members return to the free

world feeling like accepted, rehabilitated members of our community so that life won't be so hard for them either. We must love our family members no matter where they are."

Some of our children struggled with the fact that their fathers were in prison. Others had no idea who their father was. I had one mother who had two girls in the school. I needed to see the birth certificate of one of the girls. When the mother brought it in, I saw there was no father's name on the certificate, so I asked her, "Do you know who this child's father is?"

"Oh, he don't play that game, Mrs. Cartwright," she said. "He don't play putting his name on no birth certificate. If his name is on a birth certificate, the welfare people would be coming after him. They'd be after him for support. He ain't got no job. They'd be calling him down to 1801 [family court] asking him why he don't support the girls, trying to make him feel small in front of our children, when the judge knows damn well he ain't got no job."

Some names on other children's certificates meant nothing at all. I saw the name Peewee—no last name, just Peewee—listed as the father on one little boy's birth certificate. (This was another Peewee, not my friend Kitty Morris's son.)

I said to the mother, "Why is the name Peewee on this boy's birth certificate? What's the father's real name?"

She said, "Mrs. Cartwright, I don't know his real name. Everyone around here called him Peewee. By the time I found out I was pregnant, he had moved away. Peewee was all I knew."

There was a part of me that wanted to laugh out loud about this. It was comical, but it was also pathetic. Right then and there, I erased the name Peewee from the form and wrote "Paul William." I did not want this little boy going through school with other teachers and principals laughing and judging his mother, who had been left pregnant after a one-night stand. She had taken part in what I called the "Fort Lauderdale spring vacation in the city"—a week of one-night stands much like college students on spring break have in that Florida city.

"Paul William," I thought. "From now on, this boy's father's name is Paul William."

Our children's own records often caused prejudice and discomfort. We had a boy transfer into one of our fourth-grade classes who had only been at Blaine a day when his teacher came into my office and asked if I knew that the child had killed his father.

"No, I did not," I said. "How do *you* know?"

She said it was in his file, on a report he'd brought with him from his old school. The boy's mother and father had had a fight, and the boy had stepped in to protect his mother. In the scuffle, he stabbed his father in the back and his father died as a result. This was all in a report, written by the counselor at his previous school.

I pulled that report out of the boy's file, ripped it into pieces and put them in my trash can. I said, "This story stops right here. There will be no more of this boy's teachers reading about this and talking about this to each other or to anyone else."

A few of our children had court records, mostly for stealing, shoplifting or vandalism. One afternoon two plainclothes detectives came to my office with a bench warrant for one of my fourth-graders, a ten-year-old boy who had not reported to court for a hearing.

I told the officers that they would have to wait until I called the boy's mother. I said, "I don't care what the warrant says, he needs his mother with him. Would you want your child going off with two strangers alone? It would be frightening even to me. This child is ten years old, and he is going to have his mother with him if I can find her. Have a seat. It won't take long."

The police knew me. They knew I ran Blaine in my own way. And I knew them. I always stopped to talk to them whenever I saw them in the community or in the courtrooms. They understood what I was trying to do, and they trusted me.

When the boy's mother came, I called him to the office, and the police took them both away. He came back, of course, and he continued to attend Blaine even after his family moved out of the neighborhood. His court record ended that day, and he made a new beginning. The day those police officers arrived, he had already been in school two months without being absent or suspended. This was a new record for him. And he kept it going. He had a good year at Blaine, did well in his schoolwork and even had a major part in his class play. Blaine had been a new and different school experience for him. I think it truly changed his life. Eventually he had to move, and I hated to see him leave.

JUST AS A BENCH WARRANT FOR A TEN-YEAR-OLD WAS A new experience for me, I had to accept the fact that these children were witnessing violence within the walls of their own households that surpassed anything I'd ever seen on the streets when I was growing up. My parents had disagreements, but I never saw them in a physical fight, and I certainly never imagined when I went to bed at night that when I awoke in the morning I might find one of them dead.

Many of our children didn't have to imagine. They lived in a world where there was constantly some sort of battle going on, either in their own apartment or in the one next door. Some of them regularly saw their mother walk in with her nose bleeding, or saw her come out of her bedroom in the morning with her face all beaten up.

Death itself was very, very real to our children. When their parents fought, the little ones would crouch in the next room or cower in a corner, hoping and praying that when this fight was over, their mommy and daddy would still be alive.

Too many times they were not. And even more horrors awaited the children in the streets. When they were outside and saw two people arguing, they prepared to dive behind the closest car, because the guns could be coming out at any minute. If it happened to be their own father or mother out there arguing, the children didn't duck. They just prayed, the same as they did whenever there was a fight at home.

Tension works on the minds of children. It pushes them to a

point where they carry it inside them all the time. Sometimes I'd stop a child in the hall who wasn't smiling, and I'd ask, "What's the matter?" A story of violence would come out, and I would apologize. I would apologize for their pain, for the pain no child should ever have to feel.

"I am so sorry," I would say. "I am so sorry that this happened to you. This should not have happened, and nothing like it is going to happen to you here. This is your school. This is a safe place, where everybody's going to treat you nicely. We like you here. Whatever we can do to make your day pleasant, we're going to do that. We're going to try to help you smile. We're going to try to help you have a nice day."

A nice day was a rarity for girls who had to be concerned with sexual advances in their own home. We had ten-year-old girls who had learned not only how to care for their siblings but how to protect themselves from threats no child should ever face.

Home often was not a safe base for many of our children. Home too often was a place where they kept their guard up, where they looked over their shoulders and kept their legs crossed. One little girl, a fifth-grader, told me she slept in her jeans with a rope tied in a knot around her pants at night, to discourage anyone from trying to take them off. She could take that rope off and relax only after she arrived at school.

The children in our school's neighborhood lived in a world so filled with violence that they were inured to its signals. I watched them out on the schoolyard as ambulances or fire trucks raced by, sirens going full blast and lights flashing. Most of the children would not even look up. They just went on about their games. Sirens were a regular part of life, a normal thing, the same as hearing a radio or people talking. It was the background music of their world.

One morning I was driving to school when I passed a man's body lying covered in the street, two blocks from the school. There were a few people standing around looking at it, but that was it. No police. No ambulance.

I went on to the school, parked, rushed in to tell the office staff I was there, then ran back to where the body was still lying, and still no one was around except a curious crowd.

I sent one of the parents to the other end of the block with orders to steer all children to the next street. A few boys and girls had already stopped to look at the covered dead man. I didn't want any more of them seeing it.

A woman in the crowd told me she was the one who first saw the body, at about six o'clock that morning.

"Somebody must have dumped it there," she said. "I called the police, and they came about seven-thirty and put up the wood barricades. But they didn't even cover him. That's my blanket there. I covered him."

As we talked, an occasional passerby walked over, pulled back the blanket, returned it and walked on. One would have thought the body was in a funeral parlor for viewing. Those who had young men in their families checked to be sure the body was not one of theirs. About ten o'clock, it was finally taken away.

I hurried back to the school, prepared for the shock I was sure had swept through the students. I was ready to call another assembly.

When I came on the playground, the children were playing ball and skipping rope as always. I pulled one of the teachers aside and asked if she thought I needed to call the children together to talk about this incident.

"What for?" asked a little girl who overheard me. "He's not from around here. Nobody knows him."

Then she went back to her jump rope.

WHEN A VICTIM OF AN ACCIDENT OR A MURDER *WAS* "FROM around here," our children were shocked and frightened. I will never forget one Saturday morning when I heard on the radio that a man had cut off a woman's head with a machete. Even in a city as large as Philadelphia, where murders are almost an everyday occurrence, this was a particularly grotesque crime. So I was stunned when the radio report identified where the killing had occurred—two blocks from Blaine.

I came in Monday morning prepared to face children horrified by what had happened. They were. Some had actually seen the man as he stood on the front porch of his house holding the dead woman's severed head in his hand. A sight like that is something no human, much less a child, should ever witness.

Tamika Scott was also "from around here," and the day she died was one neither I nor anyone else who was a part of Blaine at that time will ever forget.

The Scotts had moved into the neighborhood at the beginning of the school year. Rowena Scott, the mother, was thirty-eight years old with eight children. Twelve-year-old Tamika was the youngest.

Tamika was a very active little girl, one of those children who are busy and bad at the same time. I occasionally had to counsel her in my office, but she just as often got hugs as scoldings. She was on the safety patrol. She played the clarinet. She was involved, she had a lot of energy and the other children loved her.

"Meeka," as her classmates called her, was one of our most popular students. Her older brother Jermaine, on the other hand, was a nightmare. Jermaine had severe emotional problems, which he acted out in violent ways. He was fifteen years old, not a student at Blaine. But he often showed up on our school grounds, out to make trouble.

"Young man," I told him the first time I encountered him, "you do not belong on this yard."

"F—— you."

Those words did not have nearly the impact on me that they had twenty years earlier, when I had first heard them as a young teacher.

"Excuse me," I said, "but you may *not* be on this yard."

"I'll be any f - - - ing place I please," he said.

I told myself, "Something is wrong with this boy. He is not

normal." I found Raymond Brooks, who supervised our playground, and told him, "Do not fool with that child. And for God's sake, do not try to touch him." Then I went to call the police.

They took Jermaine away, but a couple of days later he was back again, this time in the building. I ordered him out, and when he refused to go, I called the police again. Again they took him away.

Later that week I found Jermaine in the yard punching a little girl in the face. He was trying to hurt that child. When children fight, no one is trying to kill anyone else. Nothing, however, was holding this boy back; he was disturbed. I called the police again, but it was clear nothing was going to stop this boy until something serious happened.

Tamika had a group of girlfriends who roamed around together. One afternoon they had an altercation with some other girls from Blaine. An argument ensued, and the mother of one of the girls showed up at the house of one of Tamika's girlfriends. When the little girl answered the door, the woman began hitting her, in the presence of the little girl's grandmother. Tamika and her family were incensed.

The next day several people in the neighborhood said they had seen Jermaine walking the streets with a double-barreled shotgun in his hands.

That worried me, but I hadn't heard what had happened with the girls. I didn't know there might be a connection. And I didn't pay too much attention when several police cars came careening around the corner and past the building as school was letting out, going the wrong way on our one-way street. I, like the children, had begun to accept sirens and police cars as a part of everyday life in this community.

I gave the sirens little more than a passing thought and drove home. When I got there, my answering machine was blinking. I punched the button, and out came the voice of a child I knew who lived near the school.

"Mrs. Cartwright," he said. "Tamika got shot. I think she's

dead. The men brought the stretcher out empty. When they bring the stretcher out empty, that means the person is dead."

I called the president of our parents' organization, who told me the same story I had heard on my machine.

"I heard that her brother accidentally shot her," the woman told me, "but that ain't what the family's saying, so I ain't sayin' nothing."

As usual, Liz McCain had investigated the incident and called me later that evening with the facts.

"Tamika was shot in the head by her brother," Liz told me. "She's dead."

I left early for school the next day to plan for the commotion that was surely to follow. I arrived at school at seven-thirty to find Tamika's mother, two of her sisters and an older brother waiting for me. I put my arms around this young parent who had to plow through these circumstances, with her youngest child dead and the next-youngest locked up and charged with the killing. We all cried together, and I listened.

When they prepared to leave, I gently held the mother back, and I said to her, "I'm so sorry. You know that I loved Tamika as I love you. But we must think also about Jermaine. He is sorry and feeling very much alone. You must go to him and help him also."

I hugged her close, to share strength, I guess.

The day after Tamika was killed was one of the worst days in the twelve years that I spent at the Blaine School. Children sobbed openly as they met on the yard that morning. We brought the most mournful to my office to try to console them.

One little girl, whom Tamika had beaten up often, proclaimed, "I'm *glad* she's dead. She can't beat me up no more."

A young girl named Martha, one of Tamika's friends, walked immediately up to this girl and punched her in the face. Both of them were brought to my office in tears.

There was so much pain to sort out. Mary, the president of the parents' organization, was a friendly, motherly woman who often intervened and solved many of my office problems. She took a group of Tamika's closest friends to the supermarket to buy breakfast and dinner food to fix for the family. When they returned, they cooked and talked together. Mary soothed the group like a fairy godmother with a magic wand. Though she and I were the same age, she always seemed to me to be much wiser than I. She probably had been through more.

The staff interacted with the children as if they were all trained counselors. I didn't call anywhere for help and none was sent. No one made a phone call, mailed a card or acknowledged our loss in any way. We had no special staff of crisis counselors sent from downtown as there would have been had something like this happened at a suburban school. It was only ten minutes away from Blaine that a helicopter carrying Pennsylvania Senator John Heinz crashed in a schoolyard, killing the occupants of the aircraft and two children. That crash occurred in an affluent neighborhood, and the response to the tragedy was broad and immediate. Scraps from the helicopter were removed from the yard before the next morning, to ease the children's shock—yet dead bodies could lie for hours on the streets of Strawberry Mansion. A counseling hot line was immediately set up for families of the school where that crash occurred, yet with all the deaths we witnessed during my years at Blaine, never once was such a service offered.

I guess the assumption is that inner-city children are another species—poor minorities. Maybe it's assumed they have steel-plated psyches. Maybe they're not supposed to feel things as strongly as other children. Or maybe the general public just doesn't give a damn.

Tamika's death raised many questions for me. So did the things I eventually found out about Jermaine.

I learned that he was a special education student on suspension from the junior high school. Though the state law precluded unlimited suspension for special education children, Jermaine was out of school more than he was in school that year.

Did it have to take the killing of his sister to convince others to recognize that Jermaine had serious behavior problems and to address them? Too often schools postpone such problems or pass the buck through suspension.

Why was the special education division or the attendance division not working with Jermaine and his family?

Why was Jermaine not in school getting help?

How many other Jermaines are sitting around like powder kegs waiting to be ignited?

A FEW DAYS AFTER TAMIKA'S DEATH, HER MOTHER CALLED and asked me to go with her to the funeral parlor to help decide if the casket should be open or closed for the service. After joining other family members at the home of the grandmother—who had already gone to see the body and who felt the casket could be open—I drove Tamika's mother and two sisters to the parlor.

Tamika was clad in a beautiful white dress and was laid out in a white-and-gold-colored casket. The mortician had done wonders with her face. Though it bore little resemblance to the beautiful little girl who just a few days before had been playing on our schoolyard, it was not grotesque. I listened as the decision was made to keep the casket open for the funeral service.

I advised our student body that no one could go to Tamika's funeral without a parent. Parents who worked sent notes asking if I would take their child with me. We gathered adults to help with the many children who came to school with those notes. It seemed the entire school wanted to turn out for Tamika's funeral.

The event was heartbreaking. Five of Tamika's seven siblings were there. Two, including Jermaine, were in jail. Rowena escorted each of her children to the casket and back to their seats. She looked after her children in an almost regal fashion. They sobbed loudly. The only help Rowena was given in consoling her children was from her one-year-old granddaughter, who, seeing her own young mother—one of Rowena's daughters—crying over the loss of Meeka, patted the girl on her back.

Night was a long time coming that day and sleep even longer. As I lay awake, I thought of the phone call from the boy who had left me the first message about Tamika's death. How many teachers or principals, I thought, would know enough to draw such a conclusion? How many would understand that when a stretcher is brought out empty, that means the person inside is dead? A person has to have seen a lot of stretchers brought out to understand that pattern. A person has to have seen a lot of death.

WE SAW DEATH IN STRAWBERRY MANSION. AND WE SAW drugs as well, although they were not nearly the problem when I first arrived that they had become by the time I left. The first time I saw those two things—drugs and death—come together was in the case of Cassandra, one of our young mothers.

Cassandra had two children at Blaine and one infant at home. She was a cocaine addict. After years of seeing her let her habit rule her life, her grandmother and her children pleaded, begged and finally convinced her to go into rehabilitation. When she could not convince her husband, who also had a habit, to go with her, Cassandra tore herself from him and their devoted brotherhood of users and entered a rehab program by herself.

When she walked into my office one afternoon to take her daughter, Niema, to the clinic, she looked so beautiful I hardly recognized her.

"Cassandra," I said, "is that you? What in the world did you do to yourself? You look *wonderful!*"

"Oh, thank you, Mrs. Cartwright," she said. "I just came back from rehab. I'm clean and I'm going to stay clean."

No one could have imagined that before that day was done, Cassandra would be dead.

After taking her daughter to the clinic, she went grocery shopping and bought a pair of new sneakers for her son, then went to pick up her year-old baby from her grandmother, who had been caring for her children while she was away. After that, she and the girls went home to wait for Dorian, Cassandra's nine-year-old son, to return from school. She couldn't wait to let Dorian know of her accomplishment and to show him his new shoes.

While Cassandra was preparing the first dinner she and her children would have had together in thirty days, her husband came in. He asked to borrow some of her money. Cassandra had anticipated this, which is one reason she had spent it all on groceries and shoes.

Her husband was enraged. An argument ensued. It escalated into pushing, shoving and cursing. The children crouched together on the sofa. When Dorian saw his father pull a knife, he leapt up to intervene. His father shoved him back down and told him to stay there.

The next thing Dorian saw was his mother falling to the floor.

His father cursed, and stomped from the house as he had so many times after a fight.

Dorian and his sisters were horrified, too frightened to move. They sat there stunned, with their mother's body lying on the floor in front of them. They were still sitting there when their father returned the next morning, as he usually did after a fight. Realizing his wife was dead, he panicked. Again he left, this time to call the police, then to hide, to run, to do something, though he didn't know what.

The police responded immediately, rushing through the open door, finding the body on the floor and the three small children sitting silently on the couch.

"Is there someone else here with you?" the police asked.

The children shook their heads.

"Who can we call? Is there someone who comes when you have a problem?"

Dorian spoke.

"Call my principal," he said, holding his two sisters close. "She'll come and get us."

And I did. A counselor and I rushed to the children, who by then were across the street at their eighty-year-old great-grandmother's apartment. I took them back to the school and later to my home, to spare them the questioning of the many relatives who would want to know what had happened.

Dorian and his sister passed the baby from one to the other with experienced hands. It was evident they were used to caring for one another. They knew what the baby needed and how to prepare it for her.

I did not know what to say to these precious little victims. I could only hold them close to me that night when they joined me in my bed, sobbing uncontrollably and screaming, "I want my *mommy*, Mrs. Cartwright, I want my *mommy!*"

I patted their backs and stroked their arms as they cried themselves to sleep across my body. I cried and prayed that God would give me strength to be to these children what they needed me to be. I prayed for guidance in the handling of these fragile little souls who already had been hurt too much.

A parent from the school came to my house the next day with a collection of money and condolences from our school family. She helped me to shop and dress and prepare Dorian and Niema for their mother's funeral. We all went, and with great difficulty, we made it through the service.

Dorian and his baby sister remained with Cassandra's grandmother and he continued to attend Blaine, where I arranged for him to have counseling. During one of those sessions, the psychologist asked this nine-year-old boy, who had cared for his baby sister while his mother was alive and was now tending her after the death, to write what he was feeling.

"When I grow up," he wrote, "I will get a job.

"I will always have money.

"I will never run out of Pampers."

C H A P T E R

8

 IT WOULD BE EASY FOR A PERSON TO CONFRONT THE situation in Strawberry Mansion—the situation in the school, the situation in the surrounding neighborhood— and give it up as hopeless. I heard it all the time from people I knew.

"Why don't you quit?" they'd ask me.

"Do something else," they'd say.

"Do yourself a favor. Give yourself a break. Why put yourself through this?"

My answer would always be the same. How could I live with myself if I thought that way? The notion of bailing out never entered my mind. I never doubted that everything I wanted to do with children could be done in that school. I realized it might be more of a challenge there than someplace else, but that fact made it even more inviting to me. There was no doubt in my mind that we could do it, that we could help the children, that we could educate them, not to save them but to allow them to save themselves.

My primary question from the beginning was: "How can we

ensure that the children here at Thirtieth and Berks reach their maximum potential?" Going into their neighborhood, into their homes, stepping into some of their lives and seeing some of their horror allowed me to identify needs that had to be met to allow learning to take place, to set the table, so to speak.

First there was their pain.

From the beginning I told my teachers that we might not know what kind of life our youngsters had before they stepped into our school, we might not know what happened to them last night or what's going to happen to them tonight. But we *do* know what's happening to them *here*, I said, and every effort will be made by every one of us to make the hours between eight and four a time when our children can be children.

I think back to my own childhood, I told my staff, and I can remember so many moments of pleasure, so many moments of fun, and so very little pain. Many of our children don't have enough of those moments, I said. If they're not getting them out there, where they live, we can offer them here.

The least we can do, I said, is let the little boys and girls know—and make them *believe*—that people are going to *like* them here, that this is their school and all that goes on here is to make life better for them. Here is a place where they can smile and be happy, where they can kiss and hug and not worry that that kissing and hugging might be dangerous, that it might lead to something else.

When they are out in that hard world, I said, when they are cowering down and praying, somewhere in the back of their young minds they can comfort themselves with the knowledge that come eight o'clock in the morning the world is going to be pleasant again.

That's how it was for little Tyrone. That's how he made it through the long night, cradling his arm burnt to the bone from the hot grease his mother spilled on it. That's what kept him from just curling up and surrendering—knowing his school was going to be here for him come sunup.

That's what I told my teachers. Before anything else happens in this building, I said, it must become a beacon for the children, a haven of hope and a shelter from each of their individual storms.

That was one thing I talked about. Another was self-esteem.

You may discipline the children within the guidelines of school policy, I told my staff. You may be stern, strict, whatever your style is. But you may *never* shame a little boy or girl. You may never demean, insult or put a child down.

Then I told them the story of Fanny Q.

Fanny Q. lived next door to me when I was a young girl in Coatesville. She was the oldest of four children and lived with her two sisters in her aunt's house. Her aunt would holler out the window at suppertime for the whole neighborhood to hear: *"Fanny Quuuuu!"* Some of the children mimicked that call, ridiculing this eleven-year-old girl, who was an easy target for their cruelty. She was six feet tall, slender, and had noticeably big feet. She wore her hair in a very short, close crop cut. I don't think it ever grew longer than an inch. This made it very difficult for her to keep her hair looking nice.

It was the death of Fanny's mother that brought her to live with her aunt, who didn't have much to begin with and who just about sank under the burden of caring for Fanny and her sisters. They had a hard life, and there were stretches of time when the girls simply did not come to school for one reason or another. One of those stretches occurred during the winter. Fanny showed up one rainy day, after missing two weeks of classes. We had gym class inside that day, and the principal, Mr. Anderson, happened to walk by. He noticed Fanny and came over to our group.

"Fanny Q., where have you been?" he asked. "You haven't been to school in weeks."

Fanny was reluctant to answer in front of everyone. But she did.

"Mr. Anderson," she said, "I didn't have no shoes to wear."

The whole gym became quiet. All the kids stopped playing ball to listen.

"You didn't have shoes?" said Mr. Anderson. "That's no excuse. You could have borrowed *my* shoes. Your feet are surely big enough."

Children's laughter filled the gym. But I didn't laugh. I watched Fanny run out in tears, and I never saw her smile again.

I thought of how Mr. Anderson and some of the teachers would repeatedly tell us there was no acceptable excuse for our not succeeding at keeping clean. They'd say to us, "If you have only one dress or shirt, you can wash it every night and be clean when you come to school."

This was not realistic. Children or even adults couldn't wash every night, and Fanny Q. certainly should not have been expected to find a pair of shoes.

Few of us, in fact, had a pair of decent shoes. Many of my classmates had holes in the soles of their shoes, and I was no different. We covered the holes with cardboard and walked on our heels and toes to protect our feet.

One morning, when I could find no clean socks, I washed my socks and dried them in the oven, to escape the harsh criticism of the principal and some of the staff. When I went back for them, there were burned brown stripes from the hot oven rack on both socks. I put them on and went to school—which was a mistake.

One of my classmates was a boy named Poochie Butler. The stripes on my socks brought his attention to my feet, and Poochie began to point and laugh. Others laughed with him. I felt humiliated.

As I watched the children laughing at Fanny Q. that morning in the gym, I sensed she must have felt far worse than I had when Poochie mocked me. Poochie was a child the same as I. He was often ragged and dirty himself. Mr. Anderson, however, was the principal. No adult should ever ridicule a child. For a school principal to do it is unforgivable.

I made up my mind that day, watching Fanny Q.'s tears, that I would never hurt a child's self-respect when I became the teacher I knew I would eventually become. I felt the same way when I became a principal. And I let my teachers know I expected them to feel the same way as well.

THERE IS NO QUESTION THAT APPEARANCE GREATLY AFFECTS the way a child feels about himself. It affects his or her self-esteem, so I told my staff we were going to do all we could to help our children build that esteem. Between eight and four, I said, our children were going to be well groomed and hold their heads high. They were going to be proud of themselves and of the boys and girls around them.

The hard fact was that many of the children were *not* well groomed. Many had no clean clothing. They had nobody at home with adequate means to buy them new clothes when they needed them or to wash the ones they had on a regular basis. Some of them had no running water. Using the laundromat was prohibitively expensive for a mother with two children living on her welfare allotment of approximately $300 a month.

Urine odor was a particularly acute problem. Some of our children wet the bed or slept with other children who did. Few had pajamas. Pajamas were a luxury. Some of our kids slept in the same clothes in which they came to school.

I had to convince my staff that the solution was not to provide the children with more clothes; they'd still have dirty, smelly outfits—just more of them. What we had to do, I said, was provide a way to clean the children's clothing on a regular basis.

I had begun bringing children home with me and cleaning them there. I'd put them in the bathtub, pour in a little Clorox and some dishwashing detergent, turn on the whirlpool, toss in some toys and tell them to play a while. I'd take all their little clothes and put them in the washer. Then I'd come back and scrub them some, let them play a little more, scrub some more, then pull them out, get them dried and dressed in something warm and have them sit around and just enjoy themselves until bedtime. We'd put some sleeping bags down on the floor, they'd spend the night and next morning they'd get up with me, put on their clean clothes and we'd all come in to school together. I usually had no problem getting the permission of the parents. I took a number of children home with me who did *not* need grooming, to avoid any stigma that might be attached to the visits. The children clamored to come with me.

But the relatively few children I was able to bring home was not enough to make a real difference. What we needed, I knew, was our own washing machine at the school.

Something like this was unheard of. What would some parents say? What would the administration say? I considered the possible consequences, but I concluded that I was providing a service the children needed and I had the support that counted most—I had the support of the children and parents who would be helped immensely by the presence of a washing machine and dryer at Blaine.

So we went about buying them.

The quickest and easiest way to raise money in the community was through raffles. Most of the area residents could always find a dollar or two for a raffle ticket—the same as they could for a state lottery ticket—and they stood a lot better chance of winning something through a raffle, as well as knowing their dollars were going to a worthwhile project close to home.

But raffles were against school district policy, so if we were going to have one to raise money for a washer and dryer, it would have to be run by a committee of parents outside the school, and I insisted that students not be allowed to sell tickets, lest we invite criticism or investigation.

We offered two color television sets as prizes to the seller and buyer of the winning ticket; the raffle was a huge success. Six hundred dollars was the profit the parents made after they paid for the television sets. That six hundred dollars bought a new washer and dryer—green, our school color. When I called downtown and told them I needed someone to come out and install our new appliances, they remembered that I was the same person for whom the mayor had requested paint the previous summer. A man arrived the next morning to hook up our machines. Shortly after, our washing program was underway.

While we were raising money for the washer and dryer, we also began collecting clothing. Some was donated. Some we bought in bulk. I still stop in department stores when I see something like sweatpants on sale, and I say to myself, "God, if I was still at Blaine, I'd buy this entire *shelf* of sweats." Anything we saw that was a good deal and our kids could wear, we bought.

When they arrived in the morning, the first thing the children who needed washing did was change clothes. We had a private area set up using portable blackboards. The kids went behind the boards and changed into clean clothes. If their bodies needed washing, they could scrub themselves at the sink in the nurse's office or at the one in mine. If a child *really* needed washing, we took him or her into the mop closet, hooked a hose up to the spigot there and made a shower.

After they were clean and changed, the children put their dirty clothes in a bag, left it on a table and went to class. When they came back in the afternoon, their clothes would be back in that bag, clean, folded and fresh.

Some kids didn't come in on their own. I'd notice them out on the yard or in the hallway and steer them on in. Others would come in and mill around, just waiting for us to say something. Then there were those who would come in and tell us they needed cleaning. We'd wash their little faces and bodies, give them clean underclothes, dress them up and send them out ready to learn and play. This was for all of us. Our wash program was something of which we—the students and the staff—were proud.

Some days the washer and dryer ran all day, and almost everyone pitched in. If the secretary had a few minutes to spare, she'd stop, sort out a pile of clothes, toss them in and run a load. Nobody *had* to do it. There were some people in that building who never touched the clothes, and that was fine. There were enough people who did get involved to take care of what needed to be done: a classroom aide, a teacher, a parent, me.

Our librarian, Janet Cline, did more laundry than anyone.

She'd arrive in the morning, sign in and immediately go over to that table and start a load. The laundry room was directly across the hall from her library, so she was right there to move the loads from the washer to the dryer, to rub some soap on those extra-dirty spots. Janet loved the children and eagerly helped in every way she could.

Holidays became an especially busy time. The day before Thanksgiving we'd have forty or fifty coats come in because the parents would tell the kids, "Get your coat washed. We're going to dinner tomorrow." It was the same with Christmas. If someone wanted to take a child shopping, we made sure they had a clean coat to wear.

I brought in parents to help. I told them if they helped with the school washing, they could throw in their children's other clothes as well. Only children's clothing was allowed in the washer, but that was enough to bring several parents in to help.

Occasionally a child would resist. There was one little boy who smelled so bad his odor permeated his classroom and the hallway outside. I discovered him as I was walking down that hall, caught his scent and followed it to his classroom door. I took that little fellow down to my office and talked to him. He hadn't come to school for three or four days. He'd spent his nights sleeping with his little brothers and sisters, who wet the bed. The smell was his siblings' urine on the clothing he wore to school, the same clothing in which he slept night after night.

He did not want me to change his clothes, but I offered him no choice in the matter. I brought him down to the changing room, removed all of his clothes, put them in the machine, scrubbed him with plenty of soap and water, dressed him and sent him back to his class. I convinced him that we loved him and were helping him to look and smell better. From then on, he was a regular in our wash room.

THERE WERE OTHER SERVICES WE OFFERED AS WELL TO ADD comfort and well-being to the children's lives.

Dennis Robinson, a neighborhood teenager who had stopped by to help us with our summer cleanup, began coming in regularly to cut the kids' hair. We bought him a set of good professional clippers and let the boys know he was there for whoever needed it.

Some older girls volunteered to come in and fix our little girls' hair. They could do the cornrow style that lasted for more than one day and worked well on hair of any length or texture.

I brought a sewing machine from the Belmont School, where I had previously taught. There were many machines there, left from a defunct home economics class. I saw that torn clothing had become a big problem, with children playing tag and grabbing one another's coats or shirts. It was hard to believe how many fights we had at Belmont over two kids playing together and one accidentally ripping the other's clothing. But after I began mending those tears, we had far fewer fistfights. That problem was nipped in the bud.

We used the sewing machine at Blaine to mend rips in the children's clothing caused by staff as well as by other children. I advised my teachers never to hold a child by putting their hands directly on the child's flesh. If you must hold them, I said, get a good grip on their clothing, to avoid scratches and other injuries that could come from holding flesh. Of course, that brought with it more cases of rips and tears, which I easily remedied with that machine. Word spread about Mrs. Cartwright's sewing, and soon I was fixing more than schoolyard accidents. A little boy came in one morning, very early. He hadn't had time to be out on the yard. He was holding together the torn leg of his pants, and he said, "Mrs. Cartwright, I got a rip right up the leg here. My momma said to ask you could you run this up right quick?"

I didn't mind. If a child came to school and his pants were a size too large, and he was walking around tugging at them to keep them up, I'd just have him step into the sewing room and put a little tuck in them for him.

People would ask, "Where do you get the time to be washing and sewing? When do you do your *principaling?*" I'd tell them

I did my principaling on my feet, the same way I did everything else. It doesn't take long to put a load of clothes in a washer or to put a quick stitch in a pair of pants. Keep on the move, and those activities just become part of the flow.

Paperwork? I did my paperwork after school, between the time the children left and six o'clock, when I left. I brought no schoolwork home with me, ever. I might have brought children home with me, but no schoolwork. If I really got behind and had to catch up, which was rarely, I'd come in on a weekend and do it.

I'd often have people look at what I was doing at Blaine and say, "Sure, I could do that too if I did nothing else in my life. I could do that too if I didn't have a life outside the school." People use the phrase "Get a life." Well, I had a life. People assumed I had forfeited any sense of my own life and had sacrificed it all to tackle a situation like Blaine. Well, it was just not so. I most assuredly *had* a life. I had my home, husband, family and church. I took trips to Atlantic City. I was on the usual boards and was active in educational organizations. I enjoyed dinners out and parties with friends. The only pleasure I went without was the novel reading I had always enjoyed during the summers before I came to Blaine.

If I were not a person myself, with a real life, then I would have had that much less to show and share with the children whose lives I was trying to shape.

Get a life? Don't think a successful teacher or principal can't have one. Don't assume they can't have time for themselves as well as their job. On the contrary, it's a *must*.

THERE WERE CRITICS ALL ALONG WHO QUESTIONED WHAT WE were doing with washing machines and sewing machines and haircutting services in a public school. They said we were not a social service agency, that a school could not be all things to all children and was never intended to be such.

My answer was simple.

Someone must do these things for the children. If a child's hungry, someone must feed him. If he's dirty, someone must wash him. If his clothes need laundering, someone must clean them. For whatever reason—and there were many—we had children for whom no family or agency was taking care of such needs. So *we* did it. It didn't hurt our mission or take away from our task, the task of teaching. It helped that task. It helped to establish a sense of family in our school, which helped the children be more ready to learn.

The fact is that the age in which we live demands that we extend such efforts. We should be compelled to provide necessities for children who don't have them. We speak of how we want to help children, but then we allow ourselves to be tangled in bureaucratic nonsense and help never actually reaches those who need it.

What we did at Blaine was simple. In fact, that's another comment I often heard. People would say, "Aw, your so-called solutions are *simple*." Yes, they are. They're very simple. If the child has no clean clothes, you get him clean clothes. Do whatever it takes. It's as simple as that. If you know parents have to go to work in the morning, why wait until 8:45 to open the school doors, with kids wandering around outside since 7:30 when their parents left for their jobs? Open the school at 7:30, and if you haven't got your own people to be there to watch the kids, find others. Hire parents who don't have jobs. Give them a stipend. Forty dollars a month might not seem like much, but forty dollars would make a telephone available to a family who would not otherwise have one.

Simple. It's very, very simple. And it can make all the difference in the world for the future of the children.

I MADE CHANGES ALL OVER THAT SCHOOL WHICH ENSURED self-respect among the students. We gave each child a book bag in which to carry and store his school supplies. At first we gave out plastic grocery bags to each child to use for his books and papers. Then we obtained a supply of misprinted surplus canvas bags from a company that made them for colleges. Some kids said they wanted backpacks, so I slipped their little arms through the handles of their bags and said, "There, now you've got a *backpack*."

We set up an IOU bank, with money from fund raisers so that kids who didn't have the money for anything from a pencil to a class field trip could borrow what they needed to have the same experience and opportunities as their classmates. Even among poor children, there are haves and have-nots, there are kids who can afford certain supplies and activities and others who can't. But inside the walls of Blaine, I made sure the children were equal.

When the time for school photos arrived, I had the company offer one package—the least expensive package they had. Parents came in and asked why other schools offered a long list of packages. They asked why they couldn't get that double-exposed shot with the child's face looking both ways, how come they couldn't get that fourteen-dollar package instead of the five-fifty one we had. I said, "If you want that fourteen-dollar photograph, go on down to Sears and *get* it. If you want your child's photograph taken here, it will be the same as his classmates'."

If a child didn't have that five-fifty, we told him to get in line, and we took the money out of the IOU fund.

Everyone went on school trips. That was a mandate. No teacher was permitted to take a trip unless every child in that classroom was invited to come. I did not allow the teachers to exclude any boy or girl because of behavior. They were not permitted to use a trip as a means of punishment. I told them a trip was a learning experience, just the same as a spelling test. You don't tell a child he can't take a spelling test because he has been bad. In the same way, no child was to be left out of a trip for that reason.

As with the photographs, I did not allow expensive trips. Something like a *Sesame Street* stage production would come to town, costing eight dollars a ticket, and I would tell my teachers, "No, you may not go. Eight dollars is too much." Too many of the kids just could not afford that. Neither could our IOU fund. When teachers were really set on taking such a trip, they would raise funds themselves, through an activity such as a bake sale.

But there were plenty of trips we could afford. The biggest was our annual sixth-grade outing to New York City. This was a tradition at the school, something the kids looked forward to literally for years. We had the package fine-tuned—from the cost of the bus to the price of the kids' lunches—to a total of twelve dollars per child. That included the federal breakfast, a school-prepared lunch, the tour in the city, a snack, the return trip and three dollars each for a souvenir.

I did not allow the children to bring a dime of their own money. I went to the bank and got brand-new one-dollar bills, numbered in sequence. I wrote down the first serial number and the last, then handed out three each to every child. When we came to the souvenir booth, I checked every bill coming across that counter. Any that were out of sequence, I kept. And the word went out fast: "Mrs. Cartwright won't *let* you take any of your own money on trips."

That went right back to the issue of equality. If a child with no money has to watch a kid next to him with a pocketful of cash spending it all around, then what starts out as a good trip for everyone turns into a good trip for some and a bad trip for others.

Our trips were good for *everybody*. We fed the children. We provided drinks and snacks. And they were able to buy a little gift for their mother or grandmother, or a little something for themselves, something to remember the experience, something to take home with them.

Some of the kids chose not to spend a cent of that three dollars in the souvenir shop or anywhere. They put the money in their pocket and took it back home with them. And that was fine with me.

Just a couple of dollars was incredibly precious to some of the children. The same with some of the parents, as I found out one evening in Atlantic City.

This was a weekend evening, and I was having a night out. Suddenly I heard a voice hollering from across the casino, "Mrs. Cartwright! Mrs. Cartwright! *Hiiiiiii*, Mrs. Cartwright!"

There was one of my third-graders, Vernon Thompson, and his mother—unkempt and dressed as if they had been sleeping out on the street. I had no idea how they had come to this place or why.

Then Mrs. Thompson explained it to me.

Casinos in Atlantic City regularly ran buses from Philadelphia to their front doors. A person paid twelve dollars for a round-trip ticket to get on the bus. Once they arrived in Atlantic City, they were given eighteen dollars, the assumption being that they would spend that money gambling in the casino. But Mrs. Thompson—along with many of the other passengers on those buses—did not come to gamble. She rode the bus all that way and waited six hours to come back home to collect that extra six dollars. She brought her son along because there was no place to leave him and feel safe.

So here they were, standing in this casino waving at the one face they knew. I went over, hugged them and gave Mrs. Thompson ten dollars to buy a treat for herself and Vernon. Then, the next morning, I went to her house and helped her gather her laundry. I opened the school, and we washed.

"Mrs. Thompson," I told her, "whenever you need to wash, I want you to come over to the school.

"Then when you go to Atlantic City," I said with a smile and a squeeze of her arm, "you can *dress* to go."

C H A P T E R
9

TAKING CARE OF OUR CHILDREN'S PRIMARY NEEDS—
getting clean clothes on their backs, putting healthy food
in their bodies, comforting their restless little souls—
was an essential first step toward educating their hungry young
minds. But that's all it was—a first step.

With everything we provided for the children, we made it
clear to them that they had responsibilities also. They had to learn,
obey our rules and maintain standards both in and out of the
classroom. That washing and cleaning and sewing and feeding
was all about preparing our children to learn. In the same way,
and at the same time, I set about preparing our teachers to teach.

There was teaching at Blaine before I arrived. Much of it was
outstanding. But the prevailing attitude was that we were fighting
a losing battle, that doing enough to just get by, to survive, was all
that could be hoped for. Most of the teachers didn't expect much
of the students, and they did not demand the most of themselves.

There were thirty-six teachers on my staff when we began the 1979–80 school year. That included some who were not in the classroom, such as our reading and math specialist and our speech teachers. Among my classroom teachers, there were three I knew I could rely on as hubs for the others.

Raymond Brooks, of course, was one. He was a role model, especially among boys and young men. If there were more teachers with Raymond Brooks's dedication, there'd be a greatly improved learning environment for children. Beyond the fact that he was as solid a social studies teacher as could be found in a classroom, Raymond's bearing and his attitude toward the children were most effective. Raymond exhibited character and a presence that kids recognized immediately. They absorbed what he offered, lessons that cannot be contained in any curriculum.

Raymond grew up in Strawberry Mansion, back when it was a different place. His mother gave piano lessons in their home, and Raymond grew up with an appreciation for the fine arts. He was articulate, always professional, and had an active sense of humor. By the time I got to Blaine, he had bought and developed his own farm in New Jersey, where he raised Thoroughbred horses. He often took kids from the school out there for weekends, to give them a taste of a place beyond the sidewalks they saw every day.

Over the years Raymond gave the kids much, and they never forgot it. Grown men in their twenties and thirties—former students of his—would stop in and ask to see Mr. Brooks. They were home from the Army, or visiting from another city, or were off from their jobs and professions. They'd come by to see this man who had stayed involved in their lives long after they left Blaine. When these former students became old enough to hunt for their first job, Raymond would give them carfare to go for an interview. If they got in trouble with the law, he'd give them carfare to go see their parole officer. If a kid needed a character witness in court or a letter of reference, Raymond would go or provide the letter. He'd take a day of personal leave, if need be, to go to court with these teenagers. That cost him money he would have collected on retirement—a retiring teacher is paid in full for every personal day not used during his career. Raymond forfeited some of those days for his kids, and he never thought twice about it.

Mary Freeman was another teacher who was committed to her kids. She was six years older than I, very thin, very well groomed, precise in her dress and, even more impressively, in her speech. Mary spoke perfect English, as if she had written, rehearsed and polished every sentence before she spoke it. She never, ever raised her voice, and her students were mesmerized by her sheer presence as she guided them through a lesson. She was so smooth, so effortless, almost liquid in her delivery. Teaching flowed from Mary Freeman the way music flowed from Nat "King" Cole, and her children learned. No first-grader finished a year in her classroom without knowing how to read. When I made my formal observation of Mary, as I did with all my teachers, there were no weak spots to note, no areas that we needed to talk about improving. I just sat back and enjoyed her presentation, the same as the thirty children in her classroom—and their parents, who were often sitting in the back of the room.

Mary's reputation among parents was legendary. They called her classroom "Mary's Academy," and every mother in the neighborhood who knew Mary lobbied to have her child placed in Mrs. Freeman's class. I had my own agenda for Mary. I made a point of identifying youngsters with problems in kindergarten, for one reason or another, and I assigned them to her class. I knew that if those kids couldn't make it with Mary, they couldn't make it with anyone. My own little Tyrone—my brother's grandchild, whom I raised as if he were my son—was in Mary's room.

Verdie Brown, another of my premier teachers, was older than Mary Freeman. She was in her fifties, and very high-strung. There was nothing liquid about her. It did not take much to set Verdie off. She was very emotional, defending her point and vehemently holding forth on her opinion whenever she was challenged, whether by me, a parent or anyone else.

One morning I was in my office when I heard a loud commotion out in the stairwell. Mrs. Royal, one of our parents, came bursting through my office door, completely out of breath.

"Mrs. Cartwright!" she said, gasping. "That woman . . ."

Bang! Into the room stomped Verdie Brown, huffing and puffing just like Mrs. Royal. The two of them began yelling back and forth about a homework assignment, feathers flying. Finally Mrs. Royal, a deeply religious woman, drew herself straight up, took a deep breath and said, "Mrs. Cartwright, if I didn't have the Holy Ghost, I would kick this woman's *ass!*"

With that, Verdie leaped up, tore off her blazer, threw it on the floor and said, "Don't let *that* stand in your way!"

Those two women were ready to go ten rounds right then and there, and would have if I hadn't stepped in. I gently pushed Mrs. Royal out of my office and guided her into the ladies' room, where we discussed the situation.

Verdie was high-strung, but she did not let her temper affect her teaching. She was immersed in her craft, totally committed to what was happening with her class. That's what it took to work with the special children in her room. She taught fourth grade in the federal "Benchmark" program. This program was geared for low-achieving students—not low-ability children, but low achievers. Verdie took it as a personal challenge to bring her class around, to make them learn. She insisted that they learn. She was like a Crusader going after the Holy Grail with these kids, and they sensed that. Verdie never coasted. She never sat back and shifted to automatic. She drove herself and her kids all the time. Learn, learn, learn, every minute of the day. And the kids responded. The underachieving students in Verdie's classroom responded better to her than the so-called regular achievers did to most of their teachers.

Those three teachers were my foundation in the beginning. The next most necessary group of teachers were what I called my "career whites." These were the white teachers who stayed at Blaine year after year, keeping us out of the unreal turnover that occurred every year at some inner-city schools. These teachers were committed to Blaine and were not just there as a stepping-stone to another school.

This stepping-stone mentality was all too common among new teachers in our inner-city schools. Since most vacancies were in schools such as ours, this is where most new teachers were assigned. Many arrived with no intention of staying or committing themselves to serving the needs of the children. Some simply counted the days until they had served the minimum two years required before they could request a transfer.

Those new teachers—both black and white—who regarded their assignment to Blaine as a two-year sentence in the ghetto I called my "revolving door" teachers. It was disillusioning and disheartening to watch them come and go. Right away I decided this had to stop. I called a staff meeting that first fall and said I had no use for this business of using Blaine to get a foot in the door. I said it's not fair to the children. If you're going to be a teacher, I said, you'll teach where you are needed.

"I can't keep you from transferring out as soon as you can," I told them. "But I'm going to be here a lot longer than that, and so is the program we're putting together for this school. If you're not going to stay around, I need to know that, because I need to know how to fit you into our plans. I'm not doing any favors for anyone whose foot is in the door.

"If you're waiting to go, fine. Go on. Meanwhile, those of us who are staying will go about doing what it takes to turn this school into a good school for children, and that's going to take longer than your two years."

As I assigned teachers for the next year, I met with each one and asked how long they had been here and how long they intended to stay. If they were planning to transfer, I needed to know. Pairing teachers with classes is a delicate matter and difficult to do if it is not known who is going and who is coming.

I also made a point of indoctrinating the new first-year teachers—who were usually white, young and fresh out of college —into some basic understanding of inner-city culture. They had no firsthand knowledge other than what they might have read in the newspapers or seen on television. Most of them arrived scared to death. This was a totally alien environment to them, so I always made a point of explaining some fundamental facts they needed to understand.

One was that they must never talk about the children's mothers in an adverse manner.

"Just don't do it," I told them. "Don't say anything about a child's mother that can be construed as derogatory. Don't say, 'Why didn't your mother write you a late note?' or 'Why doesn't your mother wash your face or clothes?' or 'Why didn't your mother sign your homework?'

"If you say anything derogatory about a black child's mother, you've got a fight on your hands. You're treading on sacred ground when you put down a child's mother. You just must not do it.

"Just the two words 'your mother' will be enough to set a child off. He may not hear anything else you say but that phrase, and that will be enough to ignite his anger.

"That child might not retaliate immediately if you put down his mother, but he will retaliate," I said. "He might go outside and take a nail and scratch up your car and the others parked around it. He might put graffiti on a building, just spray his rage all over those walls. There are so many ways he'll let out his anger, and he'll do it. He'll do it if you show any disrespect for his mother."

Newcomers needed to be advised also against setting priorities for the children. To tell a child his homework is his most important job and must be done before anything else each evening is to ignore the fact that the evening's list of responsibilities for that child might include: gathering his younger siblings from wherever they are when he leaves school; searching for his mother; fixing dinner from whatever can be scavenged; supervising the younger ones and keeping them safe; watching and changing the baby; making sure there are enough diapers; finding a place to put his book bag so the little ones can't get to it and destroy his school supplies; and finally, locking up and putting the kids to sleep if Mommy hasn't shown up by bedtime.

With a list like that, homework might not have the same priority for the student that it has for the teacher.

MY "CAREER WHITES" NEEDED NO SUCH INDOCTRINATION. They had learned to understand the children and the community through years of experience. They had turned that understanding toward the task of teaching. They included Janet Schieber, Cynthia Smitt, Lori Baker, Allison Marcus, Joyce Paczosa, Frank Smallberger, Pat Hargarty, Maryanne Bell, Gloria Gordon and, most notably, Sara Brooks.

Sara was one of my most able and committed teachers. A petite woman, in her early thirties, very soft-spoken but very exact, Sara ran one of the most impressive classrooms I had ever seen. She had her first-graders on task every moment of the day, both in and out of the classroom. Sara was in her room an hour before school started, putting the day's lessons on the board and laying out her daily plan. She had every single minute planned. There was not a wasted moment in her day, not an instant when something constructive was not happening. When her class went to lunch, while they were standing in line, Sara had them going over their spelling words. When the kids went down to have their photos taken, I watched Sara stand by her students holding up math flash cards.

Sara Brooks truly believed that every child could be an A student. If a child was not making A's, Sarah believed there was a reason and there was a remedy. She even believed it in the case of a boy named Lacy Grissom.

Three weeks after the semester had begun, the special education supervisor came to Blaine to check on our special education students. One student on her list could not be found—a six-year-old trainable mentally retarded boy named Lacy Grissom. He was on the roll of a special education class upstairs, but according to that teacher, he had not reported to school yet that year. The teacher had marked him absent every day. The supervisor came into my office asking where Lacy was and if we had investigated his absence, as school policy required.

I called Lacy's home, and his mother arrived at the school in a matter of minutes, very upset. She said she knew that her son had come to school every day because she had walked him there herself. She had walked him there that morning. She demanded to know where he was that instant.

She got no argument from me. I wanted to know where he was, too.

Liz McCain happened by at that moment, heard the commotion and stepped in as usual to lend a timely hand. "Oh, you're talking about Lacy. He's in 202," she said, leading us all to Sara Brooks's classroom.

I had been in Sara's room several times that year, and I had seen her bending over this particular little boy, poking and prodding him to "Do! Do! Do!" I had seen Sara working with this little boy as he walked down the hallway, his body bent over as if he were in pain. I'd watched Sara urging him to straighten up, to walk erect.

I didn't know his name was Lacy Grissom. I didn't know he had had a heart operation as a baby and several operations after that, and that his mother considered him as fragile as a china doll. I didn't know he was classified TMR—trainable mentally retarded. I didn't know he was supposed to be in that special education classroom down the hall. Special education children were assigned from the district office, and Lacy's record had never arrived in our building. Not knowing he was classified TMR, I had assigned him to Sara's room at the beginning of the year, and he had been there ever since.

Sara didn't know any of this. She could see that Lacy was different, walking as if his limbs were welded together, his body curled up like an arthritic old man's. But she assumed he was part of the challenge I had given her, just another first-grader falling short of his potential.

No one had ever tried to get Lacy to stand up straight. No one had made him sit up at his desk, no one had ever pried his fingers open and put a pencil in there and showed him how to write. No one had imagined Lacy could do these things. But Sara could not imagine that he could *not*.

Now, three weeks into the year, this little boy was sitting up at his desk, writing his name. His mother said she knew he had been going to class and doing well, because he was coming home every night telling and showing her what he was learning.

But the woman from the district office couldn't stand for this. She was a by-the-book supervisor. As far as she was concerned, this situation was outrageous. This little boy did not belong in this room, pure and simple. It didn't matter what he was learning or how he was doing. He had been tested TMR, and that's what he was—TMR.

I said, "Look at the boy. Sara has him sitting and walking straight. He is holding his pencil and writing. He could do none of this when school opened just three weeks ago.

"Look," I said, "this boy is not TMR."

"Mrs. Cartwright," she said, "I know what the laws are. You cannot just move these kids around at your whim."

I said, "Very well. Would you please put Lacy on the list to be reevaluated?"

"I can do that," she said, "but it won't happen right away. He'll have to wait his turn like everyone else. He was just evaluated this summer. He must be placed in his assignment until a qualified evaluator assigns him elsewhere."

Then she took Lacy by the hand and led him to Room 207, the TMR class.

As soon as the supervisor left, I walked right back upstairs, got Lacy out of that classroom, returned him to Sara's room and put him back in his seat. Mrs. Grissom, Sara and I were delighted. Sara grabbed Lacy and hugged him. Then she hugged his mother and me, as tears streaked all our faces.

Lacy stayed in Sara's room until January, when he was reevaluated and assigned to an EMR—educable mentally retarded

—class. He went on through the next five years at Blaine and became one of our most visible and popular students. When break dancing became popular, Lacy went onstage in a school show and brought down the house with a performance the likes of which no one had ever seen. Here was this little boy, whose body Sara had coaxed open like a flower, spinning around that stage like a cyclone.

All I could think of was people telling us what can't be done with children.

IT WAS IMPORTANT TO ME THAT OUR ENTIRE SCHOOL FAMILY examine and plan together what we wanted for our school and that we have faith in our ability to make it all happen. What happened with Lacy was the kind of success that helped build faith. One of our teachers who inspired great faith—and faced great challenges—was Lori Baker.

Lori was a special education teacher who had graduated from a Philadelphia high school for the academically talented and later from Temple University. She was our "resource room" teacher. The resource room provided additional help to students who were assigned to the regular education program, usually from full-time special education. Children who were allowed to move into the regular education program rather than attend full-time special education classes were referred to as "mainstreamed." Lori provided them with the added help they might need to succeed in the mainstream.

She came early and stayed late, making posters and offering solutions to the children's learning problems. Among the students with whom she worked was her own special education miracle. His name was David Brooks. He had been assigned EMR, and Lori had orchestrated his move to the mainstream, where he went on to become one of our highest-achieving students. David eventually graduated from Philadelphia's High School of Engineering and Science and went on to Drexel Institute of Technology.

David provided Lori with a challenge. In a far different way, so did a student named Rene. Liz McCain had found Rene playing outside her grandmother's house during school hours one day and inquired as to why this girl was not in school. Liz brought Rene and her mother back to Blaine later that same day, took them to the health clinic for the inoculations required to begin school, and the next day Rene began her education as a student in our first grade. She was nine years old.

Rene was small for her age and did not seem remarkably out of place—until the children in her art class were asked to draw a picture of their mother. Rene drew a naked woman with developed breasts and pubic hair.

I knew then that Rene could not stay in that first-grade class with six-year-olds who rarely put even eyebrows or feet on their drawings. I put Rene in the third grade and assigned her to Lori for tutoring.

Rene worked well with Lori, staying in her room until she qualified for Verdie Brown's class through a federal program. She made remarkable academic strides, but Rene had many other problems, problems that had nothing to do with her intellect.

For one, she was a seasoned thief without a conscience. She regularly stole lunches, pencils, pens, book bags, articles of clothing and anything else that was not literally nailed down. By the time she turned ten, she had lost every bit of the innocence of childhood. Her face and eyes were those of a hardened woman of the streets. She had seen and done much in her few years. One day in class, a nine-year-old boy passed a love letter to Rene. It read:

Dear Rene,
    I love you. Do you love me? Give me some pussy?

                                     Ronald

This was a standard little love letter of the ghetto. The language was not meant to be taken literally, but not having been in school like the other children, Rene took it that way. She turned and sized up the little boy, then responded with a ridiculing smirk on her face.

"Boy," she sneered, "I ain't givin' you no pussy. Your dick is too little."

The children laughed at both Rene and Ronald, who was devastated. The classroom assistant brought Rene to the office with the same plea as the first-grade teacher who had reacted to Rene's drawing of her mother. The assistant said, "Mrs. Cartwright, Rene does not belong in a classroom with innocent little children. We are going to have to find a place for her."

The school district had no program for a ten-year-old prostitute, which is what Rene had become. She was later removed from her home, was placed in foster care and subsequently was sent to a reform school, where she became the first child I had heard of who was expelled from reform school.

MANY MEMBERS OF MY STAFF WERE SO TALENTED AND SO motivated that they needed virtually no guidance from me at all. Others required some occasional coaxing to fulfill their potential. Marie, who had a drinking problem, was one. Another staff member in the same situation—who was excellent in the classroom but whose trouble with alcohol sometimes kept her from getting there —was Beverly Kingston.

Beverly was one of the best classroom assistants we had. She could command the same attention as James Lowe. She'd just snap her fingers and the kids would scramble into line. But whereas the children were afraid of Lowe, they liked Beverly.

The trouble was, there were mornings when Beverly was not ready to get out of bed. That's when her husband would phone in to say she was sick.

Her husband was used to getting his way, and he did not take kindly to the principal herself answering the phone and forcing him to explain why Beverly was not coming to school. I always asked to speak to her, but he never allowed her to come to the phone. Finally, one afternoon, he showed up at the school, striding through the lunchroom doors in the middle of the day.

"Excuse me, sir," I said, stepping in front of him. "Can I help you?"

"No!" he said, starting to push his way past.

"Excuse me, sir," I said, stepping further in front of him. "Can I *help* you?"

"Help me with *what?*" he said.

"Can you tell me where you want to go and what you need? You may not proceed until I know what it is that you need."

He looked at me as if I were a stray dog in his path.

"You mean I've got tell you that?"

"Yes, you do."

"Do you mean," he said, smoke just about coming out of his nose by now, "I've got to take this shit from you *and* from that Cartwright bitch, too?"

"Yes, you do."

It was only after I escorted him to the office, had the secretary send for Beverly and watched Beverly begin introducing me to him that he realized who I was. He spun around like James Brown, put both hands to his head and walked briskly out of the office. The man was so small he could have left that building through the front-door keyhole.

He was back the next morning when I arrived at seven-thirty. He apologized, and we both laughed. And he was always pleasant on the telephone with me after that.

Occasionally a teacher showed up at school drunk (their lives were frequently more complicated than the children's). I was compassionate, but insisted that they go home, and I encouraged them to get help. Sometimes they did, but not everybody had the resources to seek help. And that's a shame.

I made accommodations for Beverly and Marie, and for Mr. Bailey, who had a drinking problem of his own. I kept a supply of mouthwash and clean toothbrushes in my office and let them know they were there. They used them upon request with no hassle.

◈

THEN I TURNED TO THE ISSUE OF WHAT SOME OF MY TEACH-
ers were wearing.

When the dress code for students went out the window in
the 1960s, so did the dress code for teachers. The power of the
union ensured that teachers could wear pretty much whatever
they wanted, and a few of my staff attempted to take full advantage of that freedom—more than I could possibly allow if we were
going to seriously tackle the task of teaching.

One teacher, for example, came in one morning wearing a
miniskirt so short it barely covered her crotch. I stopped her at the
door and asked why she was costumed. This woman had no
sense of humor at all.

"I beg your pardon?"

"I see you're in costume," I repeated. "Are you taking your
class skating?"

"No," she said icily, "we're not going skating."

I didn't push the issue there. But I talked about dressing
professionally—the Blaine way—at that afternoon's staff meeting.

Still, there were some staff members who were slow to
change. I had another new teacher, a young woman, who came in
wearing Bermuda shorts and slippers. Again, I could not order
her to change, but I called her into my office and laid it on the
line.

"You are perfectly free to wear whatever you want," I said.
"But you might like to know how I feel about it. It is my opinion
that your attire today is not appropriate for school. Of course,
how you look is your business. What concerns me here is what
your appearance might suggest to our children and their parents.
They may get the notion that we don't think enough of them to
dress professionally.

"Now, mind you," I said, "the decision is yours. You may
stay dressed as you are and go back upstairs, or I'll cover your
class so you may go home and change clothes."

She went home and came back beautifully dressed, and continued to dress professionally from that day on.

Covering Inetta Jones was another matter. Inetta was one of our best substitute teachers. She was in her late twenties, and amply endowed. One day she came in wearing an expensive pair of slacks and a tight Danskin top. I said, "Inetta, did you come to teach in that outfit?"

"I don't see anything wrong with it," she responded in her usual breathy voice.

I said, "Inetta, did your mother see you like that this morning?"

Inetta lived with her mother.

"Yes, she saw it."

So I called her home and spoke to her mother.

"Mrs. Jones," I said, "this is Madeline Cartwright. I'm calling to ask if you noticed Inetta's attire when she left for work this morning?"

"Yes, I saw her, Mrs. Cartwright."

"Did you feel that her attire was appropriate for school?" I asked.

She said she did not.

"But," she added, "Inetta is an adult, Mrs. Cartwright. I can't tell her what to wear."

My problem precisely. The way I resolved it was indirectly, through giving Inetta enough responsibility to match her talents.

I had taken a walk through the building early that first spring, peeking into rooms to get a feel for the school, when I came upon a classroom of SPI children—severely and profoundly impaired. These were the most extremely disabled children in our school. But there was no excuse for what I saw in that room.

One little girl was lying on the floor, her head wiggling back and forth in a closet while the rest of her body stuck out into the room like a broken doll. Several other children were sprawled across their desk seats, sound asleep. One little boy was slumped in his wheelchair, looking almost unconscious, drool dripping from his chin. Nobody was doing anything that looked like schoolwork. There was a teacher and an assistant assigned to that class, and these two women were sitting by the windows, chatting with each other. They didn't even notice me until I said, "What is going on here?"

"Oh," said the teacher, almost yawning me away, "they just had lunch, and after lunch they always have a rest period."

I didn't see one cot in that room. Not even one mattress. Just bodies strewn on the partially carpeted floor and across their desks.

"Rest period?" I said. "This is a rest period?

"What," I asked, "do they do the rest of the day?"

"Well," she said, "we have school."

I went on, but I came back another day, at a different time, and I saw the same thing.

"Mrs. Miner," I said to the teacher after several more visits, "what exactly goes on in this room?"

"Mrs. Cartwright," she answered, "you really don't understand what these children can do. These are SPI children, Mrs. Cartwright."

I said, "Mrs. Miner, if this was all that was expected of you and these children, we would not be paying a teacher's salary and paying a classroom aide to help you. We'd simply take that money and provide the children custodial care."

"Mrs. Cartwright," she said patiently, "this is all that can be done."

"No, Mrs. Miner," I said. "This may be all that you can do, and if this is all that you can do, then you need to move on to higher or lower ground and let somebody else come in and do all *they* can do."

Then I left.

Later that same day Mrs. Miner came to my office and tried to explain that she knew the children and their limits better than anyone, that they could handle only so much instruction in one day. To push them any harder, she said, would simply wear them out and frustrate them.

Again, I told her that if she felt that way, perhaps it was time for her to leave.

Mrs. Miner had good connections downtown. Within a week she had gotten a transfer, which was remarkable since school policy was that voluntary transfers were to be made only during the summer. Mrs. Miner had not even had an application on file.

The day after she left, I got a call from Jeanette Brewer, my district superintendent.

"Congratulations, Madeline," she said. "You haven't been here more than a couple of months and you've already run off one of the best teachers in that building."

"Jeanette," I said, "if that was one of my best teachers, then I'm in worse shape than I thought."

"Well," she said, "what are you going to do now?"

I already knew what I was going to do. I was going to put Inetta Jones in that classroom. I'd watched Inetta work with the kids in classes all across the building. She had the sorts of skills that I could see were ideal for working with mentally and physically challenged children. When I found that she had taken enough special education classes at Cheyney State University to be certified in the field, I arranged for a provisional assignment, pushed through her certification and immediately put her with that class.

Inetta was still a substitute in elementary education. The school district had not tested for elementary education teachers in six years and was in fact laying off regularly appointed teachers because of drops in enrollment. Inetta had not even dreamed of being a regularly appointed teacher when she walked into Blaine the morning I handed her her new assignment. But she went home that night a certified, appointed special education teacher with a class all her own.

Of course, with her new opportunity came much responsibility. Inetta had to educate herself even as she was educating the children. I told her to get every book she could find on SPI and read it. I told her to talk to every SPI teacher and supervisor in the school, to learn all she could in a hurry.

"Inetta," I told her, "the superintendent will be watching us closely. She'll be back in a few months to see what has happened, and if she finds Sonya sticking out of a closet door or Teeter over there drooling and sound asleep, we're all in trouble. If there's anything I can do to help you, let me know. But make that a class in there."

"I'll do my best, Mrs. Cartwright," she said.

Well, her best was enough. One day early the next fall, little Sonya showed up at our office door with her class's daily attendance report in hand. The secretary took it, and Sonya turned smartly and walked on down the hall back to her teacher, who waited proudly at the classroom door.

I said to my secretary, "Is that Sonya from Room 108?" I couldn't believe it. Inetta hadn't said a word about what she'd been doing with her children. She wanted to *show* me.

What she did with Teeter was even more incredible. When I first came to Blaine, this little boy had to be lifted off the bus each morning and wheeled to his class. He seemed to be in a continual stupor. But after a couple of months with Inetta, Teeter was climbing off that bus under his own power, with the bus attendant holding his arms for balance. He could walk all the way to his room unassisted, and the only problem he had was his momentum. Sometimes he'd get so excited and pick up so much forward motion that it was hard for him to stop. We had to slow Teeter down now, he was just so happy to be at school.

This was Inetta's doing. She hadn't let me down. Her class became a place where we regularly took visitors. As for her Danskin tops, she still wore those—but only on weekends.

THERE ARE TWO KINDS OF PRINCIPALS: "OFFICE" PRINCIPALS and "classroom" principals. I was the latter. The school district required two formal classroom observations to assess a teacher's performance, but I didn't need a mandate to enter our classrooms. I observed them often, and I usually did it unannounced. If what I saw was satisfactory, I discussed my observations with the teachers. When the observation period showed a great need for improvement, I would arrange for a conference with that particular teacher and give him or her a copy of my report, then do a follow-up observation. If I did not see improvement in that follow-up visit, a program designed to help the teacher would begin. Specialist teachers from our staff and the central office would be assigned to assist, and I would teach demonstration lessons to show exactly how a given concept could be presented. I found that there were very few teachers who did not evolve into solid teachers with help and encouragement.

There were some teachers who appreciated my energy and others who were threatened by it. As I began putting my program and my personality into effect, there were some staff members who complained and who began keeping anecdotal records to make a case against me: she spanks children; she lets teachers come in late and leave early; she had a raffle; she buys individual children clothes and shoes with school money; she and some of the teachers eat the school lunch without paying . . . The list went on and on.

Some of the teachers who got wind of the documentation began urging me to follow policy to the letter so that I wouldn't get into trouble. Raymond and Mary became fearful for me, since I was a new principal and they had heard stories of what happened to principals who ran into organized teacher opposition.

I was not afraid. All of my exceptions to policy were for the good of the children. I felt that I would have to take some chances if we were really going to make changes in this inner-city school. I continued to meet with the parents and children regularly so that they would always know what we were trying to accomplish.

I owed some of my fearless attitude toward job security to Malachi Robinson, a Philadelphia principal whose career I had followed. Malachi's experiences were very public and made a great impression on me.

I first heard of him when I was teaching at Belmont Elementary in 1972. He was principal of a junior high in the city. A very intelligent, outspoken man, he was involved in a bitter power struggle that year with his teachers, a fight from which he would not back down. In fact, Malachi was coming on too strong, in the opinion of the people working in the school district administration.

Mayor Frank Rizzo had recently been elected, and the administration knew that Rizzo had not backed the white superintendent against the teachers' union. They hardly expected him to back Malachi Robinson in his struggle. So they took the course of what they assumed would be the least resistance, directing Malachi to back off.

He would not.

Malachi had a record of having had some mental problems during the sixties, as a result of being beaten during a civil rights demonstration, and the union used this information to suggest he was now having a mental breakdown. Like 1972 vice presidential nominee Thomas Eagleton, Malachi watched his record of mental health treatment used against him. Is it any wonder people might be reluctant to seek help for depression and other mental conditions today, knowing their records might someday be used to destroy their careers?

Malachi stood his ground. When he would not capitulate to the union, he was ordered not to report to his building until further notice.

He was furious. The next day he arrived at school as usual. The administration expected he would and had school security and uniformed police on hand to keep him out. All three local network television affiliates had camera crews there as well, along with reporters from every newspaper in the city. Everyone had arrived for the showdown.

"Mr. Robinson," said the first reporter to approach Malachi, "we understand that you will not be allowed back into this building until you've had a psychiatric examination. Are you going to get that examination?"

The TV crews had their cameras rolling, ready to rush their tapes back for the afternoon news.

Malachi did not disappoint them.

"Just as soon as the mayor and the superintendent's *momma* gets a psychiatric examination," he said, "that's when Malachi Robinson is going to get one."

"Oh," I thought as I watched that news broadcast, "this man has lost his job right here." But the next week, Malachi was still working for the school district. The next *year*, he was still working for the school district.

I said to myself, "Well, how do you like that? They cannot fire this man."

Mayor Frank Rizzo had a reputation for being a racist. He had stripped members of the Black Panther Party on the street in broad daylight. But here was Malachi Robinson still working, which meant, evidently, that neither Rizzo nor the school superintendent could fire the man. They just could not fire him. They could not even hide him. He remained visible and outspoken.

So should I worry about a few indiscretions? In fact, Mayor Rizzo was already on my side, or at least it looked that way at the administration building, where it was known how he had helped with the painting of our school.

God, Malachi Robinson and Mayor Frank Rizzo—they were the sources of my strength.

BEFORE THE END OF THAT FIRST YEAR, I WAS PREPARED TO test all the strength my staff and I had gathered. I told my teachers we were going to make a difference in these classrooms, a clear, meaningful and measurable difference. Then I laid a bombshell on them. I told them our method of schoolwide testing was going out the window.

It was the California Achievement Test (CAT) I was talking about. The CAT was a general aptitude test much like the Scholastic Aptitude Test (SAT) used by colleges for admission. When I came to Blaine, the CAT, which gauged elementary-level reading and math ability, had been established as the adopted measuring rod for academic achievement in the Philadelphia public schools. For several years our students' scores on these tests had been steadily rising, and each year principals and district administrators across Philadelphia patted themselves on the back, pointing to the CAT scores as proof of how well they were doing.

I knew that this was all a farce. According to the CAT scores, more than half our first-graders were above the 85th percentile nationally, and even better than that compared with citywide scores. I thought, "This is ridiculous. This doesn't make sense." These scores surpassed those of the best schools in the suburbs.

So I did some investigating. I looked into our older students' records, into the scores our fourth- and fifth-graders had had over the years. What I saw made no sense at all. File after file showed a student scoring in the 90th percentile in first grade, plunging to the 50th percentile in the second grade, leaping to the 80th percentile in the third, dropping down to the 20th in the fourth, then up to the 40th in the fifth.

These were crazy numbers, roller-coaster scores. I called in a couple of teachers and said, "How can this be? How can there be a youngster scoring ninety today, fifteen tomorrow, forty here and sixty over there? What does this mean?"

They only added affirmation to what I had already concluded. They told me that the children were coached on these tests, that it was common practice, accepted and even encouraged, to get the scores up so the school would look good. Some teachers were apparently better—or more cooperative—coaches than others.

This wasn't the first time I had heard of and seen cheating such as this. When I was at Houston Elementary, I saw teachers administering a twenty-minute timed test and allowing the children to take as long as they needed to complete it. Some took an hour.

I saw teachers coaching students during a test on reading skills, doing everything but reading the correct answers aloud to the children. I even saw teachers blatantly pointing to each correct answer as they administered one of these tests.

I didn't know they had been doing this at Blaine. I still don't know exactly what went on there before I arrived, but once I saw those scores and talked to some of my teachers, I said this is going to stop. I said these tests not only mean nothing at all but they are *hurting* these children in order to benefit the image and needs of the school system. It's a sham, I said, and it's going to stop. And I didn't leave it up to my teachers alone to turn things around.

I brought my parents into it. By the time my first CAT testing was conducted at Blaine in February 1980, I had two parent-proctors in place in every classroom in that building. I gave them the directions to the test, the test numbers, a place to write the beginning and stopping time for each section of the test, and I told them to monitor any irregularities. The proctors strode up and down between the rows of desks. My teachers knew this was coming. I didn't sneak up on them. I had discussed our new testing procedure months in advance. I said there is nothing to fear, that we were going to move forward, that we would truly teach the children the concepts and skills measured by this test rather than the content of the test itself. The presence of the proctors, I told them, would ensure that their students' scores would be unquestioned.

Mr. Davis and I both walked through the building that day, looking into classrooms and watching our proctors policing the entire process. Nothing like this had ever been done in Philadelphia as far as I knew. I knew once word got out, I'd be feeling some heat from downtown.

Predictably, when those scores came back, Blaine's numbers were considerably lower than they were the previous year.

Out came a man from the district office, with the numbers in his hand.

"What are you *doing* here?" he asked.

"What do you mean, what am I doing?"

"Your test scores," he said, holding out the score sheet. "They are down."

"I saw them," I said, "and if anybody else came here and tested our children and administered the test according to the testing manual, the scores would be the same as those you have in your hand."

"Madeline," he said, "suppose other principals followed your lead. We could lose our federal funding."

"I don't know about funding," I said, "but I do know that a test like this should truly measure student achievement. I think it should be a diagnostic tool, not a political tool or a billboard contrived to deceive."

That afternoon I got a call from the office of the director of testing and evaluation. I waited for him to take me to task as well. I knew there was going to be a price to pay for what had happened, and I was ready to pay it. However, this call was different from what I expected.

"Mrs. Cartwright," he said, "there is a lot of talk down here, as you can imagine, about the test scores in your school."

"Okay," I thought, "here it comes."

"I just want to tell you," he went on, "that what you have done there is what should be done at every school in this city."

I could hardly believe my ears.

"I have been asking for years that we go out and test random grades ourselves," he said, "and the answer has always been no.

"The scores your students received," he said, "are commensurate with what they should be when they are compared to the reading and math instructional levels listed on the school plan. The math and reading levels look realistic, for once."

Then he said something I already knew was true. Still, it was nice of him to give me a warning.

"Stick to your guns, Madeline," he said. "They are going to be coming after you."

C H A P T E R

10

WELL, THEY DID COME AFTER ME ONCE THOSE ACHIEVE-
ment test results got downtown.

Of course, I knew how tainted the figures had been
prior to that. The people downtown knew that as well. But that
didn't change the fact that I was threatening to upset the entire
applecart. In an age when image and public relations are as important to school systems as they are to politicians, what I was
doing was tantamount to treason. Jeanette Brewer let me know
that. And in carefully couched language, so did a chorus of other
administrative voices.

It was obvious to me how duplicitous and how destructive
this test tampering was. It didn't surprise me recently when a
1992 nationwide study of standardized testing revealed that the
problem has reached epidemic proportions in public schools
across the country. In the face of a public outcry for higher standards and more accountability, school systems are administering
these tests more than ever before and they are rewarding or pun-
ishing principals and teachers on the basis of the results. The

stakes have become so high and the pressure so great that the test results have become total ends in themselves.

While teachers and administrators worship at the altar of the California Achievement Test or the Metropolitan Achievement Test or the Iowa Tests of Basic Skills or any of the dozens of other standardized tests available on the commercial market, their students suffer. Instruction in skills and concepts is replaced by rote memorization. Subjects not covered or emphasized on the tests—such as science, social studies and writing—are virtually ignored, as are the oral and thinking skills developed in guided classroom discussions and debates. These less testable abilities of thinking, of comprehension and of expression become casualties as they are ignored by schools obsessed with standardized scores.

I was committed to the belief that our students could do well on these tests—and on any other gauge of academic achievement —if they were taught thoroughly and completely in all subjects by committed and motivated teachers. High test scores were simply a by-product, as far as I was concerned. What mattered most to me was that our children absorb skills and concepts they could carry with them throughout their lives, not just through the end of the upcoming achievement test. If a man or a woman has the ability to read and to listen (which allows him or her to gather and absorb information) and if that person has the ability to think (to comprehend, sort out and interpret the information he or she has gathered) and if that person has the ability to write and to speak (which enables him or her to communicate the information they have to share), then that person is truly educated and able to handle anything the world might throw.

I was committed to the belief that there is no stronger weapon in this world than knowledge, and that all education should be aimed toward what the children will carry with them into adulthood. I was just as committed to the belief that the students in inner-city schools, despite the lack of resources and support systems available to children in more comfortable circumstances, could be taught as well, could learn as much and could, given a level playing field as they moved up and out into society, advance as far as their counterparts in any school anywhere in this country. These kids could do that. I knew they could. They didn't need anyone to cheat for them. They just needed a chance.

The year after those CAT results, in the fall of 1980, I fanned the administrative flames even further by rejecting one of the school district's pet projects, a pilot program called "Mastery Learning."

This was another in a seemingly endless parade of experimental teaching programs trotted out by the people downtown to show they were doing something about the well-publicized problems in our city's schools. Every few months we were asked to put something new and different in place. This string of experiments began back in the sixties, when schools responded to a critical need to improve education—and textbook authors responded to an obvious opportunity to make money. We witnessed a flood during this time of experimental texts, such as the "socially relevant" comic books that for a time replaced the traditional basal reader textbooks. These comics were supposed to be geared to inner-city kids. Instead of Dick and Jane taking Spot for a walk in the country, these books showed Johnny and his family in an urban apartment, where Johnny couldn't go for a walk because his father was asleep on the couch with a bottle of beer on the table beside him. The drawings actually showed a bottle of beer on the table. Minority teachers and parents were livid.

I don't object to any teaching method as long as it is understood that proficiency and comfort level of the teacher in using materials or methods is of paramount importance. Successful teachers and successful students use an array of methods, processes, aids and programs.

The introduction of "modern math" in the sixties frightened elementary school teachers across the country. Children came home from school confronting parents with this new vocabulary and methodology. Too many teachers heard that rote memorization was no longer good and that we no longer could "borrow" when we subtracted. Much time was lost in teaching and learning while teachers learned to use a process and language unfamiliar to them.

Many of the pilots introduced during the sixties were bought by new administrators who wanted to make their mark. The salespeople were very convincing. The new administrators played the role of patsies. Most of them did not know where the pilot originated and were reluctant to say no to the new programs. Teachers and children found themselves perpetually saddled with new material and new methods unfamiliar to them. The schools often went into a tailspin until the teachers either learned the new methods or convinced the administration to throw them out.

Meanwhile education suffered. When teachers who were successful in the classroom were told to abandon proven methods and teach these pilots, they were demoralized. They approached the new program with less enthusiasm.

Teachers should be the ones to make the decision whether or not to try a new program. These programs should be demonstrated during the summer by teachers who are thoroughly familiar with the material, not by salespeople. The targeted population of students should be selected from the school where the program is to be tried. Too many pilot programs are treated purely as products, something to be sold. The salespeople are motivated by a desire to make money, not to improve education. They are trained to package and promote their product to the most receptive buyers, who most often are the educated African-American women who make up much of the teaching staffs in inner-city schools.

There was nothing wrong with the Mastery Learning program. It, too, was designed to sell materials, but it also conceivably could improve efficiency, bring teachers and students on task and measure and increase output, with a special staff of trainers brought into each school to monitor and help develop the teachers during the regular school year.

But I didn't want to add even more changes than I had already effected that year. Our teachers were capable of teaching and their methods were working. It was as simple as that. There was no need at that time for a new pilot or a new program at Blaine. I wanted to show that our teachers and children could succeed without any special assistance. I had no doubt that they could.

I planned to say these things when I called a staff meeting in the fall of 1980 to announce this proposed program. But before I could even share how I felt, one of my kindergarten teachers, Yvonne Cauthorn, stood up and spoke for the group.

"We are so tired of being used as guinea pigs for their programs," she said. "Every year, it's 'pilot' this and 'pilot' that and 'pilot' the other. We've had so many pilots coming through here, we ought to qualify for some frequent flyer bonuses. We're just tired of it. Would they leave us alone and let us teach?"

The staff nodded in agreement as Yvonne spoke.

Yvonne was a good, solid teacher, but she was not a member of my fan club. I came on too strong for her. So that made it doubly delightful to see her standing up and bolstering my own position, giving me just what I needed.

"Well, all right then," I said. "If you all don't want this and you're sure you don't want it, we won't have it. We'll turn it down.

"But I'll tell you something," I continued. "If we turn this program down, we're going to have to show the school district that we have something better to put in its place.

"I'll take your message back," I told them, "but the burden will then be on us to produce. I'll go down to the superintendent and present our case, but then you must support me and not leave me hanging out there alone."

I then called an assembly and told the children to tell their parents that Blaine had to improve if I was going to be allowed to stay. Everyone had to study, go to bed early at night and come to school each day ready to truly learn. If they fulfilled those responsibilities, I had faith they would do well when the time came to take the test again.

◈

I WAS ALREADY OUT ON A LIMB AFTER WHAT I'D DONE WITH our CAT tests. With our opting not to participate in Mastery Learning, we were all in this together. My teachers began tackling their tasks in earnest. No longer was Sara Brooks the only one walking into the lunchroom reciting spelling words to her kids. Now everyone was working all the time. I'd stand outside the auditorium doors, watching the classes waiting in line to go in for an assembly, and I'd see the teachers going over number facts with their kids, going over geography. I'd peek into classrooms and see the children writing. Even the kindergarten and first-grade children had their stories displayed outside their doors.

The kids were enthusiastically involved in the learning process. We'd made them come to love Blaine and the people there. It was only a small step to get them to love what we were here to do. Children want to succeed. They want to achieve. They want to excel. We gave them many opportunities each day to do exactly that. We had schoolwide math contests every week, with small cash prizes which they could use to buy something from the school supply store. We publicized and posted the best work, so everyone would know and see what their classmates were doing. Tests, stories, homework, drawings—anything done well—we put on display. We made the children *proud,* not just of themselves but of one another.

We established a rainy-day lottery to keep attendance high. The percentage of attendance for each class was calculated monthly, charted and displayed in the first-floor hallway in rank order. The first eleven classes were invited to special assemblies for that month. These assemblies would often feature professional traveling theater groups.

Many children and some teachers who were not among the top eleven classes complained that this practice was not fair. One teacher said that she had a group of poor attenders in her room, and that this same group was her lowest-achieving group. She asserted that everyone knew that low achievers usually had poor attendance and that she and the other children were being penalized. I responded that this group of children was being penalized

by her attitude and low expectations. I assured her that no allow-
ance would be made for her class; that they would improve and
be included if they met together and devised a plan for improvement, and made being included in the assemblies their goal for
the next month. I must salute her professionalism, because she
went back to her class and had a discussion with the children.
Their percentage of attendance leaped from 84 percent to 91 in
one month.

In later years, attendance and lateness became an even
greater problem when many of the parents became involved in
drugs. So we suggested to children that they help each other get
up in the morning by asking a friend to knock or ring the bell for
them as they passed their houses on the way to school.

Even the youngest of students was encouraged to assume
responsibility for his or her school achievement, welfare and
safety. If the children were encouraged to look for help, they
would be less likely to sit cold and hungry in some vacant house
waiting for someone to happen along.

I didn't allow anyone in that building to utter the word
"can't." I just did not allow it. I told the children they could say
"I'm having difficulty" or "I need help." This attitude precluded
any child's abandoning hope and just giving up. During our assembly meetings we discussed how they could help themselves
and how they could help us to help them. We urged them to make
their needs known. Some were too embarrassed to ask for help. To
ease their feelings, I shared stories of "what happened to me
when I was six" if they were six, or "what happened to me when I
was eight" if they were eight, all so that maybe they would then
share their stories with me.

Making needs known became a topic of our assemblies as
well. "Children," I told them, "if you are hungry, you just ask
somebody for food and you'll get it. Go next door and knock on
the lady's door and tell her you don't have any food. If she
doesn't have any either, go to the next door. If you have difficulty,
call me. You have my phone number."

The kids had my number written on their walls right by their phones—the ones who had phones. And if they didn't know it, they could find a phone book and look it up. My home phone number had always been listed right there in the book. It still is.

We had answers to most problems the children might bring with them from home, so they had few excuses not to do what was expected of them in terms of schoolwork. By my second year there, there was not one Blaine child who walked out that door at the end of the day without a book bag and supplies to do their homework.

It was the sheer joy of pleasing me and their teachers and themselves that motivated the kids. They were vessels eager to be filled with happiness and pride. For me to be able to say, "I am so *prouuuud* of you," and to take the kids in my arms and have them feel that joy, and to have them tell me they were proud of us, too —there was no way to measure how much that meant to all of us.

WE HAD FUN, AND WE HAD FLEXIBILITY. PEOPLE ON THE outside looked at the way we did some things at Blaine and called it foolishness. They saw me start school an hour late the morning after the 76ers won the NBA championship, they heard how I announced to the kids that morning that we were all going to stay out and celebrate, they heard how our whole school stayed out on that playground and talked about Julius Erving and the team and the title and just had a wonderful hour, and they asked what that had to do with teaching.

My answer was—and is—that an hour was never more well spent than that one and others like it. Small, often spontaneous events like that are part of what makes kids want to come to school. And our kids came to school. Our attendance leaped beginning with my first year at Blaine for many reasons, not the least of which was my policy about suspensions.

There weren't any.

In Philadelphia's public schools, suspensions were a way of life. If a child was disruptive, if he wasn't doing what he was told, if he could not be controlled, if he cut classes or was chronically late, he was thrown out, put on the street, suspended. This happened to hundreds of children at a time, every day. It happened to thousands a year. It had been that way forever. I remember when I was teaching at McMichael, I would see some of my former students out on the street. I said, "Why are you not in school?" They said, "Well, I'm on suspension."

"How long," I would ask, "have you been out?"

"Two months."

Two months! That's not a suspension, I said to myself. That's expulsion. Kids were told to stay home and not to come back to school until someone called them, and no one would call. I was still seeing the same thing when I arrived at Blaine. If a child was involved in a fight or gave the wrong teacher a backward look, home he went. Home to what? To hang out on the street? This was senseless, and it was irresponsible. I told the children so. In assembly after assembly I delivered my message.

"Children," I said, "I do not believe in suspension. Suspension sends three messages: I cannot handle you, no one on this staff can handle you, and your education is not important to me.

"Now, children," I said, "I weigh one hundred sixty pounds and I'm forty-two years old. I've studied psychology and child development. I don't know anybody in this room that I'm scared of or that I can't handle. There is no one in this room whose education is not important to me. If there is one among you who doubts that, raise your hand so I can see who you are."

No hands, of course.

"Now, children," I continued, "if you misbehave in this school, you are going to have to respond to me. I might keep you in my office at recess or lunch. I might have a conference with your parents or exclude you from our recreational activities. If none of that works, I might spank you. I might do any of those things, or I might think of something totally new. But I am not going to send you home so you can eat snacks and watch television and go outside and play while the rest of us are here working and learning.

"You are going to come to school every day, whether you're

good, bad or indifferent. If I am getting up and coming here every day, so are you. It's that simple."

The point is that suspension does nothing for a child whose parents aren't at home to make good use of that suspension day. I believe educators created the practice of suspension to allow a child and his parent to have time at home together, away from other children, to discuss and work out whatever problem might exist, to plan improved behavior. Eventually, however, households with both parents working became the norm, and suspensions resulted in children being home without supervision. The original purpose had vanished.

There are instances where suspension is a viable alternative, and those instances are the cases where a child presents a danger, where he is an immediate threat to the safety of himself and others. In those situations, this alternative must be explored carefully to make sure that the home situation lends itself to behavioral changes. In cases other than that, something needs to be done in the school to adjust the behavior. A joint effort of school, home and social agencies might be required, but whatever is done must be consistent and it must address the best interest of the child.

All too often, suspension is used to remove what in most cases is no more than an inconvenience to school personnel. Problems are tossed back into a home where the parents are young, inexperienced, uneducated or otherwise unable to solve their children's behavior problems. Society can choose to help in the schools and homes now, or wait and pay more later. It costs approximately $30,000 a year to support a child in prison, plus the added costs of higher insurance rates and personal losses. It takes some extra time and resources to counsel a child and his parent; those costs are saved ten times over if the result is a better-performing student and a more promising citizen.

Problem children are problems because of the problems surrounding them. Schools need more guidance time to address these problems, and teachers need to be taught to present guidance plans. Curricula must be written to teach acceptable behavior, communication skills and problem solving. Community, home and family living skills are as important as reading and mathematics. They are all life skills.

THERE WERE, OF COURSE, TEACHERS WHO WERE SKEPTICAL of my approach to suspensions. As they saw it, they were the ones who were saddled with the troublemakers I was keeping in school. I made it clear that we—they and I—would take these kids case by case and work with each one of them, and that I was not going to allow any child to continually disrupt their class or to get in the way of the learning for the other thirty children in that room.

I knew, and my teachers had to understand, that we could not control inner-city children with fear. The danger that these children live with daily makes them immune to most school-contrived "fear authority" programs. Our children were, as they said in the neighborhood, "no strangers to danger." We weren't going to scare them into anything. What we had to do was take the time and energy to convert these children into loving, trusting, hoping, dreaming, planning, achieving young citizens by displaying all those characteristics ourselves and showing them when we dealt with the children.

I encouraged our teachers to exchange effective methods of dealing with disruptive behavior. Most agreed that isolating the offender was effective. But I objected to isolating our children *in the corner*. Imagine a teacher telling a six-year-old child to go to the corner for punishment. To a little inner-city boy, a corner is where the guys hang out. It's where the men stand and talk and have fun. It's where his mother tells his big brother that he had better not go. His other brother got into trouble for going there. His father is probably still on the corner where he met his mother. To this six-year-old boy, the corner sounds like the place to be. And here is this teacher telling him to go to the corner—for *punishment!* In his little mind, he is saying, "Where is this lady from? I wonder what else I know that she doesn't know. She sure ain't with it."

Convincing my teachers that some methods would work and others wouldn't, and that suspension was definitely one that would not, was another task that would take time. But with time, I did convince them. My policy on suspensions at Blaine resulted in no more disruption in our school than at any other school. Our policy saved more kids than I could count, most of whom might have become casualties had they been thrown out on the streets. It kept them in school, and it brought parents clamoring from across North Philadelphia to get their kids enrolled at Blaine.

Word of our no-suspension policy spread quickly through other neighborhoods. Working parents who had to either stay at home or find someone to take care of their children when they were suspended came to Blaine as soon as they heard what we were doing. Our enrollment leaped, and a lot of those new addresses were nothing but vacant lots. Parents from other areas were making up addresses to get their kids into Blaine.

But more than the absence of suspensions, what impressed and attracted these parents most was my reputation as a stern taskmaster.

"She makes the children behave," they'd say.

"The woman takes no foolishness," they said to one another, and it would get back to me.

"She takes no foolishness at all from those children. You can send your child to that school, and the lady makes them behave and learn. The children love her."

It was true. I insisted on certain behaviors. I hugged and I smiled, I kissed and I patted, but the education and welfare of the students and their young parents was my primary concern, and proper behavior was necessary to achieve our goals. I insisted on an orderly, clean, well-run school. The children, the staff and the parents did their part to deliver.

There were some who would never become comfortable with my energy. But they could see I knew what I was doing, that I wasn't asking anything of them that I would not do myself. For one, I could teach. I could take any subject, any grade, and I could walk into that room and teach a demonstration lesson.

All too many of the people passing down policies and programs into the classrooms couldn't effectively teach a lesson in hopscotch. That's why many of them left teaching and went into administration, curriculum and program writing in the first place. Many of them had never taught, and many who did were not effective teachers. Students graduating from the best education schools in this country today—places like Harvard, Berkeley and Columbia's Teachers College—become highly paid bureaucrats right off the bat. They never even come close to a classroom. Some don't even like children.

I believe that supervisors and principals should be required to spend one of every six years in a classroom, and they must be successful there in order to continue in their administrative positions. They need to stay in touch with teaching, which is what education is all about. Times change. Children change. School communities change. Administrators, supervisors and others who are influencing education need to stay in touch with these changes.

I was in touch. My teachers knew that, and it made all the difference in the world. They knew my evaluations and observations of them were reliable, that I knew what I was seeing when I watched them. They responded when I told them we needed to retrieve some of that give-and-take and sharing we had once had in those bygone days of long lunch breaks.

I said, "Everybody must join in here. If you teach and you have a particularly successful lesson, tell us about it. Spread the wealth. Share the knowledge. If you've got something that works, share it. Show the rest of us how you do it. And if you're not given to standing before a group of your peers like this, then tell it to somebody who is."

I turned to a teacher who more often than not had all thirty of her kids passing her spelling tests. In some classrooms there were only fifteen or eighteen kids passing. I said to her, "What do you *do* in there?"

She said she had developed her own personal program over the years. She had never shared it with anyone. No one had ever asked. I said, "Can you bring that program to us so that more classes in this school can have success like yours?"

Some teachers were reluctant to be singled out. Mary Freeman was one. She was embarrassed to be singled out as a teacher of demonstrated quality. She did not want me to use her name in connection with her good lessons, and she had many of them. So I shared her strategies without using her name. But most of the staff knew they came from Mary.

I saw my teachers begin spreading their methods beyond staff meetings, and I encouraged that. "If you're having a problem," I said, "seek out someone who's having success in that situation. We'll cover your class while you go watch that person."

They did. We worked together, and it happened. My teachers actually began sitting in on one another's classes, watching each other. I had not seen much of that in my career, even when I was a lead teacher and demonstrating was my job. It just did not happen back then, and I think that's because it was not encouraged. It's sometimes amazing how insular, isolated and autonomous a classroom can become, in a place as crowded as a school.

Every teacher needs a measure of space, privacy and control. But no teacher should jealously guard anything that can help others do their jobs better. We are there, after all, for the children.

FROM THE BEGINNING, AND THROUGHOUT THE TIME I SPENT at Blaine, we were there for the parents as well. Some schools perceive mothers and fathers as another inconvenience, something to be pleased or appeased as quickly as possible. That was not our attitude at Blaine. We knew parents were vital to everything we did, both in and out of the classroom. And they knew it. Not only were our parents urged and assisted to become involved in the work our children brought home from school with them, but we brought our parents in to help us with everything from washing clothes to monitoring the lunchroom, halls and playground, to serving as classroom aides, to—yes—monitoring the administration of our standardized tests.

Dr. Brewer, my district superintendent, reminded me one day that the Blaine School was not a branch of the personnel office. I probably sent more substitute classroom assistants to the board for processing than any other principal. When I compared our pupil-to-teacher ratio with that of suburban and private schools, very often ours was 100 percent more than theirs. Our children would wind up applying for the same jobs and the same places in the college freshman classes as their more advantaged suburban neighbors. To lower the pupil-to-teacher ratio would make a positive difference in our school. When our parents came regularly and demonstrated that they could contribute, I sent them to the personnel office. We were constantly recruiting.

Besides parents, we also brought other members of the community into our school family. We *were* a family, and we did what we could to meet the needs of one another. An example was Danny.

Danny was nineteen and mildly retarded. He came to the school daily to go to the store to buy lunches or sodas for the teachers. He quickly took a liking to me and always stopped to say hello or to offer to go to the store for me too. I became very involved in his errand business when one day he walked twenty blocks in the rain to get breakfast for a teacher and returned to the building soaked. I questioned why anyone would have asked him to go that far in the rain. Right there I established rules for Danny. He was only to be sent to stores in the immediate neighborhood. He had to be paid a minimum of a quarter per person. If he made a mistake, the customer absorbed the loss. I wrote this all on a three-by-five index card and instructed Danny to show it to all his customers.

Danny conducted his business pretty well. Some people continued to give him less than a quarter, but he didn't want me to say anything to them. He wanted his business to grow and was afraid of losing customers.

As I noticed Danny's pockets bulging, I pointed out to him that if the neighborhood junkies found out that he carried money, he would be an easy target for robbery or worse. I took him to the nearest bank. Once there, they told me that they had already advised Danny many times that he needed two pieces of identification to open an account. All he had was his school district ID card.

I asked to see the manager. When he came, I told him I was the principal of Danny's school and that a bank account was a part of the program for our retarded citizens. I informed him that this bank was the only bank where we were having a problem. With no further ado, he brought the necessary forms.

Danny was indeed proud and began telling me on the way back to the school the advantages of his account. "I can get my checks cashed for free," he said.

Danny soon began to hang out at the school. He became friends with the TMR teacher, volunteering in her room and helping her students to the lunchroom. A year later, a noontime aide who assisted with the TMR students at lunchtime resigned. I brought Danny on as a substitute to fill this vacancy. I did not fill the vacancy until Danny was working out well, and then I recommended him for the job.

I anxiously awaited Danny's return when he went to the school board to be processed as a permanent employee. Would they hire a young man like Danny, who was obviously special? I had my argument ready. We had graduated Danny from our Retarded Educable program. He proudly displayed his diploma in his immaculately clean public housing home, where he lived with his mother and siblings. I was ready to tell them that it was my feeling that the school system should lead all employers in the hiring of our special population. We had all of their records, the teachers who taught them knew exactly what jobs they could handle. They were already comfortable in schools. Maybe a section of the personnel office could be established with only the jobs that this population can handle.

That was my argument. The job Danny applied for was a part-time position, three hours a day at four dollars an hour. It was a start, enabling him to contribute to his support. Later, another part-time job was available that he could do concurrently. I again recommended Danny and he was selected. He holds both those jobs today, as a paid employee and contributor to his community. All of that "retarded" and "can't" business is no longer a part of his mind-set. He knows that he had some difficulty, but he knows he "can."

WE HAD PARENTS AND FRIENDS LIKE DANNY ALL OVER THE school, which helped improve school-community relations and allowed for parent-to-parent interaction. Parents and children passed one another constantly and came to know one another. Everyone had a bright "hello" to share as they walked through the halls. The separation between school and community was less pronounced at Blaine than at any other school in which I had worked. In fact, it was hard to draw a line between the two, to tell where the school stopped and the community started. Blaine *was* the community.

Some of our parents actually became students. On any given day there might be a dozen classrooms in our building with parents sitting in, ostensibly as classroom aides. Many of them were actually taking in the lessons as well, covering ground lost in their own childhoods.

One of my mothers, a mildly handicapped woman, came in to discuss placing her son in our special education program. She said she was willing to give whatever help she could to her child, and she went on to describe the problems she had had with her own education. She was still having problems with essentials in her life, she told me, because she couldn't read and she couldn't figure numbers. Her life, she said, was falling apart every day.

I asked her if she might be interested in volunteering in her son's second-grade classroom, where she could learn to add and subtract and read right along with the children. While she was doing that, I told her, she could turn off her heat at home, turn off her electricity, save on fuel and other expenses and learn at the same time. I told her she could help with the washing and use the machine for her children's laundry, and she could come down to the lunchroom and eat while she worked there as a monitor. One of the best aspects of this arrangement was that she did all this with none of the children having any idea this parent was doing anything beyond her adult duties. They had no idea she was being a student herself.

We continued to have a standing-room-only crowd for every one of our evening parent assemblies. That first night in the spring of 1979 was no aberration. Our parents kept on coming whenever the call went out, and it was more than mere curiosity bringing them back. Something was truly happening with this school, and they wanted to be a part of it. I encouraged them to bring any issues that concerned them directly to me, and if I couldn't satisfy them I encouraged them to go to even higher authorities, all the way up to the district superintendent if need be. In fact, I had the names and telephone numbers of the district school administration hierarchy posted in the front lobby for all visitors to see.

Most parents' problems, however, went no further than my office. I was able to work through almost every situation, because in most cases the parents were willing to work with me. Some, however, were not.

One was Mrs. Rogers, a young working parent. Because of her family income, Mrs. Rogers did not qualify for a totally free lunch for her daughter, one of our first-graders. With her income, small as it was, Mrs. Rogers was supposed to pay a fee of two dollars a week.

Somehow her application for the federal lunch program was incorrectly processed at the beginning of the year, and it said that her daughter qualified for free lunches. When the mistake was discovered, a correction was made, and I notified Mrs. Rogers of the change.

She would not hear of it. She marched into my office waving her free-lunch form in my face. I told her again that there had been a mistake, but she wouldn't listen. She kept chanting that she had this form and this form said her daughter was entitled to free lunches.

When she threw the form on my desk for me to see, I picked it up, tore it up, tossed it in my closet and closed the door.

"There now," I said. "There is no more form. That should end the argument."

Mrs. Rogers was livid.

"Why, you . . . you . . . you can't tear up my lunch form," she sputtered, and she stormed out of my office. In no more than five minutes she was back, this time with her husband in tow. He looked as angry as she, and he approached my desk as if he was going to turn it over.

It happened that beneath my desk was a crowbar I had borrowed from Mr. Bailey to repair the fence in front of the school. As this man loomed over me, I spoke as calmly as I could.

"The lunch form is not yours," I said. "It never was yours. It is school property, it was incorrectly filled out, and I am not going to return it to you.

"Now," I said, taking a deep breath, lifting that crowbar up and placing it firmly on the top of my desk, "is there anything else I can do for you?"

He froze. His eyes widened, and he backed away. Then he grabbed his wife by the arm and hurried out the door. The thought crossed my mind that he might be going home to get his own crowbar. When he and his wife showed up minutes later with a police officer, I was relieved.

The policeman left them in the outer office, stepped into my room and closed the door.

"Mrs. Cartwright," he said, "I've been around here for twenty-three years. I've been called into schools for children. I've been called in for parents. One time I even came in for a dog.

"But, Mrs. Cartwright," he said, "I've never had to come in for the *principal!*"

We both laughed. And when I opened the door again, the Rogers family had gone. Mrs. Rogers soon transferred her child to another school, but the legacy of that crowbar lasted long after she was gone. Word of the confrontation spread throughout the community, bringing a parade of parents into my office to see this weapon.

"Ain't nobody hardly going to mess with you," said one parent, and she was right. For years, through the many nights I worked late in that building with only one or two other women around, I was comforted and protected by the reputation I earned that afternoon.

FOR SEVERAL REASONS, THE 1982–83 SCHOOL YEAR WAS A watershed for what we were doing at Blaine. We were clearly turning around the performances of our children in the classroom. Their achievement test scores were climbing, and these were numbers we knew were reliable. Also, more of our children were coming to school than ever before—our student attendance was averaging 92 percent, highest among the thirty-three elementary schools in our district. Our teacher attendance was Philadelphia's highest—98 percent. Fifteen of my thirty-six teachers did not miss a day in 1982–83.

But the best turn of events that year both for Blaine and for the entire school district of Philadelphia was the arrival of Dr. Constance E. Clayton as the new superintendent.

Dr. Clayton was a godsend to the children of Philadelphia, who had been forced to swallow the poor examples of education perpetrated on many of the city's students. Folks who didn't want to work or who were asked to retire complained about Dr. Clayton and called her a workaholic, among other things. She *was* stern. She rarely smiled a heartfelt smile and she had a stare that could stop a train.

But I liked her. She was a brilliant educator with a vision that all children could learn and should get their fair share. She once read aloud the following poem written by a Philadelphia high school student:

Tomorrow
by Rhonda Johnson

Tomorrow, just maybe tomorrow,
I'll face it without any fears.
Tomorrow, just maybe tomorrow,
I'll go without any tears.

It's just so hard to look forward to tomorrow.
Maybe I'll be called home tomorrow.
I know that it was never promised to me.
I know that I also may see
Tomorrow.
It seems as though it gets harder and harder.
I looked for a crutch
And looking back at yesterday,
I wonder.
I keep saying I won't think about it,
But I did today.
Again I feel alone and lost,
Again I must face another day.
Maybe, just maybe I'll try again . . .
Tomorrow.

As Dr. Clayton read this poem, as she had many times before, tears welled in her eyes and trickled down her cheeks. She
wanted the most for her children—*our* children—who were to be
the future. She was warm, and she cared. She was the leader in a
school district that had long since abandoned any real feeling of
accountability for the education of the inner-city poor. She was an
African-American woman who had assumed the ultimate line authority over whites and other African-Americans who did not
want "a black for a boss, much less a black woman."

As a public servant answerable to the poor parents and children in the Blaine School community, I felt fortunate that Dr.
Clayton, a renowned, quality educator, was my superior. I'd
worked under eight superintendents by the time Dr. Clayton ar-

rived. She was the first who talked about the schools being there for the children. I had heard superintendents talk about improving the books, they talked about upgrading the buildings, they talked about adjusting the curriculum, they talked about improving test scores. But I had never heard a superintendent actually say, "The children come first. Whatever we do in this city, we must consider first and foremost its effects on the education of our children." Dr. Clayton said that, and I was impressed.

She spoke my language. In all my years as a teacher, as a union representative and as a principal, I had seen the school system approached as a business. How much money do we have? How much money will it cost? How many hours will it take? Such questions went on and on and on. Negotiation and politics displaced the subject of the children's education at every turn.

But when Connie came, the kids in the classroom became the first priority. She told the teachers they were going to begin working from a standard curriculum. She told us that teachers were no longer going to be allowed to teach social studies all day long simply because social studies was their favorite or strongest subject. She told them they were going to teach math and reading and science, and they were going to have a certain amount of time to teach these subjects each day. Teachers would be expected to cover a given amount of material by the end of the month and they would be expected to show what was learned by testing the students on that material.

This was our "pacing and planning schedule," and the teachers hated it with an undying passion. But it was music to my ears. For years, long before I came to Blaine, I had watched teachers teach pet projects or assign workbook pages to their children for weeks, then pull a canned lesson off the shelf whenever an administrator came in to observe. The principal would walk in, and the teacher would whip that lesson out and teach it like nobody's business. The impressed principal would leave, and it was back to coasting for the teacher and the class.

Well, there would be no more coasting under Connie Clayton. There were plenty of people who were threatened by these changes and who resisted them as fiercely as possible. But with me and my staff at Blaine, Dr. Clayton was preaching to the choir.

Which made it ironic that I was the only principal in the district to decline the invitation to participate in the new superintendent's first initiative. The first program Dr. Clayton pitched to our schools was called "Replicating Success," based on a nationwide study of effective schools. The idea was to collect the best ideas, innovations and approaches that each of these schools had to offer, combine them and apply them to our Philadelphia schools.

I declined the invitation. My reasons were different this time from the ones I had given when I had rejected the Mastery Learning program three years earlier. The difference was, Dr. Clayton's proposed program was *replicating* success. I felt what we were already doing at Blaine deserved replication. We were number one in the district in student achievement, number one in staff and student attendance, and both achievement and attendance were improving in an atmosphere conducive to learning. There was joy at Blaine.

We had a good program in place. That's why I declined to accept this new one. But other people were not happy with my decision.

Jeanette Brewer called me right away.

"Madeline," she said, "what is the matter with you?"

I said, "Jeanette, we have a program we're running over here that's working for us. Why should we change?"

"Madeline," she said, "I don't think you know what you're doing this time."

Harold Kurtz, who had been my principal at Belmont and who remained a close friend, called and said, "Madeline, when they told you you have an option with this program, they were just being polite. They mean for you to take the program."

A director from downtown called and told me the offices there were buzzing about the stand I was taking.

"They're saying Jeanette Brewer can't control you," the director told me. "It's putting Jeanette on the line because she has to explain to Dr. Clayton why Blaine is not included in the program."

I felt that the worst that could happen was Dr. Brewer would call and *order* me to take the program. Then I would have no choice. But as long as I did, I exercised it, and I received no ultimatum.

As that school year wore on, however, and as they began putting that program together downtown, I knew we were headed for a face-off. I was apprehensive—not afraid, but apprehensive. Dr. Clayton was out in front of the wagon, so to speak, pulling hard to improve education for all children in the city, and we at Blaine were pushing as hard ourselves, but in our own way. It might have appeared to some that we were dragging our feet and holding back the wagon. But that was not the case. We supported what Dr. Clayton was doing, and we also supported the children in our school. I believed in Connie Clayton's brilliance, determination, commitment and strength, and I believed we were singing the same song. She would see that, I was certain.

Still, as the year went on, my apprehension grew. I had no idea what Dr. Clayton thought of what we were doing. I shared my feelings with my staff, the students and the parents, urging even more commitment and involvement.

I wasn't sure when a confrontation would finally come, but there was a good chance it might be at the end of the spring, when the test results for the year came back and all the schools in our district gathered for the annual District Four Academic Achievement Awards ceremony.

The event took place after the standardized testing. The research people went through all the results, compared the schools and ranked them on the basis of the scores. Those rankings were kept totally secret until the ceremony.

I had reservations about what those scores meant in the first place, even if they were honestly achieved, and so many were not. In any event, the superintendent always came to the ceremony, so this would be my first face-to-face meeting with Dr. Clayton.

The ceremony was always a beautiful event, with candles

and flowers. This one was no different. There were short speeches, then Dr. Clayton stood and walked to the microphone. She talked about the mission and goals of the school district. Her voice was crisp, her enunciation and delivery exact. Her appearance was immaculate. She had the bearing of the Rock of Gibraltar. I admired her so.

But that day I was frightened as well. Would she make some sort of example of me for not getting in line? Was she one of those leaders who are so insecure that they take every move off of their line as a personal attack?

I heard little of what Dr. Clayton said that morning, I was so deep in thought about my career and my school. For an instant she peered over the top of her glasses and looked at me, and I could see why most folks were afraid of her.

I looked at the table and candles. I never thought this ceremony would matter so much to me. I never really liked the idea of a contest like this, with no real rules and no referee to call fouls. What this ceremony said to me was: Keep those paper programs looking good. My children were beautiful and happy and they were learning every day, but would that be enough to compete with the other schools?

I was anguished.

Dr. Clayton's speech ended, and for the first time in my life I was planning a speech for a meeting with a superior—usually I ad-libbed. I was thinking of exactly what I would say to defend all that I stood for from the attack I was certain would come.

When the last candle of the morning was lit and passed among the principals in the room, intended for the one among us whose school had shown the greatest rise in achievement in the year-end testing, no one knew where it was to stop. This was the candle coveted most by everyone in that room.

It stopped with me.

When I looked at Dr. Clayton, she was smiling.

C H A P T E R

11

GETTING THAT AWARD IN THE SPRING OF 1983 WAS THE green light we needed. It verified that what we had begun at Blaine was working, and it gave us the freedom to keep going without undue pressure from downtown.

We did keep going. It didn't take long to develop a sense of tradition in our school, a sense of achievement, of expectations and of pride. The most difficult part was getting started, putting those planks in place. But once we had done that, it fueled itself. Our older children who moved into other schools began spreading the Blaine reputation by the achievements and the attitudes they took with them. I began hearing from principals at the upper schools into which our children graduated. These principals told me that they could pick out my kids in a minute, without even asking. One told me, "They walk differently, they talk differently and they definitely work differently."

Of course they did. Our children at Blaine knew they were expected to do their homework. They knew they were expected to come to school every day, whether it was raining, blowing or snowing. They knew they were to show respect for their teachers, for one another and for themselves. They knew they were to carry themselves with pride—a pride that was earned, not awarded. They knew there was joy to be found in that building every day— joy in achievement, joy in belonging and joy in just being there. They'd absorbed these things day after day at our school for years, and they didn't just forget these established values when they moved on. These attitudes stayed with them and became a part of them.

A new administrative assistant was assigned to Blaine soon after we won that first district achievement award. Two weeks into the year she came to me and said, "I thought this school was supposed to be so special. Well, these kids are just as bad as any other kids."

I said, "What do you mean?"

She said, "My office is full of children misbehaving and giving me just as many problems as the children in the school I left."

I called an assembly.

"Boys and girls," I said, "I'd like those of you who are new to our school this year to stand up."

About thirty of the children stood.

I turned to the administrative assistant and said, "Are they your problems?"

"Yes," she said, looking out at the children, "that's most of them."

"All right then," I said. "These children are newcomers here. They have not yet learned the Blaine way. But they will, because we're going to teach them."

I explained to this new Blaine family member the Blaine way. I told her that this problem of new students not understanding our expected behavior occurred at the beginning of each school year. New children had to be oriented into their new surroundings. They needed to know what we considered acceptable behavior and what behaviors we found totally unacceptable. I had the same assemblies over and over again, to indoctrinate the new children and to remind the others of the Blaine way. Whenever anyone complained about the number of assemblies and the same messages, I asked them how many times they saw the same commercial on television or how many times they heard the same message in their churches or synagogues. Students, parents and teachers needed to be frequently reminded of the Blaine way.

I met with each and every parent and child who joined the Blaine family. I told them that I would love them and treat them as I treated my own children, and in return I demanded respect. I went over all of our rules. It was vital to go through this process with each and every child and his parents, because a school climate can be severely affected by just one or two children who are not properly assimilated. One bad apple can indeed spoil the entire bushel when it comes to the behavior of children in a school.

We watched for adverse changes in Blaine and addressed them as they occurred. To further reinforce the values we treasured, I created a school pledge, which we printed on pamphlets and cards, and posted on walls all over the school. We required the children to memorize and recite it several times a day, including each morning out on the schoolyard. Before entering the building, the children would line up and recite the Blaine pledge in resounding unison, six hundred little voices echoing up and down the narrow streets of our neighborhood:

> *I will act in such a way that*
> *I will be proud of myself and others will be*
> *proud of me too.*
> *I came to school to learn, and I WILL learn.*
> *I will have a good day.*

On rainy mornings, we would gather in the gym and begin our day by reciting the pledge there. After going to their classrooms and hearing the morning announcements, the children in each room would recite the pledge among themselves. At assemblies, we would begin with the pledge. Every child in the neighborhood knew the words by heart. Tiny two- and three-year-olds, hardly knowing how to speak, walked around with their older brothers and sisters chanting the Blaine pledge.

I reminded the children of its meaning at every opportunity. If a child misbehaved or did something foolish, the first thing I'd say was: "Are you proud of yourself right now?" They'd think about that.

I'd ask them if they thought their mother or grandmother or whoever cared for them would be proud of them, or if I was proud of them, and their little hearts would sink. Their eyes would well with water. This really meant something to them. There is nothing so infectious or so convincing as your own heartfelt enthusiasm and conviction. Kids can smell empty words and false feelings a mile away. On the other hand, there is nothing they know better than the scent of sincerity.

They knew we sincerely believed in them. That was so important, because a lot of our children had no one to believe in or to turn to but themselves.

"I'm not going to be with you all the time," I told the children. "Your mother is not going to be with you at all times.

"Children," I said, "every day you are going to have to make decisions that may well affect your lives, and you're going to have to make many of them alone. There's going to be no one looking over your shoulder helping you decide what to do.

"But this pledge can help you. Every time you've got a decision or a choice to make, remind yourself of these words and they will help you make a good decision. They will help you make the right decision."

That pledge became our rallying cry. Every year the Shriners issued free circus tickets to schools all across the city of Philadelphia. We'd take two busloads of our children to see the circus each year. One year we arrived—one hundred and twenty of our children holding hands and huddled together among the throngs of people pushing toward the Big Top entrance. When we got to the gate, I discovered I'd left our tickets back at the school. I explained to the ticket taker what had happened. No luck. He would not let us in.

So I gathered the children together and put them in two

lines, side by side, sixty pairs long. Then I had them recite the pledge.

One hundred and twenty voices rang out above the din of that crowd:

I WILL ACT IN SUCH A WAY . . .

By the time we were finished, that runway area was dead quiet. We had everybody's attention. Then I had the children do it one more time, so everyone could hear it all the way through. It was a public performance.

By then, a manager had joined the ticket taker at the gate. I asked again if we might be permitted to come in.

"By all means," said the manager, as he showed us to our seats.

IN MARCH 1984, A STORY ABOUT BLAINE'S SUCCESS AP-peared in the Philadelphia *Inquirer*, headlined "A Lesson in Commitment." Soon after that, reporters began arriving from newspapers not just in Philadelphia but in other cities as well. People seemed starved for a success story in an inner-city school. Apparently these stories were few and far between—far enough so that people were coming from out of town to see what we were doing here.

Some saw nothing but the washing and sewing machines, and that's what they wrote about. A story about Blaine was featured in *World News* magazine, one of the grocery-store tabloids. It printed a photo of me sewing a coat as several of my students watched. That's as far as that story went. But others, like the Philadelphia *Inquirer's*, looked more closely and recognized what we were doing.

And we were doing so much. Along with teaching personal and family safety, we encouraged the children and their parents to take part in community and school projects. Blaine was a part of District Four, the most densely populated of the city's eight subdistricts. A group of District Four parents began a scholarship fund named in honor of Dr. Ruth W. Hayre, who had retired as superintendent of our district. I was excited about this initiative: Scholarship Month was begun to raise money for students who graduated from schools in District Four. Here was an entire month when students would be talking about scholarship and college, two words that might never have been emphasized in their homes—or in their school, for that matter. We at Blaine began immediately to seize this unique opportunity to involve children in striving for college, even in the preschool program.

I put a scroll on my office door and announced to the children that whoever donated fifty cents to the Ruth Hayre Scholarship Fund would be allowed to sign it with my special colored pen. Everyone wanted to sign my scroll. Some of the little ones who had not started school brought in their fifty cents and made their mark. My Tyrone, who was three, was not about to be left out. He made his mark and invited visitors to the office to come and inspect it.

We continued to make Blaine serve the children and the community. We continued our efforts to stay in first place in as many areas as we could. The school district held an oratorical contest every year, with all schools urged to enter their best speakers as contestants. This was a very competitive event. Schools sent in tapes of their nominees, and the judges narrowed the finalists down to ten students, who were then invited downtown to participate in the final competition in front of a live audience.

From my first day in Blaine I began cultivating the kids for this contest—all of the kids. Again, I had assemblies to let the children know we would be going through the process of selecting the best children to represent our school in this contest. We qualified a student for the finals five consecutive years. In 1984 we qualified a girl named Felicia Lewis, and I called the kids together in an assembly to tell them about it.

"Children," I said, "we are going to be sending Felicia to represent us in this competition. When she wins, nobody's going to say 'Felicia Lewis won this contest.' They're going to say *Blaine* won it. That means us—you, me, all of us.

"We must root for Felicia," I told them. Then I brought her out to deliver her speech to her classmates, to practice for the judges she'd be facing in a few days.

The kids were so quiet during her presentation one could truly have heard a pin drop. When she finished, they burst into a mighty round of applause, just a heartfelt ovation, which was exactly how the crowd reacted at the actual competition. Felicia spoke about pride in her race, in her school, in her role models. She spoke about accomplished African-Americans, about self-respect, about being somebody, and she brought down the house— as well as the votes of all the judges.

It was no wonder Felicia won that contest. Sara Brooks was her coach, and Sara knew only success. Felicia was convinced before she left that she was going to win. She believed Sara. She believed us.

I couldn't get back to the school fast enough that afternoon.

"Children, *children!*" I yelled over the PA system. "We *won!* We *WON!!*"

Soon the whole school was screaming. Kids and teachers came out into the hall to find Felicia. Everyone was picking her up and hugging her. She was a very humble child, but there was nothing to be embarrassed about that day. We were all truly in this together.

We began making that oratorical championship an annual goal. Two years after Felicia won, we sent a student named John Payton to the finals. By then our own competition at Blaine had become very heated. We had many talented kids, all trying hard to be the one to make it downtown. We had our own series of speeches and narrowed the choice that year to John. Then I called the kids together, to assuage the ones who had lost and to rally support for our representative.

"John is going to carry the Blaine banner this year, and he's going to win," I told them. "I didn't say *might*. I said he's *going* to win.

"Somewhere in this world there is a better speaker than John Payton," I told them. "But it's stretching coincidence to imagine that that person is going to be in that auditorium next week."

Word had gotten around that the reason Blaine kids were suddenly doing so well in this contest was that their principal was so involved. So other principals began getting more involved. When I had first begun attending those finals, I'd see perhaps two or three principals in the audience. Now many more were coming, and I didn't hesitate to throw down the gauntlet. The year John Payton made the finals, I ran into Vernon Jones, one of my fellow principals, as we were entering the auditorium.

"Why, good morning, Mr. Jones," I said. "I'd like you to meet the winner of this year's oratorical contest."

John took Mr. Jones's hand and shook it like a man.

"It's nice to meet you," said Jones. "But with all due respect, Mrs. Cartwright, there must be some mistake here. Because *I* brought the winner."

He then introduced us to his student. As they turned to take their seats, Jones said, "Good luck to you, John. But you can't beat my boy."

John was nine years old, but he was big for his age, a plump little rascal and confident as could be. He won that contest that day, as I knew he would, but that wasn't the best of it. What I'll never forget was later that month when he delivered his winning speech again at a gathering of school and city officials. Dr. Clayton was there, as was William H. Gray III, our congressional representative to Washington.

Several people took the stage before John, including Congressman Gray, who was the keynote speaker. Immediately after he was finished speaking, the congressman left the room, not waiting to hear the student orators.

Now, John was a natural little ham. When he took the stage, he began by acknowledging Dr. Clayton and all the work she had done for our schools. Then he turned toward the congressman's empty chair.

"We would also like to thank Congressman Gray," John said, "wher*ever* he went . . ."

The people in that room loved it. They were amazed at that little fellow's stage presence. John did Blaine, the city of Philadelphia and Dr. Clayton proud that day and many more days that followed.

JOHN PAYTON AND FELICIA LEWIS WERE JUST DYNAMITE. But, I truly believed, so were all our kids, in one way or another. The trick was finding an outlet for the abilities and energies of each of the children. A case in point was our annual school play. One year I decided I wanted the children to do a personal favorite of mine, *The Birthday of an Infanta,* by Oscar Wilde. I just loved that play, and I asked Sara Brooks to direct it.

"Sara," I said, "I know it might be difficult, but I know the children can do it."

Sara, of course, had no doubt. She committed herself to that production the same way she committed herself to her classroom and to the oratorical contests. She had the kids carrying their scripts wherever they went. Her cast included some of our champion speakers, but Sara drew no line between them and the child with the smallest part in this play. She pushed every one of the children until they not only knew their lines but also became their characters.

That was especially true for the lead, a fifth-grader named Nikisha Jones.

Nikisha was not one of our model students. In fact, she spent more than her share of time in my office. When Sara selected Nikisha for the lead, there was a big buzz among the staff about how one of the biggest problem students in the school was selected as the star of this show.

But all Sara ever told Nikisha was how tremendous she was on that stage, which was true. Nikisha was a dramatic little girl, very theatrical off stage as well as on. That was her problem in the classroom, but Sara was able to capture that energy and put it to work with this play. When Nikisha showed disrespect for a teacher a week before the performance and was sent to my office, I told her, "Little girl, you are going out of this play."

Sara Brooks was in my office in a heartbeat.

"Mrs. Cartwright," she said, "you cannot take Nikisha out of this production. She is talented, Mrs. Cartwright. Talented people are temperamental. We must mold her and work with her. She is just too good to take out."

There was more of Sara Brooks the director speaking to me at that moment than Sara Brooks the teacher. But I listened, and when the curtain went up on that play the next week, it took my breath away. It took everyone's breath away. It couldn't have been done any better on Broadway. Everything from the costumes to the scenery was first-rate. We'd gone out and bought only the best props and materials. We didn't want the children thinking they deserved anything less than the best.

The kids played their parts like professionals. They had rehearsed that way, practicing with Sara each morning at seven-thirty. Nikisha was outstanding. When that little girl fell down on the floor and wailed, *"I am sooooooo UGLY!"* the entire audience, that wall-to-wall auditorium full of people, broke down and wept.

Not before or since have I ever seen a children's performance that surpassed the one we saw that day.

BUT EVEN AS WE WERE WINNING CONTESTS, PRODUCING plays, and pushing our grades and attendance figures higher every year, there was a shadow spreading outside our doors that threatened to undo all that we had achieved in my years at Blaine.

That shadow was crack cocaine.

I first came upon it on a warm spring morning in 1985, when Sheila, one of my third-grade girls, rushed into my office and told me Donald was out in the schoolyard "selling dope."

Donald was the brightest third-grader in the school, the highest-scoring student in his grade. He had scored in the 99th percentile on the state standardized tests. I could not imagine any of my students selling drugs on the schoolyard, let alone Donald. But Sheila had a tiny capsule of white powder in her hands. The vial was no bigger than my fingernail. She handed it to me and gave me the names of six boys who had bought similar capsules from Donald for twenty-five cents apiece. One of the boys, she said, had already eaten his.

They were all third-graders, all in the same room. I immediately called the mother of the boy who had eaten the contents of his capsule and had Raymond Brooks drive them to the hospital. Meanwhile, I collected the other children and called the Juvenile Aid Division of the police department. I told them I had a case of substance abuse on my hands.

As we waited for the JAD officers to arrive, I saw Dennis Robinson, the older neighborhood boy I'd made friends with the first summer of our cleanup, walking past the school. I opened my office window and yelled to him to come over for a minute. I told him I had something to show him.

"Can you tell me what these are?" I asked him, holding out a handful of the capsules.

"Those are crack caps," he said. "But that's not crack in them."

"And *what* is crack?" I asked him. I'd never heard the term.

"It's dope," Dennis said. "It's the stuff they're smokin' now."

I opened one of the capsules and emptied it on my desk. "Is this crack?"

"No," said Dennis, shaking his head. "Those are crack capsules, but that's not crack. Crack doesn't look like that."

"Well, what *does* it look like?"

"Like little crystals. It looks like a cracked-up mothball. It's not powdery like that."

"Well, what's this?"

"I don't know."

"Well, taste it."

"I ain't tasting that."

"Dennis, a little boy ate this stuff and I'm trying to figure out what it is. It's not going to hurt you to take a tiny taste. You can spit it out."

Dennis did what I asked as almost everyone did when I said it was for the children. He wet his finger, dabbed it in the powder and put it to his tongue.

"Tastes like flour," he said.

Now I took a taste. I tasted flour, I tasted salt . . . it was pancake mix. Little Donald had been running a scam on these kids for their quarters, all of them playing out their drug charade.

But those capsules were no charade. They were the real thing. Donald had brought them from home. His mother was collecting them to trade to a small-time distributor who offered one five-dollar vial of the drug for twenty empties. He then filled those empties with crack skimmed from his own five-hundred-dollar buy—one hundred vials at five dollars apiece. He'd take enough out of each of those hundred vials to double his profit.

Users were beginning to multiply like mushrooms across the neighborhood. We had seen all kinds of drugs in Strawberry Mansion over the years, but nothing like this. When I came out on the yard to chat and pick up trash in the mornings, I began finding more and more of these crack capsules on the ground—red, blue and yellow, the color signifying the cost and size of each ($5, $10 or $20). They were all used up, empty.

We began seeing more and more parents coming into the building, not to help us with the school, but to ask for money. Some weren't even parents. People I had never seen before walked into the office and asked for a dollar for carfare to the welfare office or fifty cents to buy some bread. What they were actually doing was scraping together the five dollars it cost to buy one of those capsules of crack.

I listened to their tales, then answered quite emphatically, "Not a dime!" Soon the pipers who routinely sat on a porch across from the school would yell to adults approaching the school doors, "Yo, bro'! She ain't givin' up nothing, not a *dime!*"

Among those I said no to were some of my regular parents, those who had been part of our program from the beginning, and this really hurt me. I had parents who were active in the school, who kept up behind their children, who kept their kids clean and kept themselves clean, who did whatever we asked them to do— and now they were into drugs. These were my "show" parents, the ones I used as models for the others, the ones whose kids were our "up" kids. I began to see some of them go down. I watched some of them turn into pipers.

Pipers. That's what they call the people who are addicted to the crack pipe. The power of that pipe, of this particular drug, is hard to comprehend. Its potency, according to the people who use it, is incomparable. The high is immediate and intense, better than an orgasm, they say—which is ironic, since the drug tends to eventually displace any sex drive whatsoever. But beyond the physical rush a crack high delivers is a sense of omnipotence, a feeling of utter clarity and confidence that makes the user feel like a god—for the ten or fifteen minutes that the high lasts. Then it's time for another hit.

It's that hunger for the next hit that turns a user into an addict, and crack creates addicts in an instant. It is that strong. It is that insidious. And it's that dangerous. It can kill in an instant, as basketball star Len Bias tragically discovered. But deaths like his and others have not kept crack off the streets.

The saddest thing to me is the fact that crack—so aptly named—has done what no other drug has been able to do in the inner-city communities. It has seduced the women, who in so many cases are the only glue holding their families and communities together. Everyone reaches for relief at some time or other. But where they might have reached for a bottle or even some marijuana before and were able to control these things, many women are now reaching for crack, and they can't control it. No one can!

To see mothers I had come to know so well and count on so

much fall victim to this drug, to watch them turn into pipers and sell out their own children's lives for those deadly crack crystals— it broke my heart.

A woman named Joanne broke my heart. Her little boy had never missed a day of school. I would have Joanne stand up at our parents' meetings and I'd say, "Her child has never missed a day. Not in kindergarten, not in the first grade, not in the second, third or fourth."

Now he was in the fifth, and he was still coming every day, but I noticed his little sister was starting to look different. Joanne didn't have much, but she always dressed her little girl immaculately—neat, clean, with all the finishing touches, the ribbons and bows matching whatever she wore. Joanne's daughter was still coming to school put together, she hadn't totally fallen apart, but those touches were gone now. Something was slipping, and I could see it happening right before my eyes.

Then I began hearing snippets from some of the parents.

"You've got to watch Joanne," they said.

"She's on that crack," they said.

Joanne was in the building on school picture day, and at the end of the afternoon we were missing two envelopes of the children's money. It didn't occur to me that Joanne might have taken it. But some of the other parents had no doubt.

Then, not long after that, Joanne came into my office to use the telephone. While she was making her call, I sat right beside her. But I did not notice her reach to the bookcase behind my desk and slip my wallet out of my pocketbook.

I didn't realize my wallet was gone until that evening, when my daughter, Jill, asked to borrow my credit card. I opened my bag, saw the wallet was missing and immediately thought of Joanne.

I drove directly to the house where I knew she lived and knocked on the door.

"Mrs. Cartwright?" she said when she opened it.

"Joanne," I said, "I need to talk to you."

"Uh, sure," she said. "Come on in."

I stepped inside and saw a man sitting in the kitchen.

"That's my father," said Joanne. This was her parents' home, not hers.

"Can we go to your room?" I asked. I wanted to speak to her alone.

Once we were by ourselves, I said, "Joanne, I don't want to talk about anything except you giving my wallet back to me. I had it before you came into my office. When you left, I didn't have it. Now I want it back."

"Mrs. Cart . . ."

I cut her off. I put my hand over her mouth and I continued.

"Joanne, don't say a word. Just get my wallet, or I am going to have to call the police and have you arrested."

She looked directly into my eyes, and I could see her surrender.

"All right," she said. "All right. All right."

She led me out without a word. We walked a couple of blocks from her home to a crack house. Joanne had me wait outside while she went in. A few minutes later she emerged with a man at her side. They had my wallet in their hands. Joanne handed it to me, and I left to come home.

All without a word.

THE EFFECT OF CRACK ON THE FAMILIES IN OUR NEIGHBOR-hood was devastating. It was tearing them apart. The Powers family, for instance, was one of the best we had. Good children, good students, both a mother and a father in the home. The grandparents were there, too. One afternoon the grandmother lumbered into my office in tears.

"Mrs. Cartwright," she said, "I was sitting in the kitchen last night with my son, just sitting there and talking like we always do, when he reached up all of a sudden and snatched my pocketbook off the table. Just snatched my pocketbook right up and ran out the door with it.

"Mrs. Cartwright," she said, "that's my *son!* It's crack that's got him and his wife."

It got a woman named Charlene as well—which is how she came to blow out the windows of one of our classrooms with a shotgun.

This was on a weekday afternoon, just after school had let out. In the building there were still teachers and children engaged in after-school extracurricular activities. I was in my office when the sound of a blast tore through the hallway outside, followed by the spray of shattering glass. Before I could even get to the door, I heard several teachers shouting out in the hallway: "They're *shooting* outside. They shot out the front *windows!*"

I hit the floor, shimmied back to my desk, reached up and pulled down the telephone by its cord. I dialed the police and told them there was a shooting here at the Blaine School.

The thing to understand about calls for help in a neighborhood like Strawberry Mansion is that help rarely arrives in time to do any good. When the police get a call from someone telling them there's shooting going on in a neighborhood like this, the last thing in the world the police are going to do is come down and get in the middle of it. They'll wait until it's over, give it some time to play itself out, *then* they'll come in and sort through the aftermath, pick through the bodies and whatever else might be lying around and begin piecing together their case. But while the bullets are flying, it is a certainty no help will be on the way.

It took a long time for help to come that afternoon. An hour after I called the police, no one had arrived. Finally I called the district's department of school security. The officer who answered happened to be a former policeman, and he convinced the police station to send someone to Blaine by telling them that this was a *school* where the shooting had taken place. He explained that it was I, the school principal, who had called and that I'd be calling the mayor and everyone else if they didn't send someone soon.

Once the police arrived, they quickly sorted out what had happened.

Charlene was about twenty-two, educable mentally retarded,

with an IQ of no more than 80. She was slow, but that hadn't kept her from getting swept up in this wave of crack. Somehow, Charlene had begun selling crack cocaine, and she'd gotten in over her head.

The way the selling worked: The supplier would give a dealer perhaps a hundred capsules. That's five hundred dollars' worth of crack. The dealer would sell them for five dollars apiece. When they were all sold, the dealer had to give five hundred dollars to the supplier, who would then give one hundred dollars *back* to the dealer as his pay.

There was a strictness to this method. The seller was not allowed to just take off his share of the money and give the supplier four hundred dollars. He had to bring him the entire five hundred. That was to assure that the seller wasn't using the supplier's money and smoking his crack. The pushers don't want *users* selling their dope. It's as simple as that.

Charlene was a user. She started selling that crack and smoking it as well. She, her sisters and one brother were all smoking some of what Charlene was selling, and when the supplier came for his money, Charlene came up short. So the man threatened her. He told her what he was going to do if he came back and she did not have his money.

There was a double-barreled shotgun in the house—it belonged to Charlene's father. Many homes in the neighborhood had shotguns. Some people had them as protection against thieves. Others were dealing drugs themselves and had the weapons to protect their investments.

When the dealer returned to Charlene's door, there were two shotgun barrels staring him straight in the eye, with Charlene behind them.

She pulled the triggers, and it was that blast of buckshot that blew out the front windows of our school.

Before the glass even hit our floor, that man was two blocks down the street, running on air and picking up speed.

❖

NOT ONLY WERE OUR CHILDREN NOW DOING WITHOUT THE food and clothing, the heat and even the housing that had already been so hard to come by in this neighborhood—all of it sacrificed by their parents for crack—but some of our children were turning into crack dealers themselves. The game Donald had played that morning on the schoolyard soon became reality for some of our children. That's how lucrative this crack business was. It was seductive in so many ways, for the sellers as well as the users, and age was no barrier.

I kept hearing kids talking in the halls about this or that little boy or even girl who had become part of the business, acting as lookouts, carrying crack or money during a deal, or even selling some of it themselves. Two of the kids I heard mentioned often were Doopah—a thirteen-year-old boy who had graduated from Blaine—and Terrance, one of our eight-year-old third-graders.

"Mrs. Cartwright," the children told me, "Terrance is helping Doopah sell drugs."

"What do you mean?"

"Terrance sits on the steps with the crack and the extra money, Mrs. Cartwright. He keeps everything on him. And Doopah stands on the corner. When the cars come by, he sells them five or ten dollars' worth or whatever. Soon as the car leaves, he goes back, gives his money to Terrance, picks up some more of those crack caps and goes on back to the corner.

"See," they went on, "that way if somebody holds Doopah up or something, they don't get everything. They only get what he's got in his hand."

"This is crazy," I thought. "This is insane, unreal."

But I knew it was real. I knew it was true. So I called an assembly. I made sure Terrance was sitting in the front row.

"Children," I began, "today we are going to talk about drugs. We are going to talk about the risks, about the dangers."

Then I took two children out of their seats and put them up on the stage steps. One of the two was Terrance.

"Now, children," I said, "here are two little boys. Let's pretend Terrance is helping this other little boy sell drugs. Let's pretend his job is to sit on the stoop of this house and hold the crack and hold the money.

"Now let's pretend that farther down the street, sitting in a stolen car, are two men, two junkies. These men are pipers, and they have no money. But they've been watching Terrance and his friend, and one says to the other, 'Man, look at that. That little kid's got what we want and a bonus, too. He's got crack *and* cash. He's got a pocketful of hits and some money to boot, and he ain't as big as a *minute.'*"

Now I pretended to be one of the pipers, creeping up on the boys. Suddenly I leaped up on the steps, grabbed Terrance, put him under my arm and literally ran out the auditorium door.

Then I came back in, still clutching that little boy as tightly as I could.

"This was an easy hit," I said, staying in character, "and all it will cost is the life of this little dummy. We can't let him go. He might tell on us. What we have to do is kill him. Yeah, *kill* him."

With that I began to choke Terrance. I mean, I really began to choke him. Tears were streaming down my face as he cried out, "Mrs. Cartwright! Mrs. Cartwright! You're *hurting* me!"

I loosened my grip, and I turned toward the children. The wetness on my face and the hurt in my eyes told them all that they needed to know.

That assembly was on a Friday. The following Monday morning Terrance's mother and father showed up at my office. They hugged me. They kissed me. And they told me they were sending Terrance to live with an aunt "down South." They wanted him removed from the drug zones, the war zones where he was in the direct line of fire.

They were sending him out of the city, they said, to save his life.

THINGS GOT WORSE. BY 1986 AND 1987 I HAD BEGUN SEEING children in our school whose behavior defied any explanation, children whose violent outbursts and complete lack of focus were unlike anything I had ever witnessed. I didn't know it at the time, but I soon learned that these were crack children, boys and girls born to mothers who used the drug during pregnancy and passed it into their embryos through their bloodstream.

The first I saw of this syndrome was a first-grader named Richard. He had been a problem in kindergarten, a very disruptive little boy, but I assumed he was just adjusting to school, that his behavior could be worked out with the right teacher. So I assigned him to Mary Freeman.

We weren't far into the fall when Mary came down to my office and said, "That little boy is just turning my room *out!*"

I said, "What do you mean?"

"I mean I can't control him, Madeline. The little boy is mean. He's hitting kids, and he's not hitting them just to hit them, the way children do. He's trying to *hurt* them. He means to bring blood. He's vicious."

"Well, Mary," I said, "the next time this happens, send the boy to me."

Mary wasn't one to ever pass her problems on if she could help it. She prided herself on taking care of her own classroom. But Richard was beyond her reach. He was in my office the next day. I talked to him as I did any of the children sent to me. Then I called his home. He lived with a foster mother. His own mother had been unable to care for him because of her crack cocaine addiction, so his care was supervised by the Department of Human Services.

"Mrs. Cartwright," the foster mother told me, "we have problems with Richard here at home, too. We're working with him, and we hope you can work with us."

So we did. When Richard's behavior got too bad, if he got totally out of hand, I'd call his foster mother, and she would come in and take him home with her. This did not help Richard, who continued hitting the other children, but it gave the teacher and the class temporary relief.

The behavior did not abate. He bloodied a little girl's nose one afternoon. The next morning he bloodied a little boy. I pulled him into my office and tried to figure out what was going on. This was a bright boy. He did his schoolwork. He had a good, solid family taking care of him at home. There was no explanation that I could see for this streak of violence. But it had to stop.

Parents of the other children were irate. "You do something or get that little boy out of here," they screamed. "If he hurts my child again, I'll do something. I'll do something, all right."

Until that point, I had held back on spanking Richard. But now I decided it was time. I called him into my office.

"Richard," I said, "did you recite your pledge today?"

He didn't answer.

I repeated the first line of the pledge. Then I asked, "Richard, are you proud of yourself?"

Still there was no response.

"Do you suppose that your mother is proud of you?"

Silence.

"Richard," I said, "you know that our school rule is that if you hit a child, Mrs. Cartwright will hit you. You just may not hit other children. Do you understand?"

He just stared at me.

"Richard, we've given you chance after chance to change this behavior, and nothing is changing at all. My only choice now is to spank you."

He kept staring at me.

I took out my ruler and hit his leg.

He didn't flinch. Didn't move a muscle. Didn't change his expression. He simply kept staring.

I hit him again.

Again he stood there transfixed, like a zombie. No emotion whatsoever in his eyes, and no movement in his body.

I said to myself, What is this? I have never seen anything like this in my life!

I sat him down, and he still didn't say a word, didn't even blink an eye. I gave him a book to read. After about a half hour, he made his first movement. He picked up the book. I allowed him to read for a while, then I took him back to his class.

I met with every staff member who had taught Richard to discuss his behavior and to compare notes. I found that most of his more violent outbreaks occurred on the schoolyard, in the lunchroom or in the auditorium. We decided that Richard would be barred from those places and not allowed anywhere where there was not close supervision.

A few days later I got another call from Mary. Richard had gotten out onto the yard and was totally out of control, trying to fight and stick another little boy with a pencil. I came right away.

"Richard," I said to him, "you know you are not to be out on this yard."

He stopped, stared straight in my face and said, "Suck my dick."

I thought, "We have to draw a line somewhere, and he has crossed that line." I slapped him right on his mouth.

He began to *cry*. This was the first time I had ever seen this child cry.

I pulled him into my arms, hugged him and said, "I'm sorry I slapped you, Richard, I'm very sorry. Do you understand that?"

"Yes," he said.

"You know I love you, don't you?"

"Yes."

"Do you love me, too?"

"Yes."

"Then give me a kiss."

And he did. The boy kissed me right there. I was shocked. I called his foster mother later that day, and we talked about what had happened. I was wracking my brain to figure this thing out.

Later, I called a girlfriend of mine who had graduated from college with me. She was now living and teaching school in San Francisco. I knew crack had been out there on the coast longer than it had been here. So I called her and told her about this new kind of child I was seeing.

"He's like a zombie," I said. "Whatever he decides to do, he shuts everything else out and does it, as if he has blinders on. If he's fighting, he continues to fight. If he's screaming and yelling, he continues to scream and yell. He's utterly impervious to anything else around him. I never know when his outbursts will occur, and when they do, it's as if he's in a trance.

"I have never in my life met a child who doesn't respond to me," I said, "but this child does not respond. He simply *does not respond.*"

"Madeline," she said, "let me send you some literature."

She sent the results of some studies done with crack babies. As I read the material, it was as if the writer had seen Richard. The behavioral descriptions fit him to a tee.

"This hit our school about five years ago," my friend told me when I called her back. "They've done studies out here, examining the brains of some of these children, and there are actually holes in some of their brains, spaces where the brain did not fully develop because of this drug.

"These are infants they've been studying, Madeline. Sometimes they seem comatose, at other times they are wracked with what seems like a seizure. You're seeing what happens as they grow older. Imagine what happens when a kid like this gets to be sixteen, he's walking down the street, he looks up and sees someone approaching and he's seized by the urge to hit that person with a brick.

"Is he just going to stay in his neighborhood and hit someone with a brick? What's to keep him from walking downtown with a shotgun?"

I read everything I could find on this subject, and there was more material coming out every day. This was a totally new phenomenon, and the doctors weren't sure what to make of it all. Stories on crack babies began appearing in the popular press—in newspapers and magazines—but the crack *children* I was seeing in our school remained almost unnoticed by the general public.

I could see that children who were physically affected by crack cocaine during gestation demonstrated, for periods of time, behavior similar to that of autistic children. They often were impervious to the world around them. They were inattentive and

unable to concentrate for more than a few minutes. Their movement seemed spontaneous and aggressive. Richard, his brother
and two other children were the only children that we had identified as "crack-infected" and "crack-affected." "Crack-infected"
children are those whose mothers used crack during pregnancy.
Children who live in a crack environment, I referred to as "crack-
affected."

There's no telling all the damaging effects that crack had on
the children as a result of its being smoked in their homes or on
their porches. We are familiar with the "contact high" experienced
by people who are around others smoking marijuana; we know of
some of its symptoms, such as hunger, giddiness or forgetfulness.
There may well be symptoms related to crack exposure that affect
learning and behavior as well.

Crack-affected and crack-infected children who continued to
live with addicted parents seemed totally uncontrolled. They
moved constantly, seemingly unable to keep still for even the
shortest periods of time. They reminded me of the wild brown
rabbits on my father's farm. They were free spirits, moving about
at will. They would dart out of the classroom and even out of the
building. When we grabbed them, they did all that they could to
get away. They would scratch, kick and bite. Since they lived with
parents who often supported their habit through prostitution,
school personnel were reluctant to physically hold on to these
children, fearing that they might be AIDS-infected. This situation
was unsafe for all involved.

The same kind of situation can be found in foster homes,
where caretakers are not trained to adequately care for crack-infected children. Crack-infected children do not respond in any
consistent manner to a given stimulus. Untrained teachers and
foster parents may find themselves unnerved by a wild crack-
infected child who may have no memory of the last violent experience.

Crack-infected children who lived in well-functioning homes
were different from crack-infected children who remained in the
crack environment. Richard's brother demonstrated less aggres-

sive behavior than Richard, who spent a longer period in the crack environment before moving into a stable foster home.

The few days that I observed the year-old crack-infected daughter of Cassandra, she was super-hyperactive. She resisted cuddling. She was civil to even her siblings only when she was hungry. Once fed, she struggled to be "free," staying in constant motion until she was exhausted and literally fell over to sleep. Extreme efforts must be made early to nurture such children into cooperative, trusting little people. I would suggest keeping them still for short periods of time, to be gradually extended until they can attend normally. They should be encouraged to sit in a chair. They could be read a story, or they could play with a desk game or watch a television story or observe fish in a tank.

Schools must plan individual education programs designed to meet the needs of these children. Their constant movements suggest to me that there should be some well-defined rigorous physical activity before and after their forced attentive periods. I would suggest that a time-out place be set up for these children so that they are not allowed to impede the progress of the class, while at the same time their needs can be addressed.

Richard received direction at home consistent with what he received at school, whereas the other crack-infected children left school and returned to a "free to do as you please" life, and the teacher had to begin almost anew each day.

Programs should be developed by a team of providers made up of the home, the school and social and health agencies to work together to plan a program that promises success for these little victims of crack cocaine before they are thought of as grown villains. I hear adults say of young children, "He knows right from wrong. He did that same thing yesterday and was punished." Yet these children may not know or remember their actions from moment to moment.

WE DID OUR BEST TO PROVIDE FOR THE CHILDREN WITH what we had. By 1989 we had half a dozen kids in the school who were clearly in the same condition as Richard. The most intense aspect of their outbursts was the suddenness of them, the sheer spontaneity, so we tried to control the conditions in which these fits began, hoping that might lessen their force.

Since Richard would almost leap from his seat without provocation or warning to hit children, we had to do something. I knew that he had to be restrained. I needed to keep him in the seat in some acceptable safe way. The idea of a car seat belt just came to me. I went to a junkyard, cut the seat belts out of several old cars and took them back to install them in these children's chairs. The children would be able to hit the release button and get out of the belts—they wouldn't be imprisoned. But the idea was to arrest the impulse, to hold the child back long enough to give the teacher a chance to get between him and the other children.

Here was a restraint that allowed the child to be free in an emergency but also thwarted his spontaneity. This restraint gave him a chance to think about what he was going to do. It gave the teacher and the children time to react to his movement, to get ready or to protect themselves from his attacks.

I didn't hear a lot of talk from other principals about this problem, and I think that was because many of them weren't aware of it. They weren't getting out into the classrooms and into the homes and identifying the elements of these kids' cases that set them apart from everyone else. They were just seeing these children arriving in their offices and they were lumping them with all the other "problem" children they had. These were just more "bad kids" who needed to be sent home.

I talked to the people at the district office. I told them something had to be done about this specific problem. There were a few other principals aware of the situation, and they were saying the same thing. But nothing came back. No program. No response.

It's still that way, and meanwhile we have children affected by crack coming through the system and walking around like sticks of dynamite. They're going to keep blowing up if something isn't done to identify and treat them.

And they won't just blow up in our schools and in our neighborhoods. They can blow up anywhere, at any time. That may be what it takes before the right people begin to notice.

We must address this problem before some innocent child or adult is seriously maimed or killed by another innocent child victimized by crack cocaine.

BY 1989 WE HAD AS MANY REPORTERS INTERESTED IN INVEStigating the seriousness of crack as there were in reporting on the success of our school. CBS News did both—first they came to Blaine and did a piece on the evening news showing the success we'd achieved with our students, then they returned and did a morning news segment on crack and kids, focusing on Richard and his foster family.

Soon after that, Philadelphia mayor W. Wilson Goode, who had pledged to visit all schools early in his term, came to visit Blaine. He brought a big entourage with him and toured the school. He was impressed with the children, and they with him. At the end of the visit, he said, "What can I do to help?"

I said, "Well, I really don't need anything in this school. The school district responds to our needs.

"The problem I do have," I said, "is the many crack houses and vacant buildings the children must walk past on their way to school.

"Our children know which houses are which," I said. "They know who the dealers are, they know who the pushers are. Those buildings are wide open, most of them condemned, and they're totally unsafe for our children."

"Come on," he said. "Let's take a walk."

So we did. Diane Cunningham, the president of our Home-and-School Association, and I led the way. We looked like a parade, Diane out in front wearing a beautiful white dress, with me, the mayor and his entourage close behind. The mayor stopped and greeted the people who were waiting on their front steps and in the windows of their homes. We walked past a vacant, abandoned building where the boards had been pulled off the door and I pointed it out. I said, "That's a crack house there. And," I said, pointing to another such building, "there's one over there." One of the mayor's assistants noted each address. She also noted the license plates of any new cars parked along the way.

As we approached a large three-story row house, where the biggest drug dealer in the neighborhood operated, there was a stretch limousine parked out front. I asked the mayor not to look directly that way, and he didn't. But his assistant took down that address and license plate number as well.

At this point, Diane had increased her pace and was down past the corner, half a block away, before we could catch up to her. When we got back to the school, she kept right on walking, straight to her home. Within a few minutes, she was back, this time wearing a bright *blue* dress.

I said, "What are you doing, Diane?" I teased her about sporting two different outfits for the mayor.

"Honey," she said, "I didn't change my clothes for the mayor. I changed so if anybody starts talking about how *y'all* were walking through the neighborhood pointing out crack houses, nobody can say Diane was there, because Diane *wasn't* there. The lady that was there was wearing a *white* dress."

Diane had even brought her camera and had her photograph taken with the mayor as proof of what she was wearing that day, if she happened to need it.

Later that afternoon, a man from the neighborhood came into my office extremely upset.

"Mrs. Cartwright," he said, "I understand you pointed out my house to the mayor as a crack house."

"I did nothing of the sort," I told him. "Whatever information you have is wrong."

"Well, I want you to know I don't have anything to do with any crack," he said. "I run a legitimate business at my house."

The fact of the matter was, this man's business was far from legitimate. I hadn't told the mayor this man's house was a crack house, but I *had* told him that I had heard this home was used to fence goods stolen by pipers. And I mentioned to the mayor that among those goods was a three-line speakerphone that had been taken from my office.

The fear that the people in the neighborhood had of the crack dealers began to make me afraid as well. The next morning I gave Dennis Robinson a ride into the neighborhood, after he had spent the previous evening at our house, as he often did.

"Mom," he said—Dennis called me Mom—"you weren't out there pointing out the houses to the mayor's people yesterday, were you?"

I said, "Dennis, I was telling the mayor to board up those vacant houses to make them safe for the children."

"Mom," he said, "the word on the street is that you've been pointing out the crack houses. And the word is you pointed out the *big* house.

"You shouldn't have done that," he said, gazing out the window. "These people don't play, Mom. You mess with them, and you're living today and tomorrow you're history."

About six blocks from the school, when I stopped at a red light, Dennis opened the door and got out.

"Mom," he said, leaning back through the door, "I'm getting out here. I can *walk* the rest of the way."

That did it. When I arrived at the school, I called downtown and had them send a security guard to keep a watch on the situation for a few days. The guard they sent had been around. He was a former police officer and was a friend of mine. He knew what was going on, and he did his best to soothe me.

"Madeline," he said, "these dealers don't care a thing about what you did with the mayor. They're used to dealing with do-gooders like you. They don't pay it any mind at all. They'd be concerned if it was the police coming around and poking in their buildings, but you don't worry them at all. You're no threat to these people, absolutely no threat."

In a way, that made me feel better—a whole lot better.

In another way, it made me feel worse.

THE ONE THING THAT WAS *NOT* SEEN IN THE NEIGHBOR-hood was children actually using crack. They sold it, they dealt it, but they did not use it. It's simple to understand why. They were watching that awful pipe grab their older brothers and sisters. They were watching it take hold of their parents and turn them into fiends before their eyes. No one knew the devastating effects of this particular drug better than our children. It made them sick. Not long ago the most insulting term that could be used about someone's mother was "bitch." But now there was something even worse to call her. Now she could be called a piper. That was the horrifying, absolute bottom of the heap.

Our children saw what this drug could do. They watched women having sex on front porches for fifty cents or bending their heads in open car doors to perform oral sex for whatever they could get—sometimes with the driver not even bothering to turn off his motor. The women performing these desperate acts were often friends and neighbors . . . and sometimes they were the mothers of our children.

I had an assembly to address the effects of crack on our children's homes and families.

"This crack is bad," I told them. "It presents the worst drug problem that I have ever encountered. Crack takes over a person and makes that person willing to do anything to get more. I know some of your family members are on it. They didn't know its devastating effect when they began using it. That's why you must stay away from it, *far* away from it. If someone is smoking crack cocaine anywhere near you, get away from it. Tell your family that Mrs. Cartwright said that they must not smoke anywhere near you or any children, and especially not near babies. It can kill you and babies. This is not a 'wait until the children go to sleep' activity. This is a *'don't do it'* activity. Tell your parents what you learn in your drug prevention classes and make sure that *you* never use drugs.

"Meanwhile, what you must remember, children, is that the drug habits those close to you might have have *nothing* to do with *you*. You have no control over what other people do, even if they are people you love. I know how it can hurt, but you mustn't let it make you think any less of yourself. Do you hear me? This has *nothing* to do with you."

Now, more than ever, we had the need to pull together, to make our school an island in a storm that had found new strength.

Now, more than ever, the strength of what we had built over the previous ten years would truly be tested.

CHAPTER

1 2

 AMID THE RISING SEA OF CRACK COCAINE, WE LOST OUR
share of casualties: among the parents who used the
drug, among the children who sold it, among the children who suffered from its effects on the grown-ups with whom
they lived and among the children whose pregnant mothers used
crack before they were born into the world. A world where no one
was making ready for them: no bassinet, no crib, no room, no
house, no doting grandparents, no college fund and all too often
no one who really cared. They were about to be born into a community where one day they would be treated as if they were the
villain rather than the victim.

Within the walls of Blaine we were able to continue building
on the foundation of pride, love, caring for one another and personal and community achievement that we had spent so long
putting into place at the corner of Thirtieth Street and Berks.

Outside of Blaine, and outside of the inner city, children
need firsthand knowledge of the horrors of substance abuse, particularly the potency and devastation of crack. We need not wait
until this drug reaches the suburbs the way we waited for it to

reach the East Coast. "Wait, there is a new drug coming from out here that will knock their socks off," was the prediction on the West Coast as the wave of crack began. That wave will reach the suburbs unless we do something to stop it.

There are too many unsupervised children looking for a thrill. I told my children at Blaine that people ride the roller coaster for a thrill. They even refuse to buckle up and they hold their hands in the air to make the ride more daring. Thrill seekers jump from planes. But in each of these instances, they expect to come out alive and in good health. To use crack is tantamount to jumping out of a plane without the parachute. The cost of the thrill is deadly. We must talk to our children. We must give them firsthand knowledge. To say, "I have warned you; I have done my part," is not enough.

The television commercial industry did not give up on commercials because people used those early ten- or twenty-second spots to refresh themselves. Those spots became the most expensive few seconds identifiable. Commercials are played over and over until we find ourselves humming the jingles or using the phrases in our conversation. We must be just as consistent and determined to get our messages heard as is the industry selling basketball shoes for $150 a pair.

Television spots with anti-drug messages have begun to proliferate and more are in the making. I serve on a national steering committee sponsored by the federal Department of Health and Human Services. As part of a nationwide alcohol and other drug use (AOD) prevention strategy, the federal government's Office for Substance Abuse Prevention (OSAP) has launched a multimedia Urban Youth Public Education Campaign called "By Our Own Hands" to prevent alcohol and other drug use by nine- to thirteen-year-old African-Americans who live in high-risk environments. This promises to be a good and worthwhile campaign. Prime-time television spots must be given to air these messages. To buy these spots is cost-prohibitive, but not to invest in the youth of our country is even more costly.

We must warn our children about the dangers of such things

as drugs, and we must correct them when their behavior becomes unacceptable or unsafe. Too many people ignore objectionable behavior in children today. I address unacceptable behavior wherever I see it. I expect children to treat me with respect and I let them know how I feel. I also intervene when I see children in danger. Not everyone does. Recently a repairman at my home saw my three-year-old grandson Jared playing with a can of insecticide and did nothing to stop him. His explanation was: "I don't say anything to other people's children." We have helped to lead children astray, but are not willing to become involved enough to help them and their parents toward safe behavior.

Not enough can ever be said about the need among children for role models. The effects of television and motion pictures are enormous. The entertainment industry has provided our children with violence and dishonor to mimic. The other day, during one of our play periods, Jared said, "Come on, Mama, let's get out of here, the cops are coming." I guessed that he had gotten this from a television program showing criminals trying to evade the law. The scene was clearly presented in such a way that my three-year-old grandson chose to be on the side of the criminals, and even worse, he tried to convince me to join that side also.

Audiences applaud *Godfather I, II* and *III*—all glorifying criminals—and then we scorn poor African-American young men and boys for wanting to be part of the Junior Black Mafia. Solid role models and self-esteem are as important to character building as food, clothing and shelter are to survival.

The salvation of this generation depends on us. Hope for the little crack victims and the victims of AIDS means hope for us all. Much help can come from the institutions of adoption and foster care. When children become members of solid families such as the one provided by Richard's foster mother, who want to love and care for children, they will get the kind of advocacy, acceptance and treatment that they need to become productive citizens. Do problems have to smack us in the face before we get involved?

▧

IF THERE WAS ONE WORD THAT UNDERLINED THE SUCCESS WE enjoyed at the Blaine Elementary School, it was involvement. Parents and the community were as much a reason for our students' achievements as the teachers and the administration. And our students *did* continue to achieve, even in the face of the ravages of crack. Our test scores continued to climb, our students continued to excel at the upper schools into which they graduated, we continued to produce winners in citywide competitions such as the oratorical contest and most of all we continued to keep our kids in school and to truly teach them while they were there.

When the Merrill Lynch Foundation decided to target ten elementary schools across the country in 1988 and give twenty-five first-graders in each of those schools full college scholarships when—and *if*—they graduated from high school in the year 2000, Blaine was the one school chosen in Philadelphia—along with one each in Atlanta, Boston, Chicago, Detroit, Houston, Los Angeles, New York, Miami and Washington.

According to the foundation, each school was selected for a combination of "good administrative leadership, an orderly environment where achievement is stressed, good student and teacher attendance rates, and parental involvement." Blaine was selected from among seven schools nominated in our district.

The process of selecting our twenty-five first-graders assured that there would be no preference given to any individual child. The name of each of our 121 first-graders was printed on a three-by-five index card. The boys' cards were put in one box, the girls' in another. I pulled twelve names from each. Then we poured all the remaining cards into one box and chose the twenty-fifth name from that. This was all done at the administration building under the watchful eye of the Philadelphia chapter of the Urban League.

Of the thirteen boys and twelve girls chosen, an interesting cross section of our children emerged. Some lived with two parents, others had one parent or foster parents; many of the children's parents were employed but several others were on public assistance. We made a profile sheet for each child so that his or her needs were readily identifiable. Richard's name was among those selected—the same Richard who was struggling with the legacy of his mother's crack habit. There was no telling what would happen with Richard, no telling if he would make it out of junior high school, much less out of high school and into college. But his selection would help Richard be special in a way that both he and his biological and foster families could be proud of and he would have an incentive to stay determined.

When the Philadelphia *Inquirer* interviewed the parents of our Merrill Lynch Scholarship winners, Richard's foster mother talked about another foster son she had, an eighteen-year-old who was getting set to graduate from high school.

"I don't know how in the world I'm going to send him to college," she said of the older boy. "But this is something I can depend on for Richard. He's going to have to study harder. Maybe I'll take a little TV away from him. But he's already come a long way."

RICHARD HAD INDEED COME A LONG WAY. WE ALL HAD. And my way took a turn when, in 1990, I was transferred from Blaine to FitzSimons Middle School, seven blocks away. The move was really no surprise. All the publicity we'd been getting at Blaine had compelled the people downtown, including Dr. Clayton, to put some of my programs—especially my success with parental involvement—into play on a wider scale. They concluded there was no better person to spread my gospel than me.

Leaving Blaine was like leaving my family, but it was time. I had prepared the children and the staff for my move. We'd brought the school and community to the point where it was a well-oiled machine, a place where the blend of care, comfort, effort and achievement had created an environment and tradition of success that could be self-perpetuating if care was taken to properly orient new staff, new parents and new children. How could I refuse to try to plant those same seeds all across the city?

I was assigned to FitzSimons for a year, then I went on to central administration to help increase and improve parental involvement for the entire Philadelphia school district: 257 schools, grades K through twelve; 180,000 children—and their parents.

It is an interesting challenge. The greatest part of the challenge is to allay fears and convince principals, school staffs and students that the active participation of parents will assist in the improvement of education.

Much of our school personnel do not want parents snooping about like unwanted mothers-in-law who know that they can do things better. They are downright afraid of the criticizing and reporting that these parents might do. They are afraid that their failures will be publicized. They do not want to share decision making. They are afraid that the parents will not become real partners in education, but evaluators instead.

Many parents are afraid of the school—afraid that school personnel don't have a dedicated interest in the education of their children. They are afraid that if decisions are made to give a little more here and a little less there, their child might be "there" and not "here." They are afraid that if they rub the wrong person the wrong way, retaliation will be felt by their child. They are leery about the quality and sincerity of the staff and administration. There are always the good, better and best teachers, and sometimes there are poorly performing teachers to whom their children might be assigned. Every parent wants the best for his children, just as the parents in Blaine all wanted Mary Freeman to teach their little first-graders.

Children are afraid of parental participation as well. All too many children are afraid that parents will come into the school to spy on them. They are afraid that their parents and the school will conspire against them. They are afraid that their parents might espouse views far too different from those of other parents. Children are afraid that parents might come into their schools and embarrass them before their peers and teachers. They are afraid. One tenth-grader told me, "I'm not bringing my mother so that these teachers can rat on me."

School boards, central administrations, field administrators, teachers and students must be made to see the advantage of parental involvement in education. This involvement must be defined in such a way that it is clear to all parties. The definition must be written out with clear and accepted rules for all "players."

Parents must be helped to be fully knowledgeable about the total school program. They must know school policy, curriculum, the instructional program, practices and procedures. And we must all move away from using one another to fulfill our own particular needs. Teachers sometimes need parents to influence the administration or the behavior of their children. Parents sometimes need teachers to grant special privileges or special consideration to their children. Administrators often need parents to influence school boards or government. We must move above and away from seeking our own individual ends and recognize that the needs that matter most are the needs we all share.

Whenever disgruntled parents came into Blaine, I said to them, "You and I are on the same side, going in the same direction, and our goals are the same: a thorough and efficient educational program in an environment conducive to learning for your child. Whatever is upsetting you is important to me also."

The sooner we accept that parents have a right to feel what they feel, that they have a right to have their perception of any situation and that we all have a responsibility to allow them to present their concerns and to clarify our actions regarding the treatment of children and the total educational program, the sooner we will see improvement in public education.

Only when the entire educational team comes to the same side of the playing field will the quality of educational delivery and reception reach its maximum. Imagine a baseball game in which only some of the players know the rules and the catcher is on the other team. Just as unthinkable is a situation in which administration, parents, teachers and students are scattered about an educational arena without mutual goals and teamwork.

Parents and school personnel must accept their roles as full team members. They must be willing and able to work out the problems of the local school at the school level. Nothing should go outside of the school until the total school team agrees that outside help is needed. Parents and governing committees should have the right to go outside the committee to other parents or to other staff of the school, but no one should go outside the total school family without concurrence from other family members.

Schools that have governing committees should be sure that these committees represent each member of the school family. These committees should remain open for observation to any and all school family members. There should be no meeting closed to any employee or parent.

School achievement assessments should be done with all parents. Parents should know what grades their individual children receive and they should also be shown the grade distribution of all children in their child's room, in the entire grade and in the entire school. The fact that an individual child scored 45 percent on a test takes on a different perspective when it is learned that the highest score in the class was 48 and the median score was 30. The child did receive a failing grade, but there is something wrong with the instructional program if the highest score is 48. A parent could not make this assessment without all of the facts. Schools too often tend to hide harsh facts that they feel will indict the teacher or the school. But these facts are not an indictment so much as a signal that a program needs review and adjustment.

It is the undue emphasis that parents place on grades that allow them to be duped into accepting a below-par school program. A lazy teacher too often gives good grades to discourage administrative and parental scrutiny. My daughter, Jill, made all A's in the fifth grade in a class where the teacher rarely taught a directed lesson or introduced a new concept. Her homework assignments were all independent projects utilizing concepts and skills she had brought with her into that grade. Careful review of the homework brought this to Earl's and my attention and we brought it to the attention of the teacher and subsequently brought it to the attention of the school administration.

There is too often fragmented or dishonest achievement reporting and sometimes no real accountability for student success.

Schools blame the parents, parents blame the schools, and all too frequently both parents and schools blame the student—his race, his socioeconomic status, his neighborhood or his family tree and his grandmother from the other side of his family. In fact, if a student is not succeeding, *the school program is not designed to meet the child's particular needs.* Pennsylvania Public Law 94-142 requires that an individual educational program be designed to meet the unique needs of each child identified as having "special needs." These requirements must be extended to each and every child who is not meeting with success at school.

Parents need to learn to assess the school program. They must look carefully at homework assignments and be sure that homework fulfills all of the functions that it is intended to do. Homework should keep parents aware of what is being taught and how well their child is processing the material. Homework was designed to be an independent activity where a child is given an opportunity to practice and apply what he has learned. Homework provides an opportunity for a child to assume and learn responsibility. Parents should provide a quiet learning atmosphere for homework and the materials needed to complete and review assignments. Parents should help their children to decide on a homework schedule where homework is done at the same time each night. Only an emergency should change that time. Whether there is a written assignment or not, the child should spend the allotted time in independent study or review. The question "Do you have homework?" should never be uttered in the school life of a student.

Homework time is not a time for parents to play tutor or play school. Parents whose temperament allows tutoring should set aside another time for it. The homework is the child's time to show the teacher how well he assumes responsibility and how well he has absorbed and assimilated what has been taught. Just as a parent would not come into the classroom and teach alongside his or her child in school, the parent should not interfere with the child's homework period unless the child invites assistance. Then and only then should the parent sit in on the homework time. Parents should review and evaluate the homework. If problems are there, make an appointment with the teacher to discuss them, with the child present—the three of you can then devise a plan to help the child perform at his maximum potential. Parents must learn to be proud of the child's effort and, secondarily, proud of the product if the product warrants it. Homework is all too often perceived by the parent as a representation of the home. It is not. Homework is evidence of the child's ability to work independently.

As homework takes the school into the home to build a home and school team, social service organizations must join the team. There must be a combining of the agencies that serve children. Health, welfare and education should all work together with representation in the building. At the time I left Blaine, we served approximately 650 children, very few of whose caretakers were not on welfare. The caseworkers assigned to these families could be housed in the school building, where they could get to know the children, see them daily and be within walking distance of their homes. Caseworkers would not have to be paid for mileage to travel or lose travel time. The school nurse could tap right into the medical centers to make sure that the children received the medical attention needed. Computer networks make all of this very possible. But all of this makes us very accountable.

The school staff and the social agency staff could work together to assess and evaluate policy and recommend policy changes. All too often policy makers make and amend policy without input from those who implement the policy or those whom it affects.

Regular physical and dental appointments could be made and supervised by the health worker who would be on the premises. Fully equipped dental trailers could be rolled right up to the school to take care of the children's teeth. Foster parent programs could be operated in conjunction with the school, where foster parents could receive training in child development as well as supervision and care of children. As families move, their social files could follow them to their new schools. This all would result in improved services for children and ensure that taxpayers' money is more efficiently spent.

Child care is just as important as food and shelter. Social agencies should arrange for young parents to have time off from their children much the same as parents of special or handicapped children are provided with hospice. I fail to see the difference between a parent with a ten-year-old whose capabilities are those of a two-year-old and a parent with an actual two-year-old. Why would one need hospice and the other not? Yet agencies offer relief to the parent of a handicapped child while a young parent with two, three or four children all under school age gets no help or relief. We need to provide help to *all* these families.

In today's society, both inner-city and suburban families are too often unwilling or unable to respond to their children's needs. Family problems are not limited to inner-city children. Kids in more comfortable circumstances have needs just as crucial as children who are less fortunate. Their choices in the morning may be about which of the family cars to drive to school or which designer outfit to wear that day, but they still may well have problems. Their problem may be a lack of communication with their parents. They may not *see* their parents. Maybe their parents are divorced. Maybe both parents work and don't get home until six o'clock, and then are dog-tired and completely unable to even fix dinner much less sit down and talk to their child about the things that might be troubling him or her, troubles that might range from difficulties writing a term paper to concerns over a friend who might be considering suicide.

The fact is that many families in today's society, whether they are in the inner city or out in the suburbs, are unable to respond to their children's needs. Try as they might, many of them are just not able to do it. Our schools need the support and involvement of the parents and families of our students, but we must also accept the fact that in many cases *we*—the schools—are going to have to be the places where a lot of these children's basic needs are met. We are going to have to accept that as a fact. We can't accept the philosophy that schools are not social service agencies. If we want to even dream of educating and guiding our children, we're going to have to feed them, clothe them, nurse and nurture them, and we're going to have to do much of that in school. Schools are going to have to become surrogate homes to a great extent, both in the cities and in the suburbs. There is just no way around it.

As for the inner cities, something can be done about the children's actual homes, something beyond the social service programs already in place. The process of abandonment we've seen in our cities has left our disadvantaged to live only among themselves. Many of the success stories, the role models, the "good" families—black and white—have moved out. Somehow, we've got to get some of them back, to show our children—and their parents—the possibilities life offers, to give them a picture of reality other than the fantasies they see on television and the grimness out on those streets.

If these "good" families have all fled and they're not coming back, maybe we should take some of our disadvantaged families and move them out into those nice neighborhoods. Maybe "mentor houses"—set up and subsidized by the state or federal government—could be established in the vacant homes in some of our cities' better neighborhoods. Disadvantaged families, sponsored by established "partner" families, could move into these neighborhoods, be given employment, have their children go to schools where the expectation is high and have these more advantaged "partner" families to work with them—to co-sign for their food stamps, to help them with shopping and setting up house, to show them how to handle a budget.

This suggestion might only be piloted for a nominal number of families, but the good it would do even one family would be worth the investment. The inspiration it would provide for others would be immeasurable.

Meanwhile, in our inner cities themselves, beyond the plethora of programs needed to nurture both opportunity and initiative in the neighborhoods, we must tend to the needs of the schools. They are the last bastion and the best hope for the future of our cities—not just for the futures of the children themselves, but for the future of the cities that surround them.

Our schools—our public schools—must be maintained and improved, for the sake of us all. It's as simple as that. They need the support that an unwilling—or *unwitting*—public has been increasingly reluctant to provide. The gap between classes—between the rich and the poor—is widening tremendously. There are now, in essence, two distinct school systems in America: our inner-city schools, which are virtually neglected and appear to be ignored, and our suburban and private schools, which are bankrolled and subsidized by parents and communities who can afford to live in these areas and send their children to these schools.

Most experts agree that our public schools today are actually more separate and less equal than they were twenty-five years ago. The tax base that funds public schools has greatly diminished in our inner cities, along with the prosperous residents and businesses that have fled. The percentage of the federal budget spent on public schools was cut nearly in half in the past decade, from 10 percent at the beginning of the 1980s to a little more than 6 percent today.

In a nation built on the premise that equal education and opportunity offers the good life to all, that figure is pitiful. It is embarrassing. And it is dangerous. We simply must be willing to spend more and do more for schools. We must build and maintain better facilities. We must entice and train better teachers by offering them more support.

Teacher training institutes can be organized that begin training teachers in junior high school and continue on through high school and college. A "Future Teacher Magnet School" would facilitate a program that would "grow" teachers with knowledge, skills and attitudes that promote quality education.

"Magnet" programs are specialized courses of study within a comprehensive high school designed to attract students from all parts of a city because of the specialized offerings. The Philadelphia school district has many such magnet schools, which feature engineering and science and the performing arts. I don't see why such schools should not offer a program for teachers. And I don't see why such schools can't be located in a building like Blaine.

When I came to Blaine, I told my husband, Earl, that it was my intention to one day turn it into a magnet school. He laughed and told me, "Madeline, Blaine would not become a magnet school if they picked up the North Pole, sat it on one corner of the yard and put the South Pole at the other end." But I believed it could. Cities need schools like this to become centers for specialized learning and instruction. Right now, these magnet schools do not provide for proportionate representation of the races. Where a school district may be approximately 25 percent white, most often the percentage of white students in the more sought-after magnet programs is 50 percent. It is my opinion that the ratio of whites to African-American to Spanish to Asian should approximate the proportion in the student population of the entire district.

Naturally this would require work not just among the students but also among the parents and neighbors who live in the communities where these students and their schools are located. When Philadelphia schools began to encourage volunteer desegregation, parents were urged to send their children to schools out of their neighborhood, to provide for a less segregated school setting. The cry from African-Americans was always: "Why should we have our children ride a bus to the white neighborhoods? Why can't they come to ours?" I said to our parents at Blaine, "Look at the vacant houses, the crack houses, the crack dealers on the corners. If you could provide a better atmosphere for your children, wouldn't you? If you could afford a better neighborhood for your children, would you want to bus them back to North Philadelphia?"

If our inner-city neighborhoods were cleaned up and made more conducive to living, then they could become centers for learning as well. Schools like Blaine could indeed become magnet schools, and among its offerings could be a future teacher training program.

We must not bail out and turn our backs on our youth and

try to separate the "haves" and the "have-nots." It won't work. It hasn't worked. The style of the have-nots has permeated suburbia. One look at the earlobes and a glance at the dance floor and it is evident there is no separation. Our children spend thirteen years in schools where children establish a culture of their own, all too often by themselves. This culture affects their speech, dress and values, and it is modeled on all sides of the tracks.

Parents who feel threatened by or fearful of the adolescent culture do whatever they can to get their children out of the schools with "these" children. One of the more recent options available is the newly touted government subsidies called "vouchers." Nothing better represents the dangerous direction of our American system of education than this proposed program.

Vouchers could spell the end to public education in our inner cities. It's as simple as that. Inner-city schools are already underfunded and operating at a deficit every year. With vouchers, the situation would only get worse. The already scant tax money going to our inner-city schools would shrink as people who have no children in these schools but whose money goes to support them will, with the voucher system, pull out their tax dollars to help pay the cost of sending their children to other schools.

The term "help" must be emphasized. No voucher system can pay the entire cost of sending multitudes of children to schools other than public schools. A bill that was recently barely defeated in the Pennsylvania state legislature would have allowed parents a $900 voucher to spend on the school of their choice, public or private. What would $900 buy? It's certainly not going to send any inner-city kid to any private school. We've got private schools in suburban Philadelphia that cost $12,000 a year. Offering an inner-city parent $900 in a situation like that is like giving that parent a two-dollar gift certificate to go shopping at Saks Fifth Avenue.

Wealthy parents, who are already paying to send their children to the school of their choice, would not be affected. The gatekeepers of their school will simply add the amount of the voucher grant to their tuition, as will all of the schools on the way down, while the marrow is sucked right out of the bones of public education—bones that hardly have any flesh left on them as it is.

The voucher will dismantle public education as assuredly as divorce has affected the American family. Public education is the only hope in the lives of most of the poor. Public education is not only a tool for the poor. An efficient public education institution serves to help middle America as well. In today's economic crunch, it is middle America that is suffering most, while trying to keep its children in private schools or while moving farther and farther from the inner city in search of adequate public schools— the only schools they can afford with or without a voucher.

Education provides the opportunity that must be afforded the poor to allow them to pull themselves out of the cycle of poverty and despair. Vouchers threaten to yank away, plow up or shut down the only real avenue of hope. It's sad. It's cynical. And it's not safe.

The voucher system simply gives up on inner-city public schools. It threatens to leave these schools to swirl down the drain. And while it promises to help middle Americans who are drowning in economic sludge, it is actually doing no more than throwing a straw to a drowning man—what looks like help is actually no more than a well-orchestrated bit of deception.

The voucher system is nothing new. It was proposed and then shelved more than twenty years ago. It has now been dusted off and put back on the table by businessmen who see money spent on education with no accountability attached to the quality of the product. These businessmen want a piece of this easy action. Where else can business take the money and not be answerable for the product? Some school systems allow business to take over their educational systems, promising no tax increases for, say, five years, with the promise from the business that their scheme will improve education. That gives the business five years to profit from the educational dollar. Then they up and walk away from an unimproved and often decimated school system, saying, "We tried. Maybe we *should* leave education to the educators."

The billions of tax dollars—*education* dollars—that would vanish this way would be the Department of Education's own savings and loan fraud.

PUBLIC SCHOOLS CAN BE EFFICIENTLY RUN INSTITUTIONS. Yes, support and resources from the local, state and federal governments are needed. But meanwhile, things can be done. City by city, school by school, classroom by classroom, child by child, things can be done. The situation can seem overwhelmingly hopeless if we do nothing but take the long, dismal view.

Yes, it can be overwhelming to ask how we're going to change the nation's schools, how we're going to change the schools in the state of Pennsylvania, how we're going to change the schools in the city of Philadelphia.

Yes, it can be overwhelming to ask what we're going to do about the teachers, what we're going to do about the children, what we're going to do about the parents, what we're going to do about their homes.

But it's not overwhelming to say I'm going to change *this* school, I'm going to help *this* teacher, I'm going to treat *this* child, *this* parent, *this* home.

When I came into the Blaine School, I didn't say I was going to dress all the kids in Philadelphia. I said I've got four hundred and fifty kids right here, and I'm going to do something about *them.* If I looked up and saw twenty-five or thirty dirty coats, I didn't stand there and say, "Oh my God, what am I going to do with all these coats!" What I did was take five coats, put them in the washing machine, take them out when they were done, put them in the dryer and stick five more in the washer. A day later, maybe two, I'd worked my way through those thirty coats.

If you've got fifteen kids with no shoes and shoes cost ten dollars a pair, that's one hundred and fifty dollars that you need. Who has one hundred and fifty dollars? We didn't have it. But we sold pretzels and we took in *fifty* dollars, and the pretzels cost twenty, so that netted us thirty. That bought shoes for three kids.

Then we'd do something else, raise a little money and buy shoes for three more.

If I went someplace to speak, I'd ask the audience if they had clothes their kids had outgrown, because I had kids who could use them. I'd bring back maybe one or two outfits, dress one or two children, do that again and again and pretty soon I had that situation in hand.

I didn't walk into that dirty building that first summer at Blaine and say we've got forty-some rooms and hallways and bathrooms to clean up here and how are we going to *do* it all! We dug in and did it one room at a time, one hallway at a time.

Which is just the way we can fix our schools all across America. Certainly there needs to be a focus on and a restructuring of our educational "system." But meanwhile lives are being lived in these schools every day. Children and teachers are coming through those doors every morning. They've got immediate needs that must be addressed, and this is how it can be done. Don't talk about systems, or cities, or other schools. Say I'm going to make *this* school a better place for teachers, I'm going to make *this* school a better place for parents, I'm going to make *this* school a better place for children.

Say I'm going to clean up that one yard out there.

Say I'm going to sweep up that one block. Not all the blocks in Philadelphia. Not all the blocks in America.

That one block.

That's what we did at Blaine.

And that's what we can do on every block in this country.

THERE ARE STILL MORNINGS WHEN I'LL DRIVE PAST BLAINE. If I'm headed anywhere near Strawberry Mansion, I'll make it a point to swing up Thirtieth Street and into the neighborhood. Kids I had at Blaine—teenagers now—come running up to the car to tell me how they're doing, to ask how I am. And they tell me about the others, about the ones who have wound up in jail and about the ones who are now in college.

Like Joanne's son, the boy who hadn't missed a day before his mother fell victim to crack. Well, he didn't miss a day after that either. Not in junior high or high school either. Now he's a student at Temple University. I stopped by to see Joanne the other day—she's still living with her parents—and she said he's doing fine.

Our "scholarship builders" are still on track, all twenty-five of them. Richard is showing promise, and with the support he's got behind him, there's no reason he shouldn't make it into and through college. The year 2000 continues to shine ahead of all those kids like a beacon.

The sight of Blaine itself never fails to give me a tug inside. The yard still looks clean, the building solid and unscarred. And if I approach at the right time of the morning, even before the school is in sight, I can hear voices, the sound of six hundred little voices rising from the yard and echoing up the street:

I WILL ACT IN SUCH A WAY . . .

Peewee is still out there every morning, standing on his stoop, waiting for a ride to his job at the hospital.

"Hi, M' Carwrigh!" he hollers. "I'm goin' to work!"

I stop, and I smile.

"I am, too, Peewee," I say. "I am, too."